RENEWALS 458-457
DATE DUE

FEB 9

WITHDRAWN
UTSA Libraries

GAYLORD   PRINTED IN U.S.A.

*The Strange Liberalism
of Alexis de Tocqueville*

The Strange Liberalism
of Alexis de Tocqueville

ROGER BOESCHE

Cornell University Press

ITHACA AND LONDON

Copyright © 1987 by Cornell University

All rights reserved. Except for brief quotations in a review, this book, or parts thereof, must not be reproduced in any form without permission in writing from the publisher. For information, address Cornell University Press, 124 Roberts Place, Ithaca, New York 14850.

First published 1987 by Cornell University Press.

International Standard Book Number 0-8014-1964-6
Library of Congress Catalog Card Number 86-29141

Printed in the United States of America

Librarians: Library of Congress cataloging information appears on the last page of the book.

The paper in this book is acid-free and meets the guidelines for permanence and durability of the Committee on Production Guidelines for Book Longevity of the Council on Library Resources.

LIBRARY
The University of Texas
At San Antonio

To Mandy

Contents

7

Acknowledgments

Finishing a project such as this is a double pleasure, because it is satisfying not only to reach the end of a road but also to thank those who have assisted along the way. For three and a half decades the Commission Nationale pour la Publication des Oeuvres d'Alexis de Tocqueville has been steadily publishing the definitive edition of Tocqueville's complete works in conjunction with Éditions Gallimard of Paris. Although the nearly herculean task remains unfinished, most of this multivolume work has been published under the direction of J. P. Mayer (*Oeuvres complètes* [Paris: Gallimard, 1951–]). Every Tocqueville scholar necessarily builds upon the efforts of the Commission Nationale, and we owe a debt of gratitude to Mayer, André Jardin, and the other editors of this edition of Tocqueville's complete works. Future Tocqueville scholars will surely benefit from more than a half-dozen volumes still to appear.

Similarly, other Tocqueville pioneers must be acknowledged by current scholars. Paul Lambert White, George Wilson Pierson, and others have gathered together large numbers of Tocqueville's manuscripts, notes, and letters relating to his voyage to North America. These are accessible to scholars at the Beinecke Rare Book and Manuscript Library at Yale University. We are extraordinarily lucky to have so many of Tocqueville's notes, because we can literally trace the thinking process behind the writing of *Democracy in America*. Very soon James T. Schleifer will publish an edited critical edition of *Democracy in America*, and at least some of this material at Yale will be available to a wider public. I certainly thank Marjorie Wynne, Re-

9

search Librarian for the Beinecke Rare Book and Manuscript Library, for giving me access to much of the Tocqueville Manuscripts Collection. I am also grateful to Alfred A. Knopf, Inc., for permission to quote from the two-volume edition of *Democracy in America* translated by Henry Reeve, revised by Francis Bowen, and edited by Phillips Bradley, copyright © 1945 by Alfred A. Knopf, Inc., subsequently reprinted in a Vintage Books edition.

Help has come from other quarters as well. Support from the National Endowment for the Humanities enabled me to do important research in Paris. Timely and generous aid from the Earhart Foundation supported my research and writing on two different occasions. Various staff members of the seemingly countless sections of the Bibliothèque Nationale in Paris gave me their full cooperation, and Occidental College—traditionally supportive of scholarly work—graciously offered me a short leave of absence to finish writing this book.

A diligent reader might discover that some ideas, sentences, and passages in this book can be found in articles and chapters I have published elsewhere. I thank the editors for allowing me to draw on the following: "The Prison: Tocqueville's Model for Despotism," *Western Political Quarterly* 33 (December 1980): 550–63; "The Strange Liberalism of Alexis de Tocqueville," *History of Political Thought* 2 (Winter 1981): 495–524; "Why Could Tocqueville Predict So Well?" *Political Theory* 11 (February 1983): 79–104; "Tocqueville and *Le Commerce:* A Newspaper Expressing His Unusual Liberalism," *Journal of the History of Ideas* 44 (April–June 1983): 277–92; "Hedonism and Nihilism: The Predictions of Tocqueville and Nietzsche," *The Tocqueville Review,* forthcoming 1987; and my introduction to Alexis de Tocqueville, *Selected Letters on Politics and Society,* ed. Roger Boesche, trans. James Toupin and Roger Boesche (Berkeley: University of California Press, 1985), pp. 1–20.

Of the many people who have helped me, I am especially grateful to Charles Drekmeier, whose depth of knowledge and breadth of curiosity have been irresistibly provocative and who for nearly two decades has kindled my fascination with the history of political thought; to Nannerl Keohane, who taught me the value and the richness of the French tradition and who read an early version of this manuscript with great care, deep understanding, and considerate suggestions; to the late Yosal Rogat, who taught me to see society as a whole, to understand how art and literature are intimately bound up with historical and political change; to Joseph Paff, who taught me how to read a time-honored political work; to Peter Breiner and Steve Sanderson, friends who helped excite an interest in the study of political ideas; to Nina Gelbart, for friendship, for encouragement, and for her scholarly example; to David Danelski, who took the time to read the manuscript closely at a crucial stage of its composition and offered some invaluable advice; and to Cathie Brettschneider and Kay Scheuer, who carefully and intelligently edited the manuscript.

Other friends who have offered encouragement, support, and suggestions along the way include James Toupin, Peng Thim Fan, David Axeen, Larry Caldwell, Marcia Homiak, Anne Howells, and Eric Newhall. Ann Manning, who must be the finest secretary in any profession, typed the manuscript with care, saving me from numerous mistakes and bringing calm and organization to my moments of frustration. But last, and certainly most, I thank my wife and best friend, Mandy, for her wisdom and patience; the light she sheds wherever she goes has enlightened my path as well.

Roger Boesche

Los Angeles, California

The Strange Liberalism
of Alexis de Tocqueville

Introduction

Too many people call Tocqueville's ideas their own. Politicians, social scientists, and political columnists all like to insert a quotation from Tocqueville, as if his words make any argument both erudite and legitimate. Scholars who befriend Tocqueville almost always claim him as an ally, one who supposedly marches under their banner and fits into some modern category of thinking. A few claim him as a fellow conservative, as either a relation to Burke or a companion in Catholic conservatism to Chateaubriand.[1] Most rush to welcome him as one of the nineteenth century's preeminent liberal theorists, quite frequently as the pluralist who best responds to Marx.[2]

This modern fight for Tocqueville's political allegiance, this wish to claim him and place him in one of our categories of political thinking, would amuse him as much as it would irritate him. Despite his repeated protests against any such identification, and his persistent admonitions to translators and readers that his was a *new* political

1. Robert Nisbet, *Twilight of Authority* (New York, 1975); Russell Kirk, *The Conservative Mind, from Burke to Eliot*, 6th rev. ed. (Chicago, 1978); John Lukacs, Introduction to Tocqueville, *The European Revolution and Correspondence with Gobineau*, trans. and ed. John Lukacs (Gloucester, Mass., 1968); Antoine Redier, *Comme disait M. de Tocqueville . . .*, 2d ed. (Paris, 1925).

2. Even those who regard Tocqueville as a liberal propose a variety of interpretations. To some political scientists, Tocqueville as liberal theorist offers a pluralist analysis of modern politics that provides an answer to Marx's class analysis. See, for example, Reinhard Bendix, *Nation-Building and Citizenship* (Garden City, N.Y., 1969); Seymour Martin Lipset, *Political Man* (Garden City, N.Y., 1963); Jack Lively, *The Social and*

view, the attempt to categorize his opinions haunted him when he was alive and has doggedly trailed him to the present day. To the end of his life, he quarreled with socialists, royalists, English utilitarian liberals, liberals of France's July Monarchy, radical republicans, and conservatives. He disliked categories then and he would dislike them now. But how can we explain this discrepancy between our wish to classify him and his belief that his ideas defied classification?

First, for reasons to be elaborated shortly, Tocqueville straddled political categories and hence embraced ideas found in almost all of them. Selecting the evidence needed to categorize his ideas narrowly therefore becomes an easy task. On the one hand, because he was an associate of several of the great liberals of his time, such as Pierre-Paul Royer-Collard, Victor Cousin, and John Stuart Mill, and because he shared their concern about protecting individuals from encroachments by the state, one can deduce that he was a nineteenth-century liberal. On the other hand, he was born and remained an aristocrat, felt most comfortable talking with royalists, intimated the dangers of equality, and seasoned his views with respect for tradition and religion. Looked at in isolation, such characteristics explain the tendency to classify him with conservatives such as Chateaubriand and Burke.

A second difficulty in interpretation arises from the manner in which he wrote. Because he wove political ideas and opinions into the

---

Political Thought of Alexis de Tocqueville (Oxford, 1962); Raymond Aron, *Main Currents in Sociological Thought*, vol. 1, *Montesquieu, Comte, Marx, Tocqueville*, trans. Richard Howard and Helen Weaver (Garden City, N.Y., 1968). A few critics regard Tocqueville as just one more liberal spokesman defending the propertied classes. For example, E. J. Hobsbawm, *The Age of Revolution, 1789–1848* (New York, 1964); Maxime Leroy, *Histoire des idées sociales en France*, vol. 2, *De Babeuf à Tocqueville* (Paris, 1950). To others, Tocqueville soundly endorsed the middle-class principle of self-interest rightly understood, arguing that a harmony of interests can knit society together. For example, Marvin Zetterbaum, *Tocqueville and the Problem of Democracy* (Stanford, 1967); R. Pierre-Marcel, *Essai politique sur Alexis de Tocqueville* (Paris, 1910); Max Lerner, "Tocqueville's *Democracy in America*: Politics, Law, and the Elite," *Antioch Review* 25 (1965–66). Finally, some argue that although Tocqueville severely criticized nineteenth-century middle-class society, he remained a liberal who ultimately had to look to this new middle class for enlightened leadership. For example, J. P. Mayer, *Alexis de Tocqueville* (Gloucester, Mass., 1966); Seymour Drescher, *Tocqueville and England* (Cambridge, Mass., 1964); Edward T. Gargan, *De Tocqueville* (New York, 1965); Harold J. Laski, "Alexis de Tocqueville and Democracy," in *The Social and Political Ideas of Some Representative Thinkers of the Victorian Age*, ed. F.J.C. Hearnshaw (London, 1933); Georges Lefebvre, "A propos de Tocqueville," *Annales historiques de la révolution française* 27 (October–December 1955); Karl Löwith, *From Hegel to Nietzsche*, trans. David E. Green (Garden City, N.Y., 1967).

fabric of his historical and analytical writings as well as his letters[3] and private notebooks, one can point to no treatise and claim it as his definitive political statement. Although he only rarely disguised his political opinions—indeed, he wished his historical writings to be "instructive," to "show" the reader how to regenerate and preserve freedom[4]—he did disperse them. Tocqueville thus seldom if ever outlined openly or completely his fundamental political convictions, his method of political analysis, his ethical assumptions, or any other such views. Consequently, interpreters must hunt for and compile exemplary passages in which he applied his most fundamental ideas if they are to build the comprehensive political statement that Tocqueville studiously avoided making all his life. But inferences of principal ideas from such examples induce errors.

Finally, we see his writings, to use his own image, through the "spectacles" of our own century,[5] whereas to understand him better we must immerse ourselves in *his* century. We must realize that Tocqueville was writing before the most important categories of our political thought had been formed. The intellectual luxury of clinging to the twentieth-century categories of Marxism, liberalism, Freudianism, structuralism, capitalism, socialism, conservatism, individualism, and so forth is one we cannot afford if we are to understand Tocqueville in his own time. To regard his work through the prism of our own contemporary categories significantly distorts his thought. Although Tocqueville was responding to many of the same political difficulties and demands that enliven or plague us, he did so without the aid—or encumbrance—of these categories. It is refreshing—even fascinating—to watch him grope for his own terminology and formulate his own ideas, provided we can extract ourselves from our own frame of reference.

When, in reading Tocqueville, we come upon such phrases as "democratic monarchy," "feudal liberty," "despotism in a democratic

3. Many of Tocqueville's most important letters have been published only in the last twenty years or so. For example, in the definitive edition of Tocqueville's complete works being published by Gallimard and referred to as *Oeuvres* (M) in this book, all of Tocqueville's important correspondence with Beaumont appeared only in 1967, his letters to Pierre-Paul Royer-Collard and Jean-Jacques Ampère in 1970, his complete letters to Louis de Kergorlay in 1977, and his complete letters to Adolph de Circourt, Francisque de Corcelle, and Madame (Sophie) Swetchine in 1983.

4. Alexis de Tocqueville, *The Old Regime and the French Revolution*, trans. Stuart Gilbert (Garden City, N.Y., 1955), p. xii; *Memoir, Letters, and Remains*, no trans. given, 2 vols. (Boston, 1862), 2: 229–30.

5. Tocqueville, *Oeuvres* (M), vol. 6, pt. 1, *Correspondance anglaise*, p. 30.

nation," or even his reference to the United States as the "New World," we sense we have set foot on foreign soil.[6] Since some of these phrases, such as "feudal liberty," appear to us inherently contradictory, his very language beckons us to enter his world of political thought and abandon ours. Similarly, words so integral to our political vocabulary—for example, *bureaucracy, socialism, individualism, ideology, culture,* or *atomization*—were just beginning to circulate in Tocqueville's time, often with strikingly different connotations. In fact, Tocqueville was one of the first writers to use the word *individualism,* and he may even have invented the word *bureaucracy.*[7] By contrast, he would have regarded some of our political expressions, such as "private citizen" or "consumer rights," as nearly incomprehensible. Furthermore, although the writers who suggest that Tocqueville despised socialism are correct, for Tocqueville the word *socialism* evoked thoughts not of Marx but of the barracks-like existence of Babeuf or Cabet, coupled with the centralized social engineering of Saint-Simon. By failing to reconstruct what Tocqueville meant when he used the word *socialism,* these writers nimbly avoid the reasons for Tocqueville's praise, in *The Old Regime,* of the medieval practice of common ownership of property in a decentralized community.[8]

To understand Tocqueville's thoughts more fully, we must recreate and rethink them, illuminating his own values and vocabulary while following his own approach to an understanding of political matters. Tocqueville told Mill that when he began an intellectual project he tried to rid himself of all preconceived conclusions about his subject. "I deliver myself to the natural movement of my ideas, allowing myself to be carried along in good faith from one consequence to another. As a result, as long as the work is unfinished, I never know precisely where I am going to arrive."[9] After delivering himself to his subject and immersing himself in it, after purposely ignoring what other authors had said about it, Tocqueville hoped to reconstruct the pattern of ideas or events without using preconceived categories that

6. Tocqueville, *The European Revolution and Correspondence with Gobineau,* pp. 102, 169; *Democracy in America,* ed. Phillips Bradley, trans. Henry Reeve, Francis Bowen, and Phillips Bradley, 2 vols. (New York, 1945), 2: 334.

7. The *Oxford English Dictionary* cites a passage from Tocqueville's first part of *Democracy* (first published in 1835 and translated by Henry Reeve into English in the same year) as its first example of the use of the word *individualism.* For Tocqueville's possible invention of the word *bureaucracy,* see George Wilson Pierson, *Tocqueville and Beaumont in America* (New York, 1938), p. 713.

8. Tocqueville, *The Old Regime,* p. 47.

9. Tocqueville, *Oeuvres* (M), vol. 6, pt. 1, *Correspondance anglaise,* p. 314.

would necessarily impose a false structure upon his subject and ultimately distort it. He ventured to "enter into the feelings" of
whomever or whatever he attempted to understand.

> You know that it is less the facts that I am looking for in this reading
> than the traces of the movement of ideas and sentiments. It is that
> above all that I want to paint; the successive changes that were made in
> the social state, in the institutions, in the mind and in the mores of the
> French as the Revolution progressed, that is my subject. For seeing it
> well, I have up to now found only one way; that is to live, in some
> manner, each moment of the Revolution with the contemporaries by
> reading not what has been said of them or what they said of themselves
> since, but what they themselves were saying then, and, as much as
> possible, by discovering what they were really thinking. The minor
> writings of the time, private correspondence . . . are even more effec-
> tive in reaching this goal than the debates of the assemblies. By the
> route I am taking, I am reaching the goal I am setting for myself, which
> is to place myself successively in the midst of the time. But the process is
> so slow that I often despair of it. Yet, is there any other?[10]

As Michelet said, one must try to "resurrect" what once was living; in
Herder's words, to understand an author "one must swim up and
down the stream of his song."[11]

Steeped in the methodology of Bodin, Montesquieu, Chateaubriand, and Guizot, Tocqueville argued that one must first seize and
experience the "true spirit of the age" in order to grasp what might
spring from that age.[12] Thus, if we adhere to Tocqueville's own method in our reconstruction of his political ideas, we must recreate the
spirit of his time and demonstrate both how Tocqueville responded to
his turbulent century and how the hopes and fears central to his
political thought arose from the aspirations and anxieties of his
generation.[13]

This latter point is pivotal, for too many of Tocqueville's interpreters have ignored the fact that he belonged to a restless generation. To

10. Alexis de Tocqueville, *Selected Letters on Politics and Society*, ed. Roger Boesche,
trans. James Toupin and Roger Boesche (Berkeley, 1985), pp. 372–73; *The Old Regime*,
p. 5. Concerning Tocqueville's methodology, see Melvin Richter, "The Uses of Theory:
Tocqueville's Adaptation of Montesquieu," in Richter, ed., *Essays in Theory and History*
(Cambridge, Mass., 1970); also Roger Boesche, "Why Could Tocqueville Predict So
Well?" *Political Theory* 11 (February 1983).

11. Jules Michelet, *Le Peuple*, in *Société des textes français modernes* (Paris, 1946), p. 25;
quoted in Robert T. Clark, Jr., *Herder: His Life and Thought* (Berkeley, 1955), p. 84.

12. Tocqueville, *The Old Regime*, p. viii.

13. I realize that I have used the word *generation* loosely because although the great
majority of writers to whom I refer are Tocqueville's contemporaries, I have stretched
this concept of a generation to include such key figures as Chateaubriand, who influ-

suggest that men are alterable only to a small degree, William James once used the enjoyable metaphor of rinsing and rinsing the bottle, but finding that the smell of whiskey remains. Too many commentators have assumed that Tocqueville emerged without the metaphorical whiff of whiskey, as if he read Montesquieu, Rousseau, and Mill and began to write, relatively unruffled by his own tumultuous era. Since he was a bright young man when Hugo's followers fought for *Hernani,* when Lamartine's *Méditations* drew sighs all over Europe, when Balzac's satires struck caustically at the new capitalist class, when young men and women all over France rushed to embrace the new religion of Saint-Simon, when men and women his own age fought at the barricades to oust Charles x in the name of liberty, how could Tocqueville have remained detached? Of course he could not. At every point, Tocqueville's political thought responded to the hopes and fears of his generation; he borrowed its vocabulary and shared its concerns. Indeed, his published writings, his letters, and his private notebooks startle us by locating Tocqueville—who scoffed at sad-eyed romantics and preferred Bossuet to Musset—precisely within this restless, Romantic generation.

How would Tocqueville proceed to reconstruct what he called the spirit of an age? When approaching his studies of North America or Algeria, he relied primarily upon observation, conversation, and subsequently a selective reading. In his historical writings on India or the Old Regime of France, however, he lacked the luxury of observation and conversation, so he pored over the statements and writings of men and women contemporary to the period of study. Following this approach, we must immerse ourselves in the writings of Tocqueville's time to synthesize those patterns that will reconstitute the age. We know that with the possible exceptions of Baudelaire and Flaubert, Tocqueville was probably familiar with the most influential writers of his time. With respect to literary figures, in one context or another he mentioned Balzac, Béranger, Chateaubriand, Dumas, Gautier, Hugo, Lamartine, Musset, Sainte-Beuve, Sand, Scribe, and Sue.[14] I have therefore attempted to illustrate the common concerns of Tocque-

---

enced Tocqueville's contemporaries, and Flaubert, who was influenced by them. In addition, I have occasionally referred to Tocqueville's "Romantic generation," even though such writers as Balzac and Baudelaire are clearly hard to classify as Romantics. Nevertheless, the term "Romantic generation" does convey what I wish, namely, that Tocqueville attained intellectual maturity along with the French Romantics and journeyed with them in many, although certainly not all, of their subsequent intellectual directions.

14. See Tocqueville, *Oeuvres* (M), vol. 6, pt. 1, *Correspondance anglaise,* p. 320, in

ville's generation by reading broadly the writings of his contemporaries and by studying closely three newspapers of Tocqueville's time:
a royalist newspaper, an opposition liberal newspaper, and a radical
newspaper owned and operated by members of the working class.

I begin this book by delineating themes that emerge repeatedly in
Tocqueville's writings and in many, but not all, of these contemporary
sources. No age of course exhibits unanimity, and even a common
vocabulary and a shared climate of opinion do not suggest political
uniformity. I merely try to show that Tocqueville and so many of his
generation shared major concerns, anxieties, assumptions, and hopes,
whether as great writers such as Balzac and Flaubert or as newspaper
editors trying to reach ordinary citizens. I do this because it helps us
to make sense of Tocqueville's thought and to see that his idea of
freedom emerged from the hopes he had about democratic societies,
whereas his idea of despotism expressed his fears. By focusing on his
conceptions of freedom and despotism, we will discover the strange
or unusual liberalism that Tocqueville offers us. As Tocqueville grap-
pled with problems of the new industrial world—problems such as a
centralized state and a citizenry that feels increasingly isolated and
powerless—he was a liberal who borrowed frequently from conservatives such as Chateaubriand as well as radical democrats such as
Rousseau. Tocqueville was indeed, as he himself maintained again
and again, a liberal of a different kind.

The dangers of such an approach, however, are immense. First of
all, my quoting Bonald and Saint-Simon, Delacroix and Lamartine,
Chateaubriand and Proudhon, often on the same page might
provoke objections that I have made them dance together when in
fact they would never have walked on the same side of the street. But
indeed, such writers often did have common concerns, though they

---

which he demonstrated his familiarity with French literature in a critique he undertook
for Mill. See also R. Virtanen, "Tocqueville and the Romantics," *Symposium* 13 (Spring
1959). Further, Tocqueville was a leading figure in publishing a journal called *Le
Commerce* in the years 1844–45, and this journal reviewed most of the authors listed
above. Finally, because both Tocqueville and Stendhal were close friends with the
literary critic Jean-Jacques Ampère, it is likely Tocqueville was familiar with Stendhal's
work. In this respect, the value of André Jardin's biography *Alexis de Tocqueville, 1805–
1859* (Paris, 1984) in linking Tocqueville to his contemporaries cannot be overstated.
For Tocqueville's regard for or contact with Chateaubriand, Lamartine, Fourier,
Michelet, Balzac, and a comparatively small intellectual elite in Paris, see especially
pages 218, 286–87, 383, 459, 362. To a lesser extent one receives the same picture of
Tocqueville's intellectual companions in Xavier de la Fournière, *Alexis de Tocqueville*
(Paris, 1981); see especially, ch. 20.

disagreed diametrically in their proposed solutions. Bonald, de Maistre, Saint-Simon, and Comte, for example, all detested the self-interested individualism of the new commercial society, yet the first two wished to revivify a feudal past, whereas the second two wanted to build a communal future.

Someone might also object that in concentrating on the anxieties of this age, I make it seem as if no one welcomed or appreciated the new era. Was there no one who praised the prosperity of industrialization, even if it brought self-interested individualism? Was there no exception to a seemingly universal disenchantment? Of course the age had its defenders and some people were content; I have tried to indicate as much. But this objection points to the heart of the problem: no empirical verification can settle this type of dispute. Knowledge of this kind demands interpretation. Some interpretations are, of course, more misguided than others. But the only evidence lies in the historical, political, artistic, and personal legacy of the epoch; yet the evidence of that heritage is itself subject to interpretation. There is no way out of the circle. Charles Taylor described this situation as follows:

> What if someone does not "see" the adequacy of our interpretation? . . . What can we do? The answer, it would seem, can only be more of the same. We have to show him through the reading of other expressions why this expression must be read in the way we propose. . . . We cannot escape an ultimate appeal to a common understanding of the expressions, of the "language" involved. This is one way of trying to express what has been called the "hermeneutical circle." What we are trying to establish is a certain reading of text or expressions, and what we appeal to as our grounds for this reading can only be other readings. The circle can also be put in terms of part-whole relations: we are trying to establish a reading for the whole text, and for this we appeal to readings of its partial expressions. . . . The readings of partial expressions depend on those of others, and ultimately on the whole.[15]

For every snippet of evidence writers include in books of this kind, they exclude thousands of pages. In the end, they can merely beckon

---

15. Charles Taylor, "Interpretation and the Sciences of Man," *Review of Metaphysics* 25 (1971–72): 6. In his unpublished notes, Tocqueville himself had an astonishingly similar answer to those who would criticize his interpretation of American democracy. It is easy to criticize particular facts, he admitted, or even individual parts of his work; but "in order to judge me it is necessary to try to do as I have done, to see the whole and to decide based on this great mass of reasons. To whoever will do that, and will not be of my opinion, I am ready to yield, because if I am sure that I have sincerely searched for the truth, I am far from regarding myself as having found it for certain." (Tocqueville Manuscripts Collection, Beinecke Rare Book and Manuscript Library, Yale University. C.V.h., Paquet No. 3, Cahier No. 3, p. 96.)

their readers to the epoch at hand, summoning them to see for themselves, hoping that author and reader will assist each other on their way to agreement. If this book does nothing more than extend the debate about the ways and extent to which Tocqueville's ideas emerged from the aspirations and anxieties of his generation, it will have served its purpose.

PART ONE

Tocqueville and His Generation

1 Anxiety in an Age of Transition

I t is perhaps not terribly significant to claim that Tocqueville lived in a time of change. Has there been an epoch in European history since the Middle Ages that one could not regard as an age of transition? It is significant, however, to suggest that Tocqueville and his generation were acutely aware of rapid changes in intellectual conventions, traditional beliefs, and social institutions. If we are to understand Tocqueville's political thought, we must explore the pervasive and anxious disenchantment that Tocqueville and other writers articulated keenly in the midst of this transformation of French society.

Arnold Hauser described the men and women of this generation in France as longing for the past while yearning for the future, because they found only disenchantment with the present.[1] Living under the twin shadows of the Great Revolution (Marat's heart still hung in a vase from the ceiling of the Jacobin Club) and the military glory of Napoleon (Mrs. Trollope reported that, years after Napoleon's demise, students traversed Paris with one hand in their coats and their hair parted like Napoleon's),[2] this generation considered the past to be glorious and spirited in comparison with the stodgy, practical world of the new bourgeoisie. In this regard, they were born too late. In contrast to this, imbued with eighteenth-century notions of

1. Arnold Hauser, *The Social History of Art*, trans. Stanley Godman in collaboration with the author, vols. 3 and 4 (New York, 1958), 3: 168–76.
2. See César Graña, *Bohemian versus Bourgeois* (New York, 1964), pp. 42–43. Graña's book and Raymond Williams's *Culture and Society, 1780–1950* (New York, 1966) very much influenced my approach to Tocqueville.

historical development (and sometimes progress), they simultaneously regarded themselves as born too soon.

This position explains the peculiar feeling that characterized this
period, namely, the feeling of being—in Hauser's words—"born between the times." Musset expressed it most succinctly when he said,
"Everything that was is no more; everything that will be is not yet.
Look no further for the secret of our troubles."[3] Similarly, Saint-
Simon wrote of "wavering between an order of things which has been
destroyed and cannot be restored, and another order which is coming
but not yet consolidated."[4] Too late and too soon, each felt condemned to live in a petty present, an age of cultural decadence on the
one hand and cultural immaturity on the other.

This attitude manifested itself in a pervasive sense of homelessness, a longing for a secure and honorable age, a dreaming of the
heroism of the past or of the possibilities of the future. Géricault's *The
Raft of Medusa* was a symbol for this homelessness, for a generation
adrift, a generation in quest of a land and a time worthy of its talent
and courage.[5] Daumier's *The Fugitives,* a painting depicting resolute
but persecuted men and women in flight, their homes behind them in
flames and the land ahead undefined, signified a generation con-
fronting the crumbling of the old and the rebuilding of the new. "An
unknown dawn is rising," declared Michelet; "it is the first morning of
a new universe."[6]

Conservative writers, of course, hungered for the institutions of
the past and saw in the rapid changes of the time a confirmation of
decadence, perhaps the eclipse of civilization. A contemporary observed of Chateaubriand that "He has no more than one idea, than
one eternal refrain which responds to all. . . . This refrain is: all is
dead, poetry is dead, glory is dead, . . . humanity is dead."[7] Not surprisingly, political radicals evinced an optimism and hope for the
future. Saint-Simon maintained that the "golden age of the human
race is not behind us but before us"; Proudhon wished for the "second dawning of flawless virtue"; and Blanqui dreamed of reestablish-
ing ancient heroism in order to leap the abyss between the old and the

3. Quoted in Harry Levin, *The Gates of Horn* (New York, 1963), pp. 79–80.

4. Henri de Saint-Simon, *Social Organization, The Science of Man, and Other Writings,*
trans. and ed. Felix Markham (New York, 1964), p. 60.

5. See Albert E. Elsen, *Purposes of Art,* 2d ed. (New York, 1967), pp. 276–77.

6. Quoted in Roger Henry Soltau, *French Political Thought in the 19th Century* (New
York, 1959), p. 116.

7. Quoted in Pierre Moreau, *Chateaubriand* (Bordeaux, 1969), p. 37. See also François-René de Chateaubriand, *The Memoirs of Chateaubriand,* ed. and trans. Robert Baldick (New York, 1961), pp. 375, 65.

new.[8] Whether a particular thinker manifested a regret for the past or a hope for the future, a persistent disenchantment with the present threaded its way through Tocqueville's generation.

Perhaps the most fundamental assumption in Tocqueville's own political thought was the recognition that the old order had collapsed and a new order was emerging. Democracy was everywhere replacing aristocracy, and the new commercial classes had supplanted a landed aristocracy desperately trying to deny that "the power, the riches, and the glory have passed forever into other hands."[9] Even though he regretted not having been born in a less corrupt and more heroic age, Tocqueville maintained that by living in an age of transition, he was able to grasp political developments more clearly. To Beaumont he wrote that his generation had witnessed the gradual "prevalence of the bourgeois classes and the industrial element over the aristocratic classes and landed property," and he wondered whether Beaumont's grandchildren would decide if this was something to be praised or condemned. Perhaps, he said, they will not be "capable of noticing what is new; because it is necessary to be at the point of division, as we are, to perceive the two routes distinctly."[10] Compelled to live between the times, Tocqueville felt that he possessed a special opportunity to evaluate the aristocratic France that was disappearing and the bourgeois France that was emerging. In a famous letter to Henry Reeve, he explained this conviction:

8. See Saint-Simon, *Social Organization*, p. 68; George Woodcock, *Pierre-Joseph Proudhon* (New York, 1972), p. 28.

9. Yale Tocqueville Collection, C.V.d., Paquet No. 6, p. 57.

10. Tocqueville, *Selected Letters*, p. 287. Tocqueville's interpretations of European history always bear the unmistakable imprint of Guizot, whose lectures on European history and the philosophy of history Tocqueville had attended from 1828 to 1830. Guizot had suggested that the history of Europe during the previous centuries had been characterized by the decline of the landed aristocracy, the movement toward greater equality, and the rise to prominence of the Third Estate, which included, of course, the bourgeoisie. All this culminated, for Guizot, first in the French Revolution and later in the rise to power of the middle class during the July Monarchy of Louis-Philippe. Throughout Tocqueville's notes one can see these themes, but one can also see him disagreeing with his mentor by contending that this struggle for equality would not necessarily end with the middle classes comfortably in power. In fact, according to Tocqueville, demands for equality would remain for the foreseeable future. "There are men who see in the Revolution of 1789 an accident and who, like the travellers in the fable, are sitting down while waiting until the river has passed. What an empty illusion! Our fathers did not see the birth of this Revolution and we will not see it end. It will roll along for more generations still with its unsettling floods. It has been more than six hundred years since it was given its first impulse." (Yale Tocqueville Collection, C.V.h., Paquet No. 3, Cahier No. 3, p. 23.) Jardin is right to suggest that much of Tocqueville's methodology for analyzing democracy in the United States came from Guizot's theories of history. (Jardin, *Alexis de Tocqueville*, p. 81.)

They alternately give me democratic or aristocratic prejudices; I perhaps would have had one set of prejudices or the other, if I had been born in another century and in another country. But the chance of birth has made me very comfortable defending both. I came into the world at the end of a long Revolution which, after having destroyed the old state, had created nothing durable. Aristocracy was already dead when I started life and democracy did not yet exist, so my instinct could lead me blindly neither toward the one nor toward the other. . . . In a word, I was so thoroughly in equilibrium between the past and the future that I felt naturally and instinctively attracted toward neither the one nor the other, and I did not need to make great efforts to cast calm glances on both sides.[11]

It is precisely because Tocqueville felt that he stood at a historically important, if highly distasteful, point of transition that he felt such a responsibility to analyze the present with an eye to depicting the various possibilities for the future. But what, in particular, characterized this age of transition?

THE UNDERMINING OF ACCEPTED BELIEFS

Toward the end of *Les Misérables,* Hugo's remarkable and hateful police inspector Javert killed himself because, after having sworn by all traditional forms of authority and having unquestioningly submitted to the dictates of society's law, he could not live when his firm beliefs dissolved; Jean Valjean, assumed to be a dangerous enemy of society, had emerged as its friend. As Hugo said of Javert, "All that he had believed was dissipated. Truths which he had no wish for inexorably besieged him; he must henceforth be another man."[12] Once more Hugo displayed his instinct for selecting an incident fated to find a sympathetic public, for this sense of losing all supportive beliefs was familiar to this generation in transition. De Staël had talked previously of "this fatal period when the solid earth seems to slip away beneath our feet. . . . We suspect everything which we formerly leaned upon."[13] Bazard and Enfantin, those odd but popular leaders of the Religion of Saint-Simon, characterized their time as a "critical" epoch when "all beliefs are overthrown, all common feelings extinguished."[14]

---

11. Tocqueville, *Selected Letters,* pp. 115–16.
12. Victor Hugo, *Les Misérables,* trans. Charles E. Wilbour with assistance from Frederick Mynon Cooper, 2 vols. in one (New York, n.d.), 2: 611.
13. Quoted in David Glass Larg, *Madame de Staël,* trans. Veronica Luca (New York, 1926), p. 200.
14. Georg G. Iggers, ed. and trans., *The Doctrine of Saint-Simon* (New York, 1972), p. 18.

It was a generation chasing a tremendous self-consciousness, a continual questioning of all that was once accepted. Indeed, Comte feared a cultural collapse brought about by "an unending discussion of the very bases of society."[15] While many argued that religious faith was crumbling Lamennais explained the increased rate of suicide by the omnipresent tendency to erect one's own "private alternative" to the dogma of the Church.[16] And the poet Nerval, declaring himself "born in days of Revolution and storms, when every belief was broken," regretted losing the capacity to believe, a capacity available only to those who were "innocent."[17]

The writers of this generation furthered, and perhaps entangled themselves in, a relentless unmasking process, a process of questioning all social and intellectual authority. Catholic conservatives such as de Maistre and Bonald regarded this process as destructive, dating it to Luther and to what they called the Protestant "revolution," which initiated this individualistic questioning of authority. Asserting that eighteenth-century French thought and the French Revolution itself sprang from such rebellious individualism, de Maistre claimed that the philosophes had destroyed "the mysterious charm of government" because they "opened their eyes to a host of objects that it was never advisable to examine, without reflecting that there are things which are destroyed in pointing them out."[18] Chateaubriand declared, "Nothing is left: the authority of experience and age, birth or genius, talent or virtue—all are rejected."[19] Above all, for these conservative thinkers, this unmasking process appeared to be boundless, bringing instability, an absence of all religious faith, and the questioning of all social and political authority.

For others less conservative, this era of change offered marvelous possibilities for a new future; every intellectual convention that this generation challenged opened new arenas for creativity. Lamartine's Romantic poetry, distinguished by an intense subjectivity, "discarded conventions" of the previous century.[20] The verbal and physical battle fought nightly by Hugo's liberal and Romantic followers for the acceptance of the majestically mediocre play *Hernani*, and hence for an overturning of the sacred "unities" of French neoclassical drama,

15. See Soltau, *French Political Thought in the 19th Century*, p. 207.

16. See Harold J. Laski, *Authority in the Modern State* (New Haven, 1919), p. 201; Graña, *Bohemian versus Bourgeois*, p. 19.

17. Gérard de Nerval, *Selected Writings of Gérard de Nerval*, trans. and ed. Geoffrey Wagner (New York, 1957), p. 147.

18. Francis Bayle, *Les Idées politiques de Joseph de Maistre* (Montchrestien, 1945), p. 101.

19. Chateaubriand, *Memoirs*, p. 371.

20. See Geoffrey Brereton, *An Introduction to the French Poets* (London, 1957), p. 99.

was dramatically symbolic of attempts to question all previous conventions and find new intellectual categories. "Let us take the hammer to theories and poetic systems," announced Hugo. "There are neither rules nor models."[21] Similarly, the classical music of Mozart and Haydn, which generally gravitated toward balance and regularity, lost ground to the dissonance, sudden irregularities, obscured and missing cadences, unstable harmony, and use of new organizing principles such as the leitmotif found in the music of Chopin and Berlioz.[22] By stressing color over line, Romantic painters transformed the purpose of art. David and Ingres, while seeking to imitate classical art, strove to capture an objective standard of beauty, to instruct the spectator in regard to some Ideal. By contrast, Delacroix disregarded "conventional illusionistic perspective," purposively using "ambiguities and distortions" for expressive ends.[23] The Romantic emphasis on color and subjective expression of emotion sprang from the observation that perception is invariably determined by a particular point of view, always distorted by our own subjectivity. "I strongly believe," said Delacroix, "that we always mix in something of ourselves with . . . the objects that strike us."[24] All these notions led in painting to a conscious overthrow of the idea of an objective standard of beauty. Delacroix asked, "What kind of beauty are you talking of? for there are several kinds: what do I say? there are a thousand of them, there is one for every eye."[25] Baudelaire claimed that beauty would vary with every historical period, and hence we need "a rational and historical theory of beauty, in contrast to the theory of a unique and absolute beauty."[26]

Because Tocqueville's writing focused on the demise of the aristocratic order and the rise of the middle classes, he assumed that a new configuration of ideas, both intellectual and artistic, would conform to the needs of a new class and a new age. In this he agreed with his teacher Guizot. Nevertheless, although Guizot thought that with the rise of the middle class, the historical development that carried it to

21. Quoted in Barrett H. Clark, ed., *European Theories of the Drama*, rev. ed. (New York, 1947), pp. 368, 379.

22. See Paul Henry Lang, *Music in Western Civilization* (New York, 1941), pp. 859–63; Hugo Leichtentritt, *Music, History, and Ideas* (Cambridge, Mass., 1939), pp. 210–11; Alfred Einstein, *Music in the Romantic Era* (New York, 1947), pp. 68, 131–38; Jacques Barzun, *Berlioz and His Century* (New York, 1956), pp. 35, 108.

23. See Lee Johnson, *Delacroix* (New York, 1963), pp. 37, 49.

24. Quoted in Elizabeth Gilmore Holt, ed., *A Documentary History of Art*, vol. 3, *From the Classicists to the Impressionists* (Garden City, N.Y., 1966), pp. 154, 165.

25. Eugène Delacroix, *The Journal of Eugène Delacroix*, trans. Walter Pach (New York, 1972), p. 706.

26. Charles Baudelaire, *Selected Writings on Art and Artists*, trans. P. E. Charvet (Baltimore, 1972), p. 392.

power would mysteriously halt, Tocqueville argued that the same questioning of assumptions basic to the aristocratic order would continue with new questions assailing bourgeois assumptions and values. Tocqueville suggested that this questioning of previously accepted values began with Luther, continued with Descartes and the philosophes, and would culminate by spreading to all aspects of nineteenth-century culture. In his unpublished notes, we find this entry: "General revolt against all authority. An attempt to appeal in all matters to individual reason. General and salient characteristic of 18th century philosophy; essentially democratic characteristic."[27] Indeed, Tocqueville argued that the unmasking process had accelerated in his own generation until large numbers of the working class possessed opinions that could lead to the "overthrow of society, [and the] breakdown of the bases on which it now rests."[28]

This political questioning, he argued, would invariably appear in intellectual realms as well; "the effect of democracy is generally to question the authority of all literary rules and conventions."[29] For example, he suggested that "the drama of one period can never be suited to the following age if in the interval an important revolution has affected the manners and the laws of the nation."[30] New intellectual conventions, Tocqueville said, must correspond to a new social structure, and in *Democracy in America* he discussed some of these changes in painting, drama, poetry, and religion.[31] Finally, like Delacroix and Baudelaire, Tocqueville recognized the necessity of subjectivity in at least one intellectual area. The famous French historian Fustel de Coulanges believed in a scientific, objective history and boasted, "Do not applaud me. It is not I that speak to you but history that speaks by my mouth."[32] By contrast, Tocqueville never denied that, in writing history, the narrative is colored with one's own subjective feelings and deeply held convictions.

For our purposes, we must recognize that Tocqueville was a political theorist who perceived himself to be writing in an age in which nothing remained unquestioned.

> When I watch everything around me, I see a spectacle unique in history; I see on all sides ancient institutions shaken; societies tremble on

27. Yale Tocqueville Collection, C.V.j., Paquet No. 2, Cahier No. 1, pp. 11, 32.
28. Alexis de Tocqueville, *Recollections*, ed. J. P. Mayer and A. P. Kerr, trans. George Lawrence (Garden City, N.Y., 1971), pp. 16–17.
29. Tocqueville, *Democracy*, 2: 87.
30. Ibid., p. 89.
31. Ibid., pp. 54–55, 77–81, 89.
32. Quoted in G. P. Gooch, *History and Historians in the Nineteenth Century* (New York, 1920), p. 212.

their foundations; not only political laws, but all that has been considered up to now as the foundation of society itself. . . . The ground of European civilization trembles . . . all is shaken, not only political institutions, but civil institutions, social institutions, the old society that we know.[33]

A Generation Disenchanted with Its Time

In an age characterized by rapid economic and political transformation, and in an era in which everything seemed to be questioned, it is not surprising to find a pervasive anxiety expressed by the writers of this time. It is more surprising to find a pervasive disenchantment, because, in retrospect, this era seems so intellectually exciting and so pregnant with possibilities. Some writers looked back at a past that seemed superior and others looked forward to a future that promised to be better, but nearly everyone seemed dissatisfied with the present. As Stendhal's character Lucien Leuwen said, "Am I doomed then to spend my life between mad, selfish, and polite legitimists in love with the past, and mad, generous, and boring republicans in love with the future?"[34]

To some, this era produced a moral disarray and a pervasive decadence. De Maistre, for example, spoke of the "countless horde of men so perverse, so profoundly corrupt."[35] Balzac, an avowed royalist but still a favorite of radicals like Marx because he depicted the disintegration of the old order so well, felt that civilization was collapsing: "The extinction of the arts, the reign of self-interest . . . I see only ruins around us."[36] Delacroix claimed in his *Journal*, "I do not know whether the world has yet seen such a spectacle: that of selfishness replacing all the virtues which were regarded as the safeguards of society."[37] Characterizing his age as "the greatest baseness in history," Delacroix suggested the arts had entered a stage of "perpetual decadence."[38] Flaubert was characteristic of this era in speaking of

33. Tocqueville, *Oeuvres complètes d'Alexis de Tocqueville*, ed. Gustave de Beaumont and referred to as *Oeuvres* (B), vol. 9, *Études économiques, politiques*, p. 570.

34. Stendhal, *Lucien Leuwen*, Book 1, *The Green Huntsman*; Book 2, *The Telegraph*, trans. Louise Varèse (New York, 1961), 1: 136.

35. Joseph de Maistre, *On God and Society*, ed. Elisha Greifer, trans. Elisha Greifer and Laurence M. Porter (Chicago, 1959), p. 91.

36. Quoted in Béla Menczer, ed., *Catholic Political Thought, 1789–1848* (London, 1962), p. 113; see also Georg Lukács, *Studies in European Realism* (New York, 1972), pp. 21–27.

37. Delacroix, *Journal*, p. 168.

38. Ibid., pp. 260, 540.

the suspicion that our middle class society of manufacturers, businessmen and bankers, of people who live on or deal in investments, so far from being redeemed by its culture, has ended by cheapening and invalidating all the departments of culture, political, scientific, artistic and religious, as well as corrupting and weakening the ordinary human relations: love, friendship, loyalty . . . till the whole civilization seems to dwindle.[39]

Finally, a radical workingmen's association in Lyons declared that in the "present state of civilization, . . . egotism . . . conducts men little by little to the point of isolation and cruelty . . . approaching the state of savages and menacing the dissolution of society."[40]

In the popular press, the sense that Tocqueville's era was a time of moral decay seemed to dominate the entire political spectrum. The liberal newspaper *Le National* said that when one looked at the "moral order," one found only "chaos," "relentless fighting," and "incurable anarchy."[41] The royalist *La Gazette de France* regarded the moral order as in complete disarray and thought that the new political economy defined by the commercial classes simply gave license to "cupidity and gross pleasures of the senses."[42] And the working-class newspaper *L'Atelier* argued that the word *liberty* must have a moral dimension and must not be allowed to justify an economic anarchy in which each person is concerned only with his or her self-interest. Such a society leads to egoism, isolation, discord, and a "depravity" of desires and passions.[43]

A generation that is disenchanted with its time is of only mild interest; indeed, the intellectual historian is more astonished when a generation exudes confidence and satisfaction. Montesquieu's declaration of happiness tugs more readily at our curiosity: "I wake up every morning with a secret joy; . . . All the rest of the day, I am content."[44] What surprises one most about Tocqueville's generation is not so much the existence of disenchantment but its extent and intensity in crossing the entire political spectrum and manifesting an extraordinary depth of feeling.

For example, Balzac, who was himself plagued by nightmares and a fear of loneliness, wrote of half the women in Paris: "external lux-

---

39. Quoted in Edmund Wilson, *The Triple Thinkers* (New York, 1948), p. 81.
40. See William H. Sewell, Jr., *Work and Revolution in France* (London, 1980), p. 215.
41. *Le National*, March 2, 1841.
42. *La Gazette de France*, January 11, 1841; July 18, 1840.
43. *L'Atelier*, May 1841; February 1841; July 1841; November 1843.
44. J. Robert Loy, *Montesquieu* (New York, 1968), p. 17.

ury, cruel anxieties within."[45] While Berlioz complained of "inner storms" Hugo experienced "black depressions."[46] Géricault lamented that life's only certainty is the inevitability that men are "born to suffer," and the young Lamennais sighed, "For me there is no longer any season but the season of tempests."[47] Even though created by Goethe over a half century earlier, Werther became a model for this generation with such questions as "have men before me ever been so wretched?"[48] Vigny clung persistently to his literary theme of the inevitability of suffering; indeed, the nobler a man is, the more he suffers, for men "were meant to be in metaphysical anguish."[49] Musset argued that one can never be a good poet without suffering, and Baudelaire—a brilliant poet—wrote, "What I suffer through being alive is inexpressible."[50] Although one might dismiss any century's occasional disenchanted genius, these sentiments surface in nearly all the writers of the time. The exceptions, such as Scribe, Meyerbeer, Dumas, and Guizot, were few and were busy profiting from the new order. For the rest, as Stendhal said, "it is hard to escape from the malady of one's century."[51]

These writers emphatically attributed their personal unhappiness, however, to the conviction that their century was small and offensive. "Everything bores me, disgusts me, offends and revolts me," Berlioz said, and Flaubert spoke of life exuding a "nauseous smell" and becoming tolerable only if one "juggles" it away.[52] In his blackest moment, Flaubert fantasied drowning the human race in his vomit.[53] If others felt less strongly, they shared a similar despair.

The most popular and financially successful poetry of this epoch, Lamartine's *Méditations*, dwelled on sadness, the emptiness of life, lost love, and loneliness; one can surmise that much of the French reading

45. Honoré de Balzac, *Père Goriot* and *Eugénie Grandet*, trans. E. K. Brown, Dorothea Walter, and John Watkins (New York, 1950), p. 149 (from *Père Goriot*); see also Levin, *The Gates of Horn*, p. 28; Félicien Marceau, *Balzac et son monde* (Paris, 1955), p. 301.

46. Barzun, *Berlioz and His Century*, pp. 60, 151.

47. Géricault quoted in Maurice Raynal, *Goya to Gauguin* (Cleveland, 1951), p. 56; Lamennais quoted in Laski, *Authority in the Modern State*, p. 197.

48. Johann Wolfgang von Goethe, *The Sorrows of Young Werther*, trans. Victor Lange (New York, 1949), p. 99.

49. Quoted in Robert T. Denommé, *Nineteenth Century French Romantic Poets* (Carbondale, Ill., 1969), p. 70; see also Brereton, *An Introduction to the French Poets*, p. 109.

50. Quoted in Martin Turnell, *Baudelaire* (New York, 1972), p. 51; for Musset see Brereton, *An Introduction to French Poets*, p. 140.

51. Quoted in Levin, *The Gates of Horn*, p. 113.

52. Berlioz quoted in Barzun, *Berlioz and His Century*, p. 189; Flaubert quoted in Graña, *Bohemian versus Bourgeois*, p. 128; and Victor Brombert, *The Novels of Flaubert* (Princeton, 1966), p. 5.

53. See Wilson, *The Triple Thinkers*, p. 85.

public shared the feeling that something was missing. Even though created in 1802, Chateaubriand's René, along with Werther, Ossian, and even Byron, became a model of suffering from what has been subsequently labeled a *vague des passions,* "an indefinite longing after an indeterminate object."[54] "What I lacked was something that would fill the emptiness of my existence: I went down into the valley, I climbed the mountain, calling out with all the strength of my desire for the ideal object of a future love that would consume me."[55] A pattern emerges; René experienced an inexplicable longing, Delacroix spoke in his *Journal* of his "unbearble emptiness," Werther lamented his "fearful void," even the young and reactionary Lamennais strove to use the Catholic Church to replenish the "void" in every person's heart.[56]

Most commonly, writers complained that life was boring. Musset identified *ennui* as the ailment of the age; Stendhal wrote "I am bored" across one of his pages; and Fourier openly pronounced that "all men are bored."[57] Chopin confessed to Delacroix that he wrote music to escape from boredom, his "cruelest torment."[58] The theme of the weariness of day-to-day living emerged in novel after novel; Emma Bovary's anguish, for example, arose from her refusal to adapt herself comfortably to a stultifying world. Although Millet's paintings of ordinary men and women suggested a strong respect for their simplicity and integrity, these paintings clearly depict labor far from heroic and romantic, labor in fact burdened with weariness and boring repetition.[59]

Loneliness was the next most common complaint, and again, Chateaubriand's René established the tone: "Alas! I remained alone, alone on earth!"[60] Delacroix told of the "inevitable loneliness to which the heart is doomed," and Baudelaire, assailed by a horror of "hideous solitude," required a companion wherever he went.[61] Flaubert confessed that he had "always locked [himself] up in a severe loneliness," and his character Madame Arnoux in *Sentimental Education*

---

54. N. H. Clement, *Romanticism in France* (New York, 1939), p. 344.

55. Quoted in Denommé, *Nineteenth Century French Romantic Poets,* p. 22.

56. Delacroix, *Journal,* p. 195; Goethe, *The Sorrows of Young Werther,* p. 92; Lamennais quoted in Clement, *Romanticism in France,* p. 199.

57. Musset and Standhal quoted in Graña, *Bohemian versus Bourgeois,* pp. 17–19, 129; Fourier quoted in Frank E. Manuel, *The Prophets of Paris* (Cambridge, Mass., 1962), p. 217.

58. Delacroix, *Journal,* p. 195.

59. Holt, ed., *A Documentary History of Art,* 3: 355.

60. Quoted in Denommé, *Nineteenth Century French Romantic Poets,* p. 23.

61. Delacroix, *Journal,* p. 52; Baudelaire quoted in Introduction by P. E. Charvet to Baudelaire, *Selected Writings on Art and Artists,* p. 16; see also Jean-Paul Sartre, *Baudelaire,* trans. Martin Turnell (New York, 1950), pp. 54, 15, 17.

confided that she could bear mere sorrow, but not her dreadful lone-liness.[62] In sharp contrast to the characters of Corneille or Racine, who usually defended a society that supported them in return, the most famous characters in the literature of this period, such as Julien Sorel, Chatterton, Vautrin, or Jean Valjean, stood opposed to society and more or less alone. Stendhal's Julien was an "unhappy man at war with the whole of society,"[63] whereas Corneille's Roderick (le Cid) saved Castile from the Moors.

Tocqueville shared his generation's despair, and in fact, one of the most understressed aspects of Tocqueville's life and thought is his personal sense of anguish. Although his aristocratic reserve partially disguised his suffering, his disguise was incomplete, and a picture of inner torment frequently emerges. While afflicted by a stomach ail-ment that reappeared throughout his life, he also suffered from what his friend Beaumont called a *mal de nerfs,* an intense anxiety.[64] During one such period he wrote to Beaumont, "There are certain moments when I am so tormented and so little master of myself," and again, "I also need your cheerfulness to make war on my black thoughts. Be-cause I do have these thoughts, and in great numbers."[65] And to his brother he wrote, "Unfortunately, the illness you want to cure is hardly curable. . . . It is this anxiety of mind, this devouring impa-tience, this need for lively and recurring sensations that we have always seen in our father. This disposition gives me a great élan in certain moments. But most often it torments without cause, agitates fruitlessly and causes those who possess it to suffer greatly."[66] Late in his life, he wrote long letters to Madame Swetchine, pouring out "mes tristesses et mes misères."[67]

Busying himself with politics and writing helped, he confessed, to thwart a mind that sought ways to torment him.[68] To Nassau William Senior, not really a close friend, he said, "I am delighted in not having a moment of the day to myself. I am naturally, perhaps, melancholy, and when I have nothing else to do, my mind preys upon itself."[69] In

62. Quoted in Brombert, *The Novels of Flaubert,* p. 14; Gustave Flaubert, *Sentimental Education,* trans. Robert Baldick (Baltimore, 1964), p. 354.

63. Levin, *The Gates of Horn,* p. 126.

64. Tocqueville, *Oeuvres* (M), vol. 8, pt. 3, *Correspondance . . . Beaumont,* p. 376. One of the shortcomings of Jardin's excellent biography of Tocqueville is his failure to describe and to analyze the anxiety that tormented Tocqueville throughout his life.

65. Tocqueville, *Oeuvres* (M), vol. 8, pt. 1, *Correspondance . . . Beaumont,* pp. 499, 336.

66. Tocqueville, *Selected Letters,* pp. 147–48.

67. Tocqueville, *Oeuvres* (M), vol. 15, pt. 2, *Correspondance . . . Swetchine,* p. 276.

68. Tocqueville, *Oeuvres* (M), vol. 8, pt. 2, *Correspondance . . . Beaumont,* p. 283; *Oeuvres* (M), vol. 8, pt. 3, p. 96.

a letter written in 1823 when Tocqueville was only eighteen, he advised a friend that the mind, "especially at our age, cannot be in motion without turning on itself, and producing moments of despair which, although without real cause, are nonetheless painful. I myself unhappily know something of this. . . ."[70] Finally, he acknowledged to his closest friend Beaumont that long solitude upset him. The prospect of "six or seven months of winter" at his chateau frightened him because he would have only his writing to distract him.[71] Even as a young man Tocqueville apparently never was able to enjoy life; for example, he entered in his notebooks on North America, "Life is neither a pleasure nor a grief. It is a serious duty imposed on us, to be seen through to the end to our credit."[72] Very late in his life he pondered his own history of unhappiness: "In my youth, I used to have a disordered mind in a fairly healthy body. Now, my mind is nearly healed, but its envelope does not lend itself any more to what is asked of it. I did not know how to be happy then; I cannot be so now. There you have the whole story of man."[73]

Tocqueville attributed his unhappiness, in part, to loneliness, a loneliness obscured by his close relationship with his wife, Marie. She was a somewhat effective antidote to his loneliness, but any separation from her Tocqueville described as "unbearable" and as generating a certain helplessness.[74] He hinted further at his loneliness in remarking how he envied Beaumont's children: "I envy you with all my heart. You cannot know how it is often heartbreaking to see oneself grow old in solitude."[75] Elsewhere, he lamented to a friend: "Because, I confess my weakness to you, loneliness has always frightened me."[76] In fact, this confession serves as a leitmotif threading its way through Tocqueville's correspondence, because over and over he complains about his "solitude" and his "loneliness."[77]

But Tocqueville linked his loneliness and anxiety to a disappointing society, because he harbored an abiding disgust for his time. In

69. Alexis de Tocqueville, *Correspondence and Conversations of Alexis de Tocqueville with Nassau William Senior, From 1834 to 1859*, ed. M.C.M. Simpson, 2 vols. in one, 2d ed. (New York, 1968), 1: 125.

70. Tocqueville, *Selected Letters*, p. 30.

71. Tocqueville, *Oeuvres* (M), vol. 8, pt. 3, *Correspondance . . . Beaumont*, pp. 153–54.

72. Alexis de Tocqueville, *Journey to America*, ed. J. P. Mayer, trans. George Lawrence, rev. ed. (Garden City, N.Y., 1971), p. 155.

73. Tocqueville, *Selected Letters*, p. 324.

74. Tocqueville, *Oeuvres* (M), vol. 8, pt. 3, *Correspondance . . . Beaumont*, p. 374.

75. Ibid., p. 434.

76. Tocqueville, *Oeuvres* (M), vol. 15, pt. 2, *Correspondance . . . Swetchine*, p. 268.

77. For example, Tocqueville, *Oeuvres* (M), vol. 18, *Correspondance . . . Circourt*, pp. 34, 43, 102, 269.

the most literal manner, he felt estranged from the new commercial society, like a stranger with tastes and habits different from those of the surrounding world. "Solitude in a desert often appears to me less harsh than this sort of solitude amidst men."[78] To the Countess de Circourt he wrote:

> Have you not noticed while travelling, Madame, the impression that one receives upon arriving in the morning in a strange town where everything is new and unknown to you—the men, the language, the mores; you are in the midst of a crowd, and nevertheless, you are more overwhelmed by the feeling of solitude than if you were in the heart of a forest. This is precisely what often happens to me in the midst of my compatriots and my contemporaries. I sense that there is hardly any point of contact between their manner of feeling and thinking and mine. I have kept lively tastes that they no longer have; I still love passionately what they have ceased to love; I have a more and more invincible repugnance for what suits them more and more. It is not only the times that have changed; it is the entire race that seems to have been transformed.[79]

He described the July Monarchy as hastening to become "depraved," and in the Second Empire he sought a way to live in the midst of "our dunghill without sensing too much the bad odor."[80] After only one year in the Chamber of Deputies, he looked upon his parliamentary life "avec ennui et dégoût," because he saw in this life only petty interests and ambitions. "I would like a state of revolution one hundred thousand times better than the wretchedness that surrounds us."[81] Tocqueville despised the France of his time because it flourished on the ruin of his most noble hopes and had betrayed the vast potential of the French nation. An "infinite sadness" arose from comparing "what we imagined, desired, hoped for our country during all those years with what we see."[82]

One irony about this widespread disenchantment has become familiar to intellectual historians who have studied the last several centuries. The first part of the nineteenth century in France was a period of rapid economic growth and even a modest extension of prosperity.[83] Yet those who expressed dissatisfaction were almost always

78. Tocqueville, *Oeuvres* (M), vol. 15, pt. 2, *Correspondance . . . Swetchine*, p. 268.
79. Tocqueville, *Oeuvres* (M), vol. 18, *Correspondance . . . Circourt*, p. 103.
80. Tocqueville, *Oeuvres* (B), vol. 9, *Études économiques, politiques*, p. 382; *Oeuvres* (M), vol. 8, pt. 3, *Correspondance . . . Beaumont*, p. 89.
81. Tocqueville, *Oeuvres* (M), vol. 15, pt. 1, *Correspondance . . . Corcelle*, p. 138–39.
82. Tocqueville, *Oeuvres* (M), vol. 8, pt. 3, *Correspondance . . . Beaumont*, pp. 350–51.
83. Sewell, *Work and Revolution in France*, pp. 146–54.

from the very middle classes who benefited most from this prosperity. It is an irony noted by the French writer d'Auvenel late in the century: "Never, never has this French people of ours been so happy as it is today, and never has it believed itself more to be pitied. Its grievances have grown with its comfort; and in proportion as its condition became better it deemed itself worse. The mark of this century, favoured among all centuries, is to be dissatisfied with itself."[84] Tocqueville and his generation were among the first writers on the European continent to encounter the emerging capitalism, and in articulating their dissatisfaction they suggested that a certain disenchantment might be the inseparable companion of bourgeois society.

84. Quoted in J. H. Clapham, *The Economic Development of France and Germany, 1815–1914*, 4th ed. (Cambridge, 1936), p. 406.

2 Individualism, Isolation, and the Fragmentation of Society

When writers of Tocqueville's generation attempted to analyze the reasons for their anxiety and their disenchantment, one theme appeared again and again: the rapid transformation of social institutions accompanied by the pervasive questioning of all accepted beliefs had led to a collapse of traditional ties and hence to egoism and individual isolation. Immersed in the political assumptions of Locke and Mill, modern readers might be tempted to understate the vigorous resistance of Tocqueville's generation to a new economic and political ethos that praised individualism. In fact, Tocqueville himself, widely regarded as nineteenth-century France's finest defender of modern liberalism, criticized individualism for "destroying" all virtues and becoming "at length absorbed in downright selfishness."[1] Once again the resistance to this new individualism came from writers who traverse the entire political spectrum. Bonald argued that the rise of bourgeois individualism signified a loss of affection among men, and de Maistre longed for the previous "paternal communication" between those who ruled and those who served.[2] At the other

1. Tocqueville, *Democracy*, 2: 104.
2. Bonald, Louis Gabriel Ambroise, Vicomte de, *Oeuvres complètes*, vol. 2, *Économie sociale et oeuvres politiques* (Migne, 1859), p. 113; de Maistre quoted in Elio Gianturco, "Joseph de Maistre and Giambattista Vico" (Ph.D. dissertation, Columbia University, 1937), p. 19. In fact, modern social historians, in comparing France with England, find a great deal of "paternalism" in the employer/worker relationships during nineteenth-century French industrialization. See, for example, Peter N. Stearns, *Paths to Authority*, (Urbana, 1978), ch. 4.

end of the political spectrum Leroux apparently invented the word *socialism* just to counteract the English word *individualism*.[3]

INDIVIDUALISM AND THE PRIVATIZATION OF LIFE

Certainly the new individualism had its defenders. Having exiled herself in England, de Staël suggested that liberty meant the "triumph of individualism."[4] When the Abbé Sièyes defined a nation as a "unity of combined individuals," he expressed the same sentiment.[5] De Staël articulated the conviction of most English liberals in declaring that fulfilling the interests of individuals is the proper goal of a political order. "Individual interests are the only real interests."[6] Similarly, Guizot argued that liberty attracts people only because it extends material advantages, a position Tocqueville regarded as demeaning. The literature of this period incessantly expounded the theme of the individual alone against a hostile society that loomed as an enemy, as a threat to one's private freedom. As Vigny said, "In truth I tell you: man is rarely wrong and the social order is always."[7] Stendhal declared "the only thing of value in this world is the self," and his characters struggled to protect their individual selves through withdrawal, deception, and dissimulation. When Stendhal used his pseudonyms, and when he declared "I wear a mask with pleasure," he claimed that he did so to protect his individuality from a hostile world.[8]

The praise of individualism emerged with the extolling of private rights and with a deemphasis of public duties. Constant suggested that "individual liberty" is the "true modern liberty"; but when examined, Constant's idea of liberty entails the unhindered independence of individuals to enjoy the pleasures of a private world. "The goal of the ancients was the sharing of social power among all the citizens of

3. Donald D. Egbert, *Social Radicalism and the Arts* (New York, 1970), p. 125.
4. J. P. Mayer, *Political Thought in France*, 3d rev. ed. (London, 1961), p. 16.
5. Quoted in ibid., p. 2. For a good discussion of this peculiar belief that a nation must discourage the existence of associations and "corporations" of any kind, because a nation is merely a large unity of individuals, see Sewell's discussion of policy toward workers' corporations during the French Revolution. Sewell, *Work and Revolution in France*, ch. 4, pp. 62–91.
6. Quoted in Leroy, *Histoire des idées sociales en France*, 2: 169.
7. Quoted in Clement, *Romanticism in France*, p. 258.
8. Quoted in Victor Brombert, *Stendhal: Fiction and the Themes of Freedom* (New York, 1968), pp. 8, 89–91.

44 Tocqueville and His Generation

the same homeland. That was what they called liberty. The goal of moderns is security in private enjoyments, and they call liberty the guarantees accorded by institutions to these enjoyments."[9] When Stendhal's Lucien Leuwen rented an apartment, he exclaimed "Here I am free."[10] Similarly, Vigny rejoiced over a "magic circle" that surrounded him, separating him from a troubled and troubling world.[11]

Two widely different thinkers detected this trend of emphasizing private rights over public duties in the architecture of the nineteenth century. Bonald lamented that in the age of Louis XIV, architects concerned themselves with the exterior (public), whereas nineteenth-century architects concentrated their attentions only on the interior (private); he suggested that his century had attempted to carve out a space in which to be free, free—according to Bonald—to pursue economic gain and private pleasure while ignoring public duty.[12] Walter Benjamin, in his habit of discovering in the particular something that illuminates a whole era, noted that private homes assumed more importance in the France of Tocqueville's time. Just when Paris began to assign street numbers to houses, a practice reflecting an attempted extension of social control, the home came to be considered a place of refuge from this society, an attempt to establish and to express one's individuality by collecting and protecting one's things. "For the first time the living-space became distinguished from the place of work." In collecting things, in privately accumulating commodities, middle-class individuals sought to define themselves as owners and consumers, and thus the house became a "kind of case for a person and [embedded] him in it together with all his appurtenances."[13] Nevertheless, to glorify the private world, to see it as a place in which to be free and safe from society, is to isolate people and to confirm that ties once enjoyed in a previous epoch have been severed.

Consider the world of dance. With the passing of the aristocratic order, the waltz replaced both the *contre* and the minuet. The eclipse of the minuet reflected the slow extinction of the tightly knit aristocratic community. In learning the minuet, one simultaneously learned the manners and ideology of an aristocratic community; one dance manual, for example, consumed sixty pages in explaining the

9. Henri Benjamin Constant de Rebecque, *Benjamin Constant,* ed. Olivier di Borgo (Paris, 1965), pp. 98, 97.
10. Stendhal, *Lucien Leuwen,* 2: 339–42.
11. Quoted in C. Wesley Bird, *Alfred de Vigny's Chatterton* (Los Angeles, 1941), p. 24.
12. Bonald, *Oeuvres complètes,* 2: 29.
13. Walter Benjamin, *Charles Baudelaire,* no. trans. given (London, 1973), pp. 167–68.

bow of the minuet by itself, because in mastering the bow, one mastered so much of the demeanor required in aristocratic society. The waltz, easier to learn and needing only two people in order to dance, reflected the fragmentation of society and more fully suited the energy and individualism of the rising bourgeoisie.

> The decline of the choral dance is a cause and an indication of the social development. The choral dance, communal dances, demand a compact social order; they require an association in the dance which is something more than mere correct execution of a series of figures and movements. . . . The triumph of individualism in the nineteenth century inevitably raises the couple dance to the leading position and allows the choral dance to fall back. The latter is now devoid of content—a weak attempt to impose upon a chance gathering of a few dozen guests a communal feeling.[14]

This one change in customs mirrored the larger change in society. Self-interested individuals, as Hauser said, found themselves released from the traditional ties of church, family, trade corporation, class, and community; extracted from these ties, individuals became increasingly "free" to enter the economic world of the marketplace.[15]

EGOISM AND ISOLATION

The single word that seems to appear most often in analyzing this trend toward privatization is *egoism*. Conservatives, liberals, and radicals criticized the new commercial order for what appeared to be an alarming acceptance of self-interest. The royalist newspaper *La Gazette de France*, in declaiming against the moral decay of middle-class society, argued that "individualism, isolation, and all their consequences are the basis of this system," and it mourned the loss of traditional ties that had led to mutual, if paternalistic, assistance among individuals.[16] The glorious French nation, claimed the *Gazette*, had been delivered to a systematic debasement, a debasement that had gone beyond the old maxim of "divide and conquer" to a new corollary suggesting that one now needed simply to "corrupt and conquer." How had this happened? "It is by degradation; it is by destroying in man the noble sentiments of nation, honor, disinterestedness, love of virtue, and devotion to the public good; it is a

14. Curt Sachs, *World History of the Dance* (New York, 1937), pp. 389–99, 438.
15. Hauser, *The Social History of Art*, 4: 12, 47.
16. *La Gazette de France*, January 25, 1840.

development of egoism, by directing men to sensual pleasures."[17] Surprisingly, one finds a similar despair in the liberal newspaper *Le National* whose readership was certainly the new middle class profiting from the policies of the July Monarchy.[18] "Deprived of all moral unity, profoundly indifferent to general interests, broken up and reduced to powder like the sand of the seas by the most narrow egoism, the French people is a people in name only."[19] France, declared *Le National*, had fallen "prey to a thousand passions of egoism," and the popular maxim of *chacun chez soi, chacun pour soi* was only one example of this encouragement of egoism.[20] Finally, the working-class newspaper *L'Atelier* argued that the ethos of *laissez-faire* and *chacun pour soi* had caused the atomization or dissociation of society. "People show us the egoist becoming richer, and they tell us to do as he does. The egoism that they seek to excite in us with a shocking perseverance is the most detestable sentiment to which a man can yield; it is the sentiment of the most powerful dissociation. And dissociation is anarchy."[21]

The writers of Tocqueville's generation expressed the same fear of egoism and isolation that one finds in the popular press of the time. Baudelaire's poetry was largely a reaction to his fear that the ties between individuals had collapsed, to be replaced only by a society witnessing a multitude of "exiles."[22] Saint-Simon, Fourier, Lamennais, and Comte lamented both the disappearance of a close community and the emergence of a society of self-interested individuals. "Society is today," claimed Saint-Simon, "in a state of extreme moral disorder; egotism is making terrible progress, everything tends toward isolation."[23] Or as Enfantin and Bazard put it, "It is impossible to see anything else in society but an aggregate of individuals without ties or relationships, having nothing to motivate their conduct but the impulses of egotism."[24] In almost all these French writers, one can uncover Carlyle's fear that the cash payment would become the "sole nexus" among men.[25]

17. Ibid., October 17, 1842.
18. See Irene Collins, *The Government and the Newspaper Press in France, 1814–1881* (Oxford, 1959).
19. *Le National*, January 9, 1840.
20. Ibid., January 11, 1842; January 1, 1842.
21. *L'Atelier*, November 1840; January 1841.
22. Quoted in Turnell, *Baudelaire*, p. 234.
23. Quoted in Frank E. Manuel, *The New World of Henri Saint-Simon* (Notre Dame, Ind., 1963), p. 284.
24. Quoted in Manuel, *The Prophets of Paris*, p. 159.
25. Thomas Carlyle, *Selected Writings*, ed. Alan Shelston (Baltimore, 1971), from "Chartism," p. 193.

In Balzac's *Eugénie Grandet*, money supplanted the traditional ties of husband to wife, brother to sister, and even master to servant. Balzac claimed that gold had become God, whereas "the softer emotions of life occupied only a secondary place."[26] Contemplating and gazing at gold constituted M. Grandet's only pleasures, as he subsisted oblivious to all feelings for his wife and his daughter. Near death, M. Grandet still struggled to awake "on the day and at the hour when the rents were due," and he daily whispered to his family, "Show me some gold!" so addicted had he become to his accustomed pleasure. All who entered his world were either oppressed or corrupted. His wife was "reduced to a state of complete serfdom," and his servant Big Nanon defended "her master's property like a faithful dog." (Or, as Rastignac was advised in *Père Goriot*, "Use men and women only as horses for your coach.") Even though in another era their instincts for affection and goodness might have flowered, in the end all Balzac's characters in *Eugénie Grandet* accustomed themselves to living as M. Grandet did. Learning the value of self-interest and money, M. Grandet's nephew, once a good-hearted chap, became a slave trader. The world was remade in the miser's image, and Eugénie, once a wonderful young lady, ultimately loved only money and adopted the "impassive countenance" of her father. Money had taught "distrust of feelings to a woman who was all feeling." As M. Grandet said, "Life is a business."

When Goriot sorrowfully muttered that if he had had money, he would have been loved, Balzac was expressing his fear that love and affection would become, or had become, a "commodity sold to the highest bidder" in the marketplace.[27] Of his striking character Baron de Nucingen, Balzac claimed, "Natural love, artificial and self-regarding love, vain and decorous love; casual love, decent, conjugal love, love on the fringes, the baron had paid for them all, known them all, except true love."[28] The fear that all ties among individuals had been severed centered on the family, an institution of central importance in French thought since Bodin. Thus, when Balzac announced, "The family no longer exists today; there are only individuals," and when Delacroix scoffed "What used to be called the *family* is today a vain word," they were indicting their society harshly.[29] Without the ties of

26. Balzac, *Père Goriot* and *Eugènie Grandet*, p. 323. See pages 467–68, 302, 311, 81, 487, 496, and 465 for the quotations that follow in the text.

27. Quoted in Martin Turnell, *The Novel in France* (New York, 1951), p. 243.

28. Honoré de Balzac, *A Harlot High and Low*, trans. Rayner Heppenstall (Baltimore, 1970), p. 83.

29. Menczer, ed., *Catholic Political Thought, 1789–1848*, p. 113; Delacroix, *Journal*, p. 393.

family, society crumbled; as Goriot said, "Everything collapses if children do not love their parents."[30]

In part, we can now answer one of the questions posed in the first chapter. Why did this generation have such a preoccupation with loneliness? The collapse of most traditional ties left individuals isolated from one another, which was one source of that pervasive disenchantment that has accompanied industrial societies for a century and a half. If we, in our time, have attempted to adapt ourselves to such a life, the men and women of Tocqueville's generation resisted any such resignation.

The concern about the isolation of individuals reappeared ceaselessly in the literature of this period. In his poem *The Horn*, Vigny depicted an awesome, empty black forest in which "lone travellers" at great distances from one another listened for the faint sound of another horn, a powerful metaphor for the chasms separating people.[31] In another passage, Vigny wrote that "moral solitude is the sad certainty that each individual is as if walled within himself."[32] Stendhal abundantly seasoned his works with images of walls and hedges that separated town from country, men from men, class from class. Flaubert described his character Frédéric in this manner: "Thinking about his friends, he felt as if there were a great, dark gulf separating them from him."[33]

On the other hand, when people did congregate, these gatherings seemed to be composed of strangers, a theme first noted by Rousseau who suggested that "People think they come together in the theater, and it is there that they are isolated."[34] Similarly, a character in Rousseau's *La Nouvelle Héloïse* confessed his horror at these assemblies of strangers. "I enter with a secret horror on this vast desert, the world, whose confused prospect appears to me only a frightful scene of solitude and silence. . . . For my part, I am never alone but when I mix with the crowd."[35] Fascinated by anything that induced people to act or anything that brought them together, Daumier painted railroad passengers, theater crowds, juries, and riots.[36] With the excep-

---

30. Quoted in Levin, *The Gates of Horn*, p. 205.

31. Alan Conder, ed. and trans., *A Treasury of French Poetry* (New York, n.d.), pp. 157–59.

32. Quoted in Bird, *Alfred de Vigny's Chatterton*, p. 22 (my translation).

33. Flaubert, *Sentimental Education*, p. 147.

34. Jean-Jacques Rousseau, *Politics and the Arts*, trans., ed., and introduced by Allan Bloom (Ithaca, 1968), pp. 16–17.

35. Jean-Jacques Rousseau, *Eloisa*, no trans. given, 4 vols. (London, 1776), 2: 25–26.

36. See Oliver Larkin, *Daumier* (New York, 1966), p. 122.

tion of the latter, however, the individuals who gathered were indifferent to each other, and even in the midst of assembling, they concentrated only on their own affairs. Whereas we have become accustomed to these gatherings of "exiles," as Baudelaire called them, Tocqueville's generation had not. Michelet, for one, found them horrifying and protested the "savage isolation even in cooperation."

> Machines (I do not except the most beautiful, industrial, administrative) have given to man, among so many advantages, one unfortunate faculty, that of uniting man's forces without need of uniting hearts, of cooperating without liking each other, of acting and living together, without knowing each other; the moral power of association has lost all that the mechanical concentration gained.[37]

People seemed to come together frequently in this new urbanized society, but less frequently as an enjoyable end in itself and more so as a means to satisfying private interests.

Not surprisingly, a longing for a cohesive community, for some sort of existence that knitted people together, emerged in the ideas of a variety of political thinkers. Bonald, for instance, admired the fact that in the Middle Ages, "Europe could be considered like a single family . . . a society joined by a common interest."[38] The Saint-Simonians sought to transcend the present "critical epoch," an epoch characterized by egoism and by an absence of common beliefs, and wished to attain a new "organic epoch" of collective existence and cooperation. Michelet used the word *association* for a collective organization that overcame egoism and individualism.[39] Believing that people should cooperate and not compete, should care for one another and not remain indifferent, such writers declared individualism to be an "unnatural" state. Fourier claimed that "the individual is an essentially false being," and Lamennais declared that "man alone is only a fragment of a being."[40] Radical workers' associations, often called mutual aid societies, drew heavily on the tradition of trade corporations under the Old Regime; they very consciously set about to organize themselves in order to overcome what they regarded as the

---

37. Michelet, *Le Peuple*, p. 129; see also Elliott Mansfield Grant, *French Poetry and Modern Industry, 1830–1870* (Cambridge, Mass., 1927), p. 44. Arriving in England from a more rural Germany, Engels experienced a similar horror of these crowds of strangers, indifferent to one another. See Benjamin, *Charles Baudelaire*, p. 58.

38. Quoted in Manuel, *The New World of Henri Saint-Simon*, p. 401.

39. Michelet, *Le Peuple*, p. 221.

40. Fourier quoted in Egbert, *Social Radicalism and the Arts*, p. 134; Lamennais quoted in Leroy, *Histoire des idées sociales en France*, 2: 443.

isolation and egoism of the July Monarchy. A Parisian shoemaker, for example, called for workers' associations that would "create bonds of amity." Without associations, "corporations" would "dissipate and dissolve . . . annihilate themselves in the individualism and egoism of isolation."[41] Symbolizing the human need for cooperation, the Saint-Simonians under Enfantin formed a well-organized community (which became something of a spectacle for curious Parisians) in which the vests customarily worn had buttons in the back—requiring a friend to help oneself dress reminded individuals of their interdependence.[42]

TOCQUEVILLE'S ANALYSIS OF THE NEW ISOLATION

How did Tocqueville respond to the collapse of traditional ties among individuals? Although he noted that the traditional and hierarchical family was disappearing, Tocqueville did not seem as concerned about this development as did Balzac, for example. The relations of family members to one another had altered in the nineteenth century, and "paternal authority" had become "impaired"; this led, however, to more "natural" and "affectionate" relations between, for instance, father and son.[43] Indeed, the ties of the less extended family of the nineteenth century needed to be strengthened, according to Tocqueville, because as citizens in other areas of society became more isolated from one another, people would have to rely more heavily on the family for affection. "Democracy loosens social ties, but tightens natural ones; it brings kindred more closely together, while it throws citizens more apart."[44] It was this tendency of nineteenth-century society to "throw citizens more apart" that Tocqueville worried about most. Like Bonald and de Maistre, he claimed that the aristocratic society of the Middle Ages offered examples of communities in which individuals were concerned about one another and not merely about their narrow self-interests. Unlike Bonald and de Maistre, Tocqueville deplored the hierarchical elements of the Old Regime; rather, in praising the communes of medieval France, which he compared with the participatory democracy of New England townships, Tocqueville

41. See Sewell, *Work and Revolution in France*, p. 212.
42. David Owen Evans, *Social Romanticism in France, 1830–1848* (London, 1951), p. 24.
43. Tocqueville, *Democracy*, 2: 202, 205. Lively gives a good assessment of Tocqueville's belief in the decreasing moral authority of the family in *The Social and Political Thought of Alexis de Tocqueville*, p. 77.
44. Tocqueville, *Democracy*, 2: 208.

revealed his preference for a community in which all members, regardless of economic class, could participate.[45] In making this contrast between the unity among individuals that he found in the Old Regime and the atomization of society he saw all around him, Tocqueville displayed his distaste for the latter, a distaste we have seen in so many writers of his era. Even though he knew the world could not return to an aristocratic past, even though he preferred ties of equality to ones of hierarchy, he confessed an admiration for the "sweet and paternal relations" of previous centuries.[46]

In sharp contrast to liberals such as de Staël or Constant, with whom he is often associated, Tocqueville deplored the trend toward individualism and the acceptance of self-interest as the force primarily responsible for directing society. He noted that individualism was a modern development. "That word 'individualism' which we have coined for our requirements, was unknown to our ancestors, for the good reason that in their days every individual necessarily belonged to a group and no one could regard himself as an isolated unit."[47] Defining individualism as the practice of withdrawing from public action in order to enjoy a private existence with family and friends, Tocqueville attributed such individualism to "erroneous judgment." Although he thought individualism was not strictly speaking identical to selfishness, Tocqueville argued, as we have seen, that in the long run the two became synonymous; like selfishness, individualism destroyed all the virtues of "public life."[48] In Tocqueville's opinion, those who extol individualism, those who encourage citizens to separate themselves from public affairs in order to accumulate goods and private enjoyments, might nourish a new despotism, because after individuals vacate the public sphere, a suffocating government will surge forward to accept new forms of authority. Tocqueville sought what he called a "healthy" individualism that resulted not from submerging oneself in a private world but from participating in a group or community that has a public purpose. In such a group, one

45. Tocqueville, *The Old Regime*, pp. 18, 47–48, 131.

46. Tocqueville, *Oeuvres* (B), vol. 7, *Nouvelle correspondance*, p. 436.

47. Tocqueville, *The Old Regime*, p. 96. For Tocqueville's disagreement with Constant, see Jean-Claude Lamberti, *Tocqueville et les deux démocraties* (Paris, 1983), pp. 75–76.

48. Tocqueville, *Democracy*, 2: 104. For a superb discussion of the effects of individualism and egoism on democratic citizenship, see Lamberti, *Tocqueville et les deux démocraties*, pp. 192–98, 220–27, 238–43. For another excellent discussion, and for an insight as to how Tocqueville struggled with these terms, see James T. Schleifer, *The Making of Tocqueville's "Democracy in America"* (Chapel Hill, 1980), pp. 177, 228–30, 240–43, 250–59.

acquires self-confidence and gains knowledge from acting with others, eventually developing the personal courage necessary for a truly independent, individualistic moral stance.

Tocqueville lamented that the people of his time were in a state of "dispersal" that threatened to make them strangers to one another; "each is retired and as if buried in his private affairs."[49] This dispersal, resulting from the fragmentation of society, would leave a political vacuum, and the government alone would become active. "It is the government alone that has inherited all the privileges of which families, guilds, and individuals have been deprived."[50] In the Old Regime, the privileges of families, guilds, parishes, and trade corporations had managed to check any attempt at a thorough despotism; "as long as family feeling was kept alive, the opponent of oppression was never alone; he looked about him and found his clients, his hereditary friends, and his kinsfolk."[51] In Tocqueville's era, however, only a conglomeration of powerless individuals confronted the state. Under the Second Empire, Tocqueville joked to Beaumont that he was staying near the royal dogs, the only assembly in France that could make itself heard.[52] In a letter written in 1840 to Royer-Collard, Tocqueville wrote, "I have never seen a country in which the first manifestation of public life, which is the frequent contact of men among themselves, is less to be found."[53] And in *Democracy:*

> What strength can even public opinion have retained when no twenty persons are connected by a common tie, when not a man, nor a family, nor chartered corporation, nor class, nor free institution, has the power of representing or exerting that opinion, and when every citizen, being equally weak, equally poor, and equally isolated, has only his personal impotence to oppose to the organizing force of the government.[54]

Certainly he saw the problem of atomization, the problem of the dissolution of ties, from a political perspective, and he was clearly part of his generation in fearing this development.

Similarly, Tocqueville dissociated himself from de Staël, Constant, and Guizot, all of whom equated political freedom with the freedom

49. Tocqueville, *Oeuvres* (M), vol. 8, pt. 1, *Correspondance . . . Beaumont*, p. 538; Tocqueville, *Oeuvres* (B), vol. 7, *Nouvelle correspondance*, p. 288.

50. Tocqueville, *Democracy*, 1: 11.

51. Ibid., p. 340.

52. Tocqueville, *Oeuvres* (M), vol. 8, pt. 3, *Correspondance . . . Beaumont*, p. 250.

53. Tocqueville, *Oeuvres* (M), vol. 11, *Correspondance . . . Royer-Collard . . . Ampère*, p. 89.

54. Tocqueville, *Democracy*, 1: 340.

found in one's private life. Like Aristotle, Tocqueville suggested that the household—the private realm—was a place of servility, and that only a servile society could spring from urging people to seek the bulk of their satisfactions in the private sphere. His was a world, however, in which the private realm, even the domestic realm, had taken precedence, aided by an acquisitive or commercial ethic that taught both men and women, especially women, that life's satisfactions lie not in public duty but in a private one.

> Far more often, I must confess, I have seen domestic work and work on behalf of the home, which transformed little by little a man, to whom nature had given something of generosity, disinterestedness, and greatness, into an ambitious, cowardly, vulgar, and egotistical person, who, in the affairs of his country, ultimately could envision only the means of rendering his private situation comfortable and convenient; and how did this happen? By daily contact with an honest woman, a faithful spouse, a good mother to the family, but a woman to whom the grand notion of duty in political matters, in its most energetic and elevated sense, had always been, I do not say fought against, but ignored.[55]

In a democratic country, people never "shut themselves up in a narrow selfishness, marked out by four sunk fences and a quickset hedge."[56] In the France of his time, "public life has no object," and because of this, people "close themselves up within themselves."[57] He scoffed at his countrymen who, even though war was possible, remained unconcerned with such a public event as long as they could still manage, as Beaumont put it in a letter to Tocqueville, a good price for their beef.[58] Indeed, despotism strives to "[immure] . . . each in his private life,"[59] separating individuals from each other until they have lost the capacity to act together. Once the public domain is abandoned, a new despotism will thrive, eventually seeping into every private home. The fragmentation of society, the isolation of individuals, the dissolution of old ties—these are the requisite conditions, as we will see later, for a new and qualitatively different despotism.

55. Tocqueville, *Oeuvres* (M), vol. 15, pt. 2, *Correspondance . . . Swetchine*, p. 298.
56. Tocqueville, *Democracy*, 1: 260.
57. Tocqueville, *Oeuvres* (M), vol. 11, *Correspondance . . . Royer-Collard . . . Ampère*, p. 112.
58. Tocqueville, *Oeuvres* (M), vol. 8, pt. 3, *Correspondance . . . Beaumont*, p. 259.
59. Tocqueville, *The Old Regime*, p. xiii.

3 Powerlessness: From an Age of Heroes to an Age of Machines

The fragmentation of society engendered the general sentiment, again reflected by writers of all political persuasions, that individuals were powerless and confronted by historical or economic forces beyond their control. Napoleon's failure established the tone for this belief, and he added to it by claiming after Waterloo, "It is fate," an idea repeated years later when Hugo, speaking of the same battle, contended that "a power above man controlled that day."[1] Hugo expressed this same sentiment more fully in his poems: "Vast forces shape our darkened destinies/ And naught diverts them: they must take their toll."[2] One of Balzac's characters sighed, "We are all playthings of some unknown and Machiavellian power," and de Maistre argued that man is "merely a tool of God."[3]

Accompanying this sensation that people were playthings of powers beyond their control was a feeling that individuals were insignificant. Balzac wrote that the "chariot of civilization," like a Juggernaut, is barely held back by a broken heart and then moves on; Hugo talked of a single man tumbling overboard, ignored by a ship that proceeded without pause.[4] The most forceful and haunting image of

1. Napoleon quoted in Felix Markham, *Napoleon and the Awakening of Europe* (London, 1954), p. 148; Hugo, *Les Misérables,* 1: 347.

2. Quoted in Conder, ed., *A Treasury of French Poetry,* p. 185.

3. Honoré de Balzac, *A Murky Business,* trans. Herbert J. Hunt (Baltimore, 1972), p. 198; de Maistre quoted in Gianturco, "Joseph de Maistre and Giambattista Vico," p. 208.

4. Balzac, *Père Goriot* and *Eugénie Grandet,* p. 4; Hugo, *Les Misérables,* 1: 95.

this feeling of insignificance, however, came from Nerval in his story *La Main enchantée*. Before being hanged, a man asked if he might say a few prayers: "But the executioner replied that the folks stationed there had their chores to do and that it would not be proper to keep them waiting, especially for such a paltry spectacle: a single hanging."[5]

The insignificance and powerlessness of individuals was a recurring theme in the popular press. The liberal newspaper *Le National* declared that isolation and egoism had left each person alone and powerless, and the new commercial classes had condemned the "immense majority" to serfdom in the factories—a new "slavery."[6] The working-class newspaper *L'Atelier* argued that workers could organize effectively only if they realized that, at present, isolation had delivered each one to an "individual powerlessness," making active association the only possible means for reform.[7] Finally the royalist *La Gazette de France* proclaimed France to be a nation of "Lilliputians," led by "the smallest men of the world" who were but "pygmies compared to the giants" France had seen. Moreover, "these powerless men who, in the eyes of the crowd seem to direct Fate, are all simply controlled by Fate." Indeed, the *Gazette* suggested that the leaders under the July Monarchy might well resemble children who lead lions by a leash, eventually to be devoured later when the lions are aroused.[8] In sum, argued the conservative writers of the *Gazette*, one could depict the moral and political state of affairs in France in one word: "powerlessness."[9]

"Things Are in the Saddle"

This same feeling surfaced in the political and social thought of this period, persuading writers of this generation that history makes its journey under its own power, that men and women are powerless while someone or something else is the primary actor. Consider Sismondi's famous claim: "We searched, and while we found in our century the triumph of things, man seemed to us more badly off than ever."[10] As the historian Mignet said, things, not men and women, are

5. Quoted in Angel Flores, ed., *An Anthology of French Poetry from Nerval to Valéry*, new rev. ed. (Garden City, N.Y., 1958), p. 6.

6. *Le National*, January 9, 1840; September 29, 1841.

7. *L'Atelier*, January 1841; February 1841.

8. *La Gazette de France*, January 2, 1840; July 7, 1843.

9. *La Gazette de France*, November 15, 1843.

10. Quoted in Emile Durkheim, *Socialism and Saint-Simon*, ed. and introduced by Alvin W. Gouldner, trans. Charlotte Sattler (Yellow Springs, Ohio, 1958), p. 73.

active. "How consistently things act, how they accomplish themselves necessarily and make use of men as means and of events as occasions! From the beginning of the French Monarchy it is less men who have guided things than things which have directed men."[11] Indeed, the world of this generation appeared to have inverted itself: things (objects) had become actors (subjects). Likening himself to a dry leaf swept along upon the wind, Chateaubriand's René clearly felt himself to be like an object, impelled by external forces.[12] Sartre claimed that Baudelaire wished to be an object, attaining the security of a mere thing while renouncing his responsibility as a subject.[13] Delacroix suggested that men "are the passive instruments of circumstance"; Balzac declared "the surroundings command."[14] In Stendhal's *Charterhouse of Parma*, Fabrice was borne along by event after event, rarely choosing his course of action, something seen quite literally when his horse ran beyond his control and carried him into the Battle of Waterloo.[15] Finally, de Maistre stated that Providence stood behind all human actions; in the formation of constitutions "human action is so far circumscribed that the men who act become only circumstances."[16]

To the men and women of this generation, theirs was an age of rules, regulations, and routine, an age when all citizens passively adhered to the directions of external forces. In England, Carlyle labeled it the mechanical age. "Were we required to characterize this age of ours by any single epithet, we should be tempted to call it, not an Heroical, Devotional, Philosophical, or Moral Age, but, above all others, the Mechanical Age. It is the Age of Machinery, in every outward and inward sense of the word . . . all is by rule and calculated contrivance."[17]

The writings of Tocqueville's generation were replete with forebodings about machines and technology. In the opening pages of *Le Rouge et le noir,* Stendhal juxtaposed the peaceful countryside to the harsh, horrible noise of a nail factory that seemed to tyrannize over the women working there.[18] In Vigny's poetry, particularly in *La Maison du berger,* his famous diatribe against the railroads, the fear

11. Quoted in Gooch, *History and Historians in the Nineteenth Century,* p. 193.
12. Denommé, *Nineteenth Century French Romantic Poets,* p. 23.
13. Sartre, *Baudelaire,* p. 79.
14. Delacroix, *Journal,* p. 168; Balzac quoted in Marceau, *Balzac et son monde,* p. 346.
15. Stendhal, *The Charterhouse of Parma,* trans. Margaret R. B. Shaw (Baltimore, 1958), p. 62.
16. De Maistre, *On God and Society,* p. xxvi.
17. Carlyle, *Selected Writings,* "Signs of the Times," p. 64.
18. Brombert, *Stendhal: Fiction and the Themes of Freedom,* pp. 62–63.

consistently emerged that machines would dominate people.[19] The
poet Pommier suggested that decisions about the whole process of
invention and production, decisions at least as important as parliamentary issues, took place well beyond anyone's conscious control.[20]
Michelet contended that people were becoming passive while acted
upon by machines.

> What humiliation, to see, in front of the machine, man fallen so
> low! . . . The head turns, and the heart sinks, when, for the first time,
> one goes through these fairy-houses, where the iron and the copper,
> dazzling, polished, seem to go by themselves, have the appearance of
> thinking, of willing, while the weak and pale man is the humble servant
> of these giants of steel.[21]

Bonald, too, feared that individuals would eventually resemble machines; the worker "passes his life in caves and attics; and, having
become a machine himself, he exercises his fingers, but never his
mind."[22] Although the machine itself drew much attention, it represented a more comprehensive fear, the fear that people would in fact
become incapable of influencing their own destiny. As Michelet put it,
the new society would only bring new forms of servitude—workers to
machines, clerks to their desks, shopkeepers to competition, the rich
to their riches.[23]

This same fear of human beings dominated by external forces and
mechanical things can be seen in painting; Constable and the landscape painters depicted individuals as spectators rather than actors.[24]
In Corot's landscapes both buildings and nature dwarf the people,
and Corot's colors and shapes communicate the feeling that men and
women are passive and acted upon. In *Le Beffroi de Douai,* the buildings of the town dwarf the tiny men, and in such works as *A Woman
Reading, Reverie,* and *The Letter,* people are passive while nature alone
seems alive and active.[25] In Théodore Rousseau's *Sunset near Arbonne,*
the sun is tremendously active, transforming with its light the entire
countryside; the men and women present are merely components of

19. Brereton, *An Introduction to the French Poets,* p. 116; Grant, *French Poetry and
Modern Industry,* p. 28.

20. Grant, *French Poetry and Modern Industry,* p. 31.

21. Michelet, *Le Peuple,* p. 59.

22. Bonald, *Oeuvres complètes,* 2: 240.

23. Michelet, *Le Peuple,* pp. 40, 55, 91, 106, 123, 128.

24. Hauser, *The Social History of Art,* 3: 220; Edward Lucie-Smith, *A Concise History of
French Painting* (New York, 1971), pp. 197–99.

25. Maurice Sérullaz, *Corot* (Paris, 1952), passim; Charles Sterling and Margaretta
Salinger, eds., *French Paintings,* vol. 2 (New York, 1966), passim.

this altered countryside. In his *The Forest in Winter at Sunset,* perhaps Rousseau's most important work, the forest grows rapidly and jungle-like, strangling every object in its way. As one commentator put it, Rousseau "aimed at creating an imposing vision of the life of growing things, indestructible in their chaotic vitality as earth itself, majestically dwarfing humanity."[26]

All this differed sharply from the previous century. To take but one example, David, when imprisoned in Belgium, painted a landscape from his room. Although some of its symmetric and geometric nature can be attributed to his portraying the outskirts of a city, the painting communicates the feeling that people had ordered nature for their own benefit, that people had mastered nature and not vice versa. He borrowed his technique from Poussin, but his confidence came from the Enlightenment. Similarly, Bonald regretted replacing the more symmetric and designed French gardens with the less or-dered and more natural English gardens, and indeed this question of the merits of English and French gardens was raised frequently in the literature of this period. Although for some people the English gar-den was more "natural," for others, such as Bonald, the English gar-den demonstrated that people no longer had confidence in them-selves to shape nature and society to conform to their own needs.

The rise of the novel, an art form preeminently concerned with private interests and aspirations, by itself signified this sense of powerlessness. The characters of Corneille and Racine saved nations and became the heroic objects of public acclaim, whereas the charac-ters of Balzac and Flaubert became the victims of the forces imping-ing on their private lives. As Hannah Arendt stated:

> The elevation of chance to the position of final arbiter over the whole of life was to reach its full development in the nineteenth century. With it came a new genre of literature, the novel, and the decline of the drama. For the drama became meaningless in a world without action, while the novel could deal adequately with the destinies of human beings who were either the victims of necessity or the favorites of luck.[27]

Beyond this, it was feared that people would more and more experi-ence the world at one distance removed. Stendhal claimed that mod-ern man, if walking by a house on fire, would choose to ignore it and forego its fear and excitement, all in order to read about it in the newspaper the following day.[28]

26. Sterling and Salinger, *French Paintings,* 2: 84–85.
27. Hannah Arendt, *The Origins of Totalitarianism,* 2d rev. ed. (New York, 1958), p. 141.
28. Quoted in Graña, *Bohemian versus Bourgeois,* p. 111.

An Age of Insignificant People and Petty Ambition

Throughout this period, men and women perceived themselves as small in relation to men and women of past ages. Bonald claimed that in the past "there were great persons and beautiful sentiments; in our time, there are obscure persons and small passions."[29] In his terrifying poem, *Les Petites vieilles*, Baudelaire depicted several old women who, after a full life in the France of his time, were buried in coffins no bigger than a child's.[30] Gautier captured this feeling in his poem about a spring. A spring bubbled up from the ground, announcing itself to the sunlight with great ambitions of becoming a river.

> Bathing the valleys, rocks and towers.
> And I shall embroider with my foam
> Stone bridges, aye, and granite quays;
> I'll bear great steamers which will roam
> And smoke upon the boundless seas.

But such dreams were destined to fail in nineteenth-century France.

> But the cradle is neighbor to the tomb;
> The future giant perishes small:
> No sooner born than it meets its doom
> In the near-by lake that engulfs it all![31]

No line could better sum up this generation's feeling of insignificance than "the future giant perishes small"; in their own eyes, theirs was an age of powerless, mediocre individuals, an age of dwarfs.

Comparing themselves with a romanticized image of Frenchmen of the eighteenth century, with the giants of the Revolution, and with the heroes of Napoleon's armies, these writers of the nineteenth century erected a standard by which they could judge their age to be petty and servile. Consider Michelet: "Man, poor and alone, surrounded by immense objects, enormous collective forces which drag him along, without him understanding them, feels himself weak, humiliated. He has none of that pride that formerly rendered his individual genius powerful."[32] Referring to the pensioners of Napoleon's army, Vigny declared, "These men seemed to us the survivors of a giant race which was dying out, man by man, and forever"; Baude-

---

29. Bonald, *Oeuvres complètes*, 2: 29.

30. Charles Baudelaire, *Flowers of Evil*, trans. Jackson Mathews et al., ed. Marthiel Mathews and Jackson Mathews (New York, 1955), p. 89.

31. Quoted in Conder, ed., *A Treasury of French Poetry*, p. 225.

32. Michelet, *Le Peuple*, p. 145.

laire remembered fondly "that race of strong men, the last of whom
we knew in our childhood."[33]

The desire for glory, courage, or creativity was not lacking; many
a young man shared Delacroix's sentiment when he said, "I will be the
trumpeter of those who do great things."[34] Although the desire to
perform great deeds persisted, the opportunity seemed lost, because
the philistines of their age bartered the chance for glory to obtain the
petty pleasures of accumulating possessions. As Stendhal's Lucien
Leuwen said, "What could be more stupid and meanly bourgeois?
What a ferocious passion for anything connected with money! And
these are the progeny of the conquerors of Charles the Bold!"[35] Juxtaposed to the small passions of their age, the aristocracy of the past,
however oppressive these writers judged it to be, seemed courageous
and enlightened. Nerval, in his poem *Nobles et valets*, portrayed the
"mighty" noble of the past whose children had become "cringing,
greedy, and degraded," a collection of "frail fellows, corsetted, wearing chest-pads and false calves."[36]

The potential greatness of individuals never blossomed because
bourgeois culture did not provide a fertile soil from which their potentials might surface. It was, as Rousseau said of his own age, "an age
when it is impossible for anyone to be good."[37] Stendhal's Lucien,
who—we are told—would have been a great man in another age,
became somewhat laughable in the July Monarchy.[38] Again, in *Lucien
Leuwen*, "The colonel, who was once a brave soldier, under the magic
wand of the *Juste-milieu* is transformed into a filthy policeman."[39]
When Lucien journeyed to the provincial town of Nancy early in the
book, he passed through an almost surreal area of barren, stony, flat
land; Stendhal commented that "nothing could possibly grow in that
barren and stony ground," a powerful metaphor suggesting that the
fertile culture required to produce great statesmen, courageous soldiers, and exceptional artists was desolate.[40] In a similar way, Stendhal argued that this culture stunted the intellectual and creative
growth of women, for in the July Monarchy their only function was to

33. Alfred de Vigny, *The Military Necessity*, trans. Humphrey Hare (London, 1952),
p. 119; Baudelaire, *Selected Writings on Art and Artists*, p. 374.
34. Delacroix, *Journal*, p. 41.
35. Stendhal, *Lucien Leuwen*, 1: 298.
36. Nerval, *Selected Writings*, p. 189.
37. Rousseau, *Eloisa*, 1: lv.
38. Raymond Giraud, "Romantic Realism in *Lucien Leuwen*," in Victor Brombert,
ed., *Stendhal* (Englewood Cliffs, N.J., 1962), p. 66.
39. Stendhal, *Lucien Leuwen*, 2: 7.
40. Ibid., 1: 34.

bear children and display the goods purchased by their husbands. Stendhal, however, disputed the bourgeois claim that this was the "natural" status of women, that women were less able and less capable of intelligent concentration. "A Paris idler who once took a walk in the Versailles Gardens concluded that, judging from all he saw, the trees grow ready trimmed."[41] In a better culture, in a better era, both men and women would more become more creative and more intelligent.

Not surprisingly, having seen that the writers of this time regretted not being able to live in the past, and having witnessed their despair at being forced to live in a century so undistinguished, we find they often looked to the future. Nerval said, "They will come back, those Gods whom you forever mourn/ For time shall see the order of old days reborn."[42] The most famous and eloquent statement of this feeling was one by Saint-Simon: "The most absurd belief places the Golden Age in the past. It is the future alone which holds it in store. Giants will return, not giants in stature, but giants in the power of reasoning. Machines will replace the arms of men."[43] When Vigny likened poems to bottles cast at sea destined for future travelers who could understand the message, and when Stendhal talked of writing for the men and women of the twentieth century, they were expressing this hope that the future would be more grand.

This feeling that the age was petty generated a curious fascination with war and crime. The clue to understanding the significance of this fascination emerged in Stendhal's worry that individuals would no longer have the courage and passion needed to commit a great crime.[44] Wrenching people from an existence of boredom and routine, crime displayed all the passions that individuals seemed to be losing. Looking to the lower classes that contained the only individuals capable of such acts of energy and passion, Stendhal declared that "in France it is the galleys that bring together the most remarkable men." After a well-educated but very poor man named Laffargue had murdered his mistress, Stendhal said, "Probably all great men will henceforth emerge from the class to which M. Laffargue belongs."[45] Balzac's inimitable Vautrin, described as a "man of the people in revolt against authority," furnished another example of this fascination with crime. Vautrin was a man "constrained to live outside

41. Quoted in Simone de Beauvoir, "Stendhal or the Romantic of Reality," in Brombert, ed., *Stendhal*, pp. 147–48.

42. Quoted in Flores, *An Anthology of French Poetry*, p. 12.

43. Quoted in Manuel, *The New World of Henri Saint-Simon*, p. 191.

44. Hauser, *The Social History of Art*, 4: 39.

45. Quoted in Levin, *The Gates of Horn*, pp. 115–16.

the world into which the law forbade him ever to enter again, drained by vice and by furious, by terrible oppositions, but endowed with a force of soul which devoured him." In short, preoccupied not with the domestic virtues of a family and a comfortable home, not with the routine life of the bourgeois world, Vautrin was a man of passion. "For him, Lucien was more than a son, more than a beloved woman, more than a family, more than his life, Lucien was his revenge," a revenge on a corrupt and petty world.[46] As long as men of such passion live, Balzac seemed to be hinting, the world would not be devoured by the pettiness of the Gobsecks and the Grandets. Crime, in this sense, was a cause for hope.

Indeed, we can see a similar idea in the statement made by Julien Sorel to a startled Mathilde: "In a word, Mademoiselle, must a man who wants to drive ignorance and crime off this earth pass through it like a whirlwind and do evil indiscriminately?"[47] Regardless of how much these Frenchmen shuddered at the oppressions committed by their aristocratic ancestors, regardless of how much they condemned the crimes of the giant figures of the Revolution, some seemed secretly to harbor a sense of pride that these, their ancestors, had the courage and passion to transform the world, actions that towered above the insignificance and pettiness of their own century.

TOCQUEVILLE'S FEAR OF POWERLESSNESS

Once more, Tocqueville shared his generation's concerns. For example, despite the fact that several of his relatives had been guillotined in the Terror, we never once find the sort of denunciation of the Revolution, or even of the Terror, that we might expect. Indeed, he greatly admired the year 1789: "It was [a year] of incomparable grandeur, it will never be effaced from the memory of mankind. All foreign nations witnessed it, applauded it, were moved by it."[48] Even though Tocqueville disapproved of the Terror, in a strange way he too was proud that his country was capable of what he considered a grand crime. Discussing the exhausted France of 1799, he wrote, "Men thus crushed cannot only no longer attain great virtues, but they seem to have become almost incapable of great crimes."[49] In an early work on Sicily he wrote, "distorted by oppression, that hidden strength reveals

46. Balzac, *A Harlot High and Low*, pp. 337, 91.

47. Stendhal, *Scarlet and Black*, trans. Margaret R. B. Shaw (Baltimore, 1953), pp. 309–10.

48. Tocqueville, *The European Revolution and Correspondence with Gobineau*, p. 86.

49. Ibid., p. 125.

itself only by criminal acts."[50] Although the crimes themselves did not attract him, the capacity to commit them did, precisely because the passion and energy needed to commit great crimes can often accomplish great good. By contrast, the routine and petty virtues of bourgeois society could attain, he felt, only mediocrity.

If Tocqueville did not share Stendhal's enthusiasm for lower-class crime (indeed he talked of curing it[51]), he did exhibit a fascination with war. Certainly Tocqueville recognized and expounded the pernicious effects of war: it is murderous, it centralizes governments, it destroys freedom. But whereas Turgot, Condorcet, Comte, Saint-Simon, Constant, and Guizot looked forward to the day when the commercial instinct would replace the aristocratic military instinct, Tocqueville more often shared with the artists of his generation that longing for personal courage manifested in the military grandeur of ancient France. It is true that he acknowledged in one passage that "commerce is naturally the enemy of war," but consider this surprising sentence in *Democracy:* "I do not wish to speak ill of war; war almost always enlarges the mind of a people and raises their character."[52] Later in his life, after reading about the Crimean war, he wrote to Reeve about the "profound emotion" he was experiencing. "What gigantic efforts! What energy, what manly and heroic virtues come spontaneously from the breast of these societies which seemed to be sleeping in well-being."[53] Further, when in 1840–41 it appeared that France might go to war as a result of some badly handled diplomatic affairs, Tocqueville wrote to Beaumont that certainly war was not desirable, and if begun, France would again stand alone against the rest of Europe and probably lose. "These wise reflections do not prevent me, at the bottom of my heart, from seeing all this crisis with a certain satisfaction. You know what a taste I have for great events and how tired I am of our little democratic and bourgeois pot of soup."[54] Tocqueville considered war as one means of wrenching a society from an infatuation with the routine affairs of private life, by thrusting people out of their petty affairs, by forcing them to cooperate, by bringing forth leaders with courage and imagination, and by compelling individuals to think of the public good.

The most striking example of this sentiment emerged in a letter written to Mill in 1841 at a moment when war threatened to break out

50. Tocqueville, *Memoir*, 1: 129.

51. See Roger Boesche, "The Prison: Tocqueville's Model for Despotism," *Western Political Quarterly* 33 (December 1980).

52. Tocqueville, *Oeuvres* (B), vol. 9, *Études économiques, politiques,* p. 194; *Democracy,* 2: 283.

53. Tocqueville, *Oeuvres* (M), vol. 6, pt. 1, *Correspondance anglaise,* p. 148.

54. Tocqueville, *Selected Letters,* p. 143.

between France and England. In France, Tocqueville wrote, three possible positions in regard to this war were taking shape: one group wanted war either for its own interests or for the revolution that might issue from it; another group desired to avoid war at any cost, largely because of fear; the third group, Tocqueville's own, found itself somewhere in-between. Although he did not approve of the first group desiring either war or revolution, he considered the second group to be even "more perilous." Strangely, he began the letter by assuming that Mill would agree with him.

> I do not have to tell you, my dear Mill, that the greatest malady that threatens a people organized as we are is the gradual softening of mores, the abasement of the mind, the mediocrity of tastes; that is where the great dangers of the future lie. One cannot let a nation that is democratically constituted like ours and in which the natural vices of the race unfortunately coincide with the natural vices of the social state, one cannot let this nation take up easily the habit of sacrificing what it believes to be its grandeur to its repose, great matters to petty ones; it is not healthy to allow such a nation to believe that its place in the world is smaller, that it is fallen from the level on which its ancestors had put it, but that it must console itself by making railroads and by making prosper in the bosom of this peace, under whatever condition this peace is obtained, the well-being of each private individual. It is necessary that those who march at the head of such a nation should always keep a proud attitude, if they do not wish to allow the level of national mores to fall very low.[55]

He continued by stating that the government made threats, and then, when war seemed probable, "a large part of the middle class gave an example of the weakness and the egoism that is peculiar to it. It asked loudly that they yield, that war be avoided at all cost. The stampede was general, because the example had come from the top. Do you believe that such circumstances could be repeated without wearing out a people?" In Tocqueville's opinion, France could not become submissive; in order to maintain its own sense of pride, it was sometimes necessary to go to war. Otherwise, by losing its self-confidence, its sense of historical purpose, and its grandeur, France would take steps toward becoming a country of "material enjoyments and small pleasures."

In response, Mill was shocked that Tocqueville would stress the importance of national glory, or at least the "low and grovelling" idea of national glory that the French nation (and by implication

---

55. For this quotation and the next two in the text, see ibid., pp. 150–52.

Tocqueville) displayed. National glory, claimed Mill, is not a "bois-terous assertion of importance" but "industry, instruction, morality, and good government." Indeed, the rest of the world considered French leaders to be "sulky schoolboys" displaying "simple peurility."[56] Although both Mill and Tocqueville desired a pros-perous, well-governed country, Tocqueville felt that a nation without pride, absorbed in its private pursuits and its commercial prosperity, would attain no greatness because it lacked that sense of self-impor-tance that would impel it to achieve some historical purpose. Stable government and prosperous industry *can*, although they do not al-ways, suffocate all sense of purpose, because tranquillity, prosperity, and the atomization of society can lead to sterility and an anxiety about the smallest political change. For this reason Tocqueville had minimal enthusiasm about the commercial spirit replacing the mili-tary spirit. Although he never sought war, he acknowledged that war could engender greatness, whereas avoiding war in order to ensure prosperity condemned a nation to the petty pursuit of mere wealth.

This sentiment becomes more understandable when we recognize that Tocqueville shared the belief that individuals of his time were small and petty. "There has never been anything smaller than our time."[57] It is a century of "grand movements . . . in the middle of which each man feels himself so weak and so small."[58] In his note-books on America he wrote, "Why as civilization spreads do outstand-ing men become fewer?" and "We have not yet met a really outstand-ing man."[59] With the passing of great figures, the French nation had lost the courage, the self-reliance, and the public spiritedness of its ancestors, virtues replaced by mere covetousness and vanity. "Our fathers observed such extraordinary things that compared with them all of our works seem commonplace."[60]

Likening the petty people of his time to "dwarfs" riding on a wave, Tocqueville argued that each individual was powerless: "We live in a time and in a democratic society where individuals, even the greatest, are very little of anything."[61] The French busy themselves with petty concerns that torment and stultify those with grand ambition. The political world of his day, characterized by "pettiness," "unsightly passions," and a "swarm of microscopic interests," could boast only of

56. Tocqueville, *Oeuvres* (M), vol. 6, pt. 1, *Correspondance anglaise*, pp. 337–38.
57. Tocqueville, *Oeuvres* (B), vol. 7, *Nouvelle correspondance*, p. 196.
58. Tocqueville, *Oeuvres* (B), vol. 9, *Études économiques, politiques*, p. 115.
59. Tocqueville, *Journey to America*, pp. 161, 290.
60. Seymour Drescher, ed. and trans., *Tocqueville and Beaumont on Social Reform* (New York, 1968), p. 137.
61. Tocqueville, *Oeuvres* (M), vol. 8, pt. 2, *Correspondance . . . Beaumont*, p. 369.

small people and unimportant events that could not foster "noble emotions" but instead could only "torment, agitate, and persecute one's life at each instant."[62]

Thus, Tocqueville looked to the past for examples of greatness. Consider his discussion of Plutarch. Although the French of Tocqueville's time were often as learned and as powerful as the ancient Greeks, the Greeks had a remarkable ability, even in the midst of their weaknesses, never to abandon the sentiment of "beauty and moral loftiness." Upon reading Plutarch's description of ancient times, Tocqueville wrote: "What strikes me the most about our days is not that people do such small things, it is that they do not better conceive the *theory* of grand things."[63] The men about whom Plutarch wrote were not perfect, Tocqueville said, "but they are grand, and, in our century, it is grandeur for which one is so bold to hunger."[64]

Similarly, the eighteenth century furnished a past example that compared favorably with the pettiness of the present. "It is difficult to conceive the degree of pride in these forefathers of ours. When one reads the literature of the time, one is amazed at the tremendous opinion that Frenchmen of all ranks had at that time of their country and of their race, at their superb self-confidence."[65] In this discussion of the eighteenth century, however, it is easy to discern where Tocqueville placed the blame for the pettiness of his own age: namely, on its commercial character. "The French were not yet a manufacturing, a commercial, a proprietary people; their material interests did not yet coincide with the tranquillity of State. They had not yet fully acquired the taste for material comforts; they were more preoccupied with ideas and sentiments."[66] Tocqueville longed for a better past, in part because he longed for personal glory. Even in 1848, despite his disapproval of the February Revolution, he wrote Beaumont that "Perhaps such a moment will present itself in which the action we would undertake could be glorious."[67] In a letter to Royer-Collard in 1841 he stated:

> It seems to me, however, that in other times and with other men, I could have done better. But will the times improve? And will the men we see, will they be replaced by better or at least by *worse*? I would be

62. Tocqueville, *Oeuvres* (B), vol. 7, *Nouvelle correspondance*, pp. 196–97.

63. Tocqueville, *Oeuvres* (M), vol. 11, *Correspondance . . . Royer-Collard . . . Ampère*, pp. 60–61.

64. Tocqueville, *Oeuvres* (M), vol. 15, pt. 1, *Correspondance . . . Corcelle*, p. 97.

65. Tocqueville, *The European Revolution and Correspondence with Gobineau*, p. 84.

66. Ibid., p. 109.

67. Tocqueville, *Oeuvres* (M), vol. 8, pt. 2, *Correspondance . . . Beaumont*, p. 13.

disappointed about this last change for the country, but not for myself. Because the true nightmare of our period is in not perceiving before oneself anything either to love or to hate, but only to despise.[68]

Like so many of his generation, Tocqueville dreamed of "other times" and "other men."

But the belief that he was living in an age of mediocrity, isolation, and pettiness led him to the conviction that all were rapidly becoming powerless in the face of political and historical developments. In a letter written in 1851 he complained that "the most salient characteristic of the times is the powerlessness of both men and of governments on the general movement of both ideas and political events."[69] This powerlessness sprang from the social atomization that deprived people of the habit of acting together. Admiring the ability of Americans to cooperate with one another, Tocqueville paused to compare this trait with the characteristics of Europeans, preeminently the French. In Europe, argued Tocqueville, individuals regarded themselves as "settlers" who were "indifferent" to the decisions of their communities. The condition of streets and churches, the practices of police and juries—all were of no concern; the European "looks upon all these things as unconnected with himself and as the property of a powerful stranger whom he calls the government."[70] In a speech before the Chamber of Deputies in 1842, Tocqueville scoffed at those who felt that France was most endangered by turmoil and agitation in the streets; a greater danger was the growing privatization of society that separates individuals and renders each one powerless. "More and more," he said, "each seems to retire into himself and to isolate himself." Provinces, departments, and districts all seemed to regard politics as a game in which one gains some advantage of self-interest, and as a consequence each citizen ignored public concerns, retiring into a private sphere and into the "contemplation of his individual and personal interest."[71] This isolation nourished the ever-present sensation of powerlessness.

> When the inhabitant of a democratic country compares himself individually with all those about him, he feels pride that he is the equal of any one of them; but when he comes to survey the totality of his fellows and to place himself in contrast with so huge a body, he is instantly overwhelmed by the sense of his own insignificance and weakness. The

68. Tocqueville, *Selected Letters*, p. 155.
69. Tocqueville, *Oeuvres* (M), vol. 15, pt. 2, *Correspondance . . . Corcelle*, p. 48.
70. Tocqueville, *Democracy*, 1: 96.
71. Tocqueville, *Oeuvres* (B), vol. 9, *Études économiques, politiques*, pp. 375–76.

same equality that renders him independent of each of his fellow citizens, taken severally, exposes him alone and unprotected to the influence of the greater number.[72]

Thus Tocqueville, like so many of his contemporaries, linked the
sense of powerlessness both to the severing of traditional ties and to
the subsequent encouragement of individuals to pursue mainly private interests.

One last point should be mentioned. Tocqueville revealed a personal ambivalence toward the idea that his age was dominated by fate
or historical forces that people could not control. On the one hand, he
used this kind of argument when he suggested that the historical
tendency toward more equality was irreversible; he even went so far
as to say that "the gradual development of the principle of equality is,
therefore, a providential fact."[73] On the other hand, when his contemporaries argued in a similar fashion that "things are in the saddle"—to use Emerson's phrase—that fate or God or material forces
were rendering people powerless to direct history, he objected stren-
uously. As a very young man he wrote that any arguments of historical determinism were "false and cowardly doctrines, which can produce only weak individuals and faint-hearted nations."[74] Historians
of democratic times, he argued, tend to attribute historical change to
forces beyond human control, whereas historians of aristocratic times
see all historical developments as the result of the "particular will and
character of certain individuals."[75] The tendency of historians in
democratic ages to deny the ability of individuals to direct history—
the tendency, that is, to suggest that factors of race or climate or
economic forces determine everything and human will nothing—
arises from the very sense of individual insignificance and powerlessness characteristic of democratic times.

When, on the contrary, all the citizens are independent of one another,
and each of them is individually weak, no one is seen to exert a great or
still less a lasting power over the community. At first sight individuals
appear to be absolutely devoid of any influence over it. . . .

Historians who live in democratic ages . . . deprive the people themselves of the power of modifying their own condition, and they subject
them either to an inflexible Providence or to some blind necessity.[76]

72. Tocqueville, *Democracy*, 2: 11.
73. Ibid., 1: 6.
74. Quoted in Mayer, *Alexis de Tocqueville*, p. 5.
75. Tocqueville, *Democracy*, 2: 90.
76. Ibid., pp. 90–93.

Individuals, Tocqueville argued, have the opportunity to combine and to act, and for this reason he scoffed at historians who claimed that unseen forces determine events, thus "banishing men from the history of the human race."[77] For this reason Tocqueville reacted angrily to his friend Gobineau's book that maintained racial characteristics foretold the inevitable decline of Europe. The public acclaim and even welcome of this book, he told Gobineau, was no sign of its accuracy, only a symptom of an age in which men and women, feeling themselves to be powerless, sought to explain events by invoking forces beyond their control. While this book was emphatically wrong it was also dangerous, because such a fatalistic argument reinforced France's prostrated belief about itself. The consequence of Gobineau's argument was "a very great contraction, if not a complete abolition, of human liberty."[78]

Yet despite his anger, Tocqueville's own ambivalence surfaced in other passages where he spoke of the same powerlessness of individuals and a similar belief in determining forces. For instance, in writing to Beaumont he discussed how freedom might be restored to France under the Second Empire; instead of suggesting that one use political organization, he looked at some accident of history to overturn the Empire. "An unforeseen circumstance, a new turn of affairs, any accident can lead to extraordinary events that would force each to come out of his hole."[79] In his study of India, Tocqueville claimed that England conquered India not because of the particular people involved but because of a series of historical needs and impersonal historical forces. In a remarkable statement for one who denied that external forces dominated men and women, he claimed that "in the long run, institutions are always stronger than men."[80] Finally, in discussing European colonization of the world, he wrote to Reeve that in the nineteenth century, "the men are small, but the events are great."[81]

Tocqueville's ambivalence is not hard to explain. He found his century dull, detestable, dwarfish—a century in which individuals felt powerless because they had become isolated and had lost all habits of acting together. When confronted by writers such as Gobineau who seemed to encourage a passive acceptance of fatalism, Tocqueville

---

77. Tocqueville, *Recollections*, p. 78.
78. Tocqueville, *Selected Letters*, p. 298.
79. Tocqueville, *Oeuvres* (M), vol. 8, pt. 3, *Correspondance . . . Beaumont*, p. 543.
80. Alexis de Tocqueville, *L'Inde*, in *Oeuvres* (M), vol. 3, *Écrits et discours politiques*, p. 467.
81. Tocqueville, *Oeuvres* (M), vol. 6, pt. 1, *Correspondance anglaise*, p. 58.

reacted bitterly, trying to encourage his contemporaries to shoulder a sense of pride, purpose, and belief in the efficacy of political action. We will see later that his discussion of the concept of freedom was, in large part, a reaction to the pettiness and sense of powerlessness that he felt were characteristic of his age. In all these sentiments, Tocqueville proved himself again to be part of his generation. But he agreed with them even further when they blamed the troubles of their age on the new commercial classes.

4 Belittling Bourgeois Society

Historical studies indicate that the July Monarchy, despite being called a "bourgeois monarchy," was in reality an oligarchy composed of landowners—a high percentage of whom, however, had purchased their land from profits made in commerce or industry. Moreover, social historians object to using the word *bourgeoisie* interchangeably with the term middle class, as if these entities were the same. In fact, the industrialists of the July Monarchy mixed traditionalism with free-market liberalism, the mentality of the old bourgeois with that of the new middle-class entrepreneur, and finally a paternalistic sympathy toward workers characteristic of the Old Regime with a harsh workplace discipline appropriate to rapid industrialization.[1] Historical studies notwithstanding, the overwhelming *perception* of Tocqueville's generation was that the bourgeoisie had come to power and that this class was strongly unified by a common ethic and common interests. As a result, Tocqueville's generation sought to blame its problems on the practices and ethos of the new bourgeois society. For this reason, the present study has dropped all attempts both to distinguish between the bourgeoisie and the middle class and to demonstrate the enormous variety in attitudes and practices among French industrialists of this period.

1. Alfred Cobban, *A History of Modern France*, vol. 2, *From the First Empire to the Second Empire, 1799–1871*, 2d ed. (Baltimore, 1965), p. 98; Stearns, *Paths to Authority*, pp. 3, 108–10, 134, 181–82. Tocqueville himself consciously borrowed from Guizot's discussion of the middle class, confessed that he found the phrase "middle classes" entirely too vague, and frequently used the word *bourgeois* and the phrase "middle class" interchangeably. (See, for example, Yale Tocqueville Collection, C.V.k., Paquet No. 7, Cahier No. 1, pp. 21–22.)

FEAR OF THE NEW MIDDLE-CLASS SOCIETY

In the popular press, the blame for society's ills fell constantly upon the new middle class. The working-class newspaper *L'Atelier*, advocating a "deliverance from capitalist servitude," complained that the word *freedom*, used nobly by the ruling bourgeoisie, only supported those who were responsible for the pettiness and deterioration of France. "In our day, how is freedom understood by this high bourgeoisie that so often clamored for it, if not as the ability to squander away the national fortune and to keep the people in perpetual industrial serfdom?"[2] Even *Le National*, a liberal newspaper with an audience composed of middle-class readers profiting from the new capitalism while seeking mild reforms, was cynical about what it called the new "oligarchy of the bourgeoisie" or the "aristocracy of capitalism."[3] The doctrine of *"chacun chez soi, chacun pour soi"* seemed to *Le National* to be a "stupid maxim of egoism," and all the prosperity brought by the new capitalism did not make up for the political and moral decay.[4] "Among the material advantages that have been promised to France, in exchange for moral and political advantages that still have not been given to the country, the railroads have always held a prime spot. Whenever one speaks of national honor, of the rights of citizens, of the emancipation of the working classes, the newspapers that support the present ministry respond with dithyrambs about the railroads."[5]

The harshest indictment of the new bourgeois society came from the conservative newspaper *La Gazette de France*. Claiming that the bourgeoisie constituted a new aristocracy with a monopoly on government, the *Gazette* blamed the middle class for everything from business decline to the alleged corruption of philosophy and literature.[6] In the *Gazette* one seems to find the pent-up and vicious anger of an aristocracy that had been supplanted in historical struggles and now despised its enemy.

> We have a government of the middle class: this phrase explains our entire decline. At all times, in France, it is in this class that one has found the petty and vulgar ideas against which the instinct of grandeur inherent in the national spirit has protested. "This is bourgeois" was always a sentence of disdain used to characterize triviality of manners, of language, or of actions. Indeed, the sentiments carried in the calcula-

2. *L'Atelier*, January 1844; May 1841.
3. *Le National*, September 29, 1841; January 24, 1844.
4. *Le National*, January 1, 1842.
5. *Le National*, October 22, 1841.
6. *La Gazette de France*, June 28, 1840; November 7, 1842.

tions about money, in the intellectual mediocrity, in the mercantile spirit, in the narrow and fearful egoism that seeks to find a material advantage in everything and places interest above honor—these sentiments have always been antipathetical to the French character.[7]

Remarkably, the *Gazette* continued by saying that the *sans-culottes* of 1793 did less harm to the public interest than the practical "cupidity" of the bourgeoisie, because although "France has a horror of blood, it has an even greater horror of filth."[8] In the eyes of the *Gazette*, the emergence of the bourgeoisie was the final sign of the nation's decline; it quoted Bacon to the effect that in a nation's youth the military rules, at its height one finds a rule by wisdom (i.e., an aristocracy), and in a nation's eclipse "business and the mechanical arts flourish."[9]

Imbued with a sense of powerlessness, troubled by a conviction that theirs was a century of pettiness, Tocqueville's generation rebelled in two different ways against the ascent of the middle class to both economic and political power. First, the literary men and women responded to the new order with an expression of intellectual disgust, a hunger for a past age thought to be more intellectually profound, and a wish to have been a writer or a great conversationalist in an eighteenth-century salon. Exemplifying this view, Stendhal's Julien Sorel contended that great men in past ages had to vanquish danger and fear, but who, in previous centuries, ever had to struggle against disgust? "Man's will is strong; I read it everywhere, but is it strong enough to overcome disgust like this? . . . Who but myself can understand the ugliness around me!"[10]

The second route was more political. Having embraced the ideas of people such as Saint-Simon and Fourier, many of the young writers and artists of France dreamed not of recreating the past but of constructing a future.

What passed from Saint-Simon and Fourier into the writings of the Romanticists was their criticism of society, of its customs, usages, and morality, of its selfishness and greed as exemplified in the wealthy bourgeoisie . . . of its oppression of women to whom it refuses equality with man, of its toleration of idlers and parasites who live at the expense of those who work, of corruption . . . ; and in the second place, their insistence on the need of a reform which should broaden the moral and intellectual, the social and economic base of the state so as to provide justice and equality for the masses.[11]

7. *La Gazette de France*, March 21, 1841.
8. Ibid.
9. *La Gazette de France*, May 4, 1843.
10. Stendhal, *Scarlet and Black*, p. 199.
11. Clement, *Romanticism in France*, p. 251.

Of the two revolts against the bourgeoisie, the former walked the sidewalks of Flaubert and Baudelaire, and the latter led to the doorstep of Blanquism, anarchism, and Marxism. Although Tocqueville occasionally sympathized with the social critiques of Saint-Simon and Fourier, to an even greater extent he shared the disgust, expressed by the artists and writers of his generation, for the new bourgeois society. But why such a disgust?

A World in Which Everything Is for Sale

To begin with, the writers of this time felt that art and "civilization" were passing from the world. Delacroix, for one, deplored the loss of intelligent conversation, an authentic art to those Frenchmen recalling the salons of the previous century. "The people who pride themselves on being high society are practically unaware of the extent to which they are deprived of real society. . . . It is a rare thing to find people with minds."[12] The decline of art was a recurrent theme of Delacroix's *Journal,* and he complained frequently of a "decadence of the works of the mind."[13] Lukács remarked that the eclipse of culture was Balzac's greatest fear; Balzac's character Cousin Pons, an art collector commenting on Dresden China, said "they manufactured wonderful things in those days, such as will never be produced again."[14] In one introduction to *Flowers of Evil,* Baudelaire proclaimed that "no respect for humanity, no false modesty, no conspiracy, no universal suffrage will ever force me to speak the unspeakable jargon of this age."[15]

But what engendered this "unspeakable jargon," this loss of intelligence and culture? Perhaps we can find the key in a statement by Ruskin, who argued that those who entered business, those who strained to secure markets for their goods, would create tastes by manipulating tastes. "But whatever happens to you, this, at least, is certain, that the whole of your life will have been spent in corrupting public taste and encouraging public extravagance. . . . Your life has been successful in retarding the arts, tarnishing the virtues, and confusing the manners of your country."[16] The commercialism fostered by the ruling middle classes became identified as the enemy. While

12. Delacroix, *Journal,* p. 471.
13. Ibid., p. 217.
14. Honoré de Balzac, *Cousin Pons,* trans. Herbert J. Hunt (Baltimore, 1968), p. 50.
15. Baudelaire, *Flowers of Evil,* p. xii.
16. Quoted in Williams, *Culture and Society,* p. 144.

Berlioz contended "trade and art are mortal enemies," Vigny claimed "spiritual man [is] smothered by a materialistic society."[17] Similarly, Balzac's character Lucien suffered great ridicule when he announced he wanted to be a great writer, because, as his critics said, he still clung to "his illusions" about art, refusing to realize that literature was a "business proposition."[18]

Art became commercialized partly because of the new economic status of the artist. No longer directly dependent on a portion of the wealthiest classes, the artist drifted alone, attempting to sell his work in the marketplace.[19] No longer the champion of the Church or of a dominant landed class, no longer the frequent defender of established social values, the best artist often became the misunderstood genius expressing a personal awareness of suffering, whereas the worst artist became a mere salesman profiting from a hectic, urban market.

When Courbet promised himself that he would make a living "without ever painting, even as much as can be covered by a hand, only to please anyone or to sell more easily," he was expressing a widespread conviction that writers and artists must resist the transformation of all valuable things, including art, into commodities.[20] Just as Berlioz burned a symphony fearing that it was so different and unappealing that it might impoverish him, Schubert wrote certain music for his more learned friends and other music for financial success. Lamartine consciously prostituted his prose (though never his poetry) to pay off his debts.[21] In some cases, writing became a profitable business; Dumas's *Capitaine Paul* was so popular that it increased the circulation of the newspaper in which it was published by 110,000 in just three weeks![22] Entertainment, not art, assumed the central position; Scribe, who openly viewed the theater as a "financial institution," declared that when he had outlined the plot, he "had nothing more to do," and this was a claim from the most popular

17. Berlioz quoted in Barzun, *Berlioz and His Century*, p. 386; Vigny quoted in Jean Giraud, *L'École romantique française: Les doctrines and les hommes* (Paris, 1927), p. 121.

18. Honoré de Balzac, *Lost Illusions*, trans. Herbert J. Hunt (Baltimore, 1971), p. 354.

19. Hauser, *The Social History of Art*, 4: 6; Einstein, *Music in the Romantic Era*, pp. 10–16, 37.

20. Quoted in E. H. Gombrich, *The Story of Art*, 11th ed. rev. (New York, 1966), p. 385.

21. Rey M. Longyear, *Nineteenth-Century Romanticism in Music* (Englewood Cliffs, N.J., 1969), p. 94; Einstein, *Music in the Romantic Era*, p. 39; Brereton, *Introduction to the French Poets*, p. 96.

22. Albert Joseph George, *The Development of French Romanticism* (Syracuse, 1955), p. 153.

playwright of this era.[23] Moreover, it was widely known, and eventually proved, that Dumas sequestered an army of writers to churn out stories fast enough for maximum profit. (A popular joke of the time pictured Dumas asking his son, "Have you seen my latest work?" and the son replying, "No, father, have you?")[24] Finally, uniting himself with Scribe to produce a financially successful opera for the middle class, Meyerbeer, as one writer states, "used his great gifts to conceal with superb craftsmanship the emptiness of an art devoid of artistic integrity."[25] When Rossini realized what kind of opera the Parisian public was admiring, he quit in disgust and retired to Italy.[26] In sum, these writers felt, in Balzac's words, "we have no more works; we have products," or as Sainte-Beuve claimed, "money, money, one cannot say how much it is truly the nerve and the god of literature today."[27]

In addition to art, this generation of writers and artists feared that all cherished principles and traditions would be considered valuable only if they proved useful and profitable. Mourning the loss of the brave French soldiers who had vanished in Russia, Chateaubriand offered a terrible but powerful image of some profiting from the courageous death of others.

> Who gives a thought to those peasants left behind in Russia? . . . I am perhaps the only person who, on autumn evenings, watching the birds from the north flying up in the sky, remembers that they have seen the graves of our fellow countrymen. Industrial companies have gone out into the wilderness with their furnaces and their cauldrons; the bones have been turned into animal-black: whether it comes from dog or man, varnish is the same price.[28]

Stendhal satirized the idea that profit and utility should be the only criteria for action and value when his character M. de Rênal stated, "I have my trees cut to provide shade. What else is a tree made for, I can't imagine, especially when, unlike the useful walnut, it does not bring in money." Stendhal continued by saying that in a town so lovely, one might assume that the townspeople were sensitive to beau-

23. Quoted in Neil Cole Arvin, *Eugene Scribe and the French Theatre, 1815–1860* (Cambridge, Mass., 1924), pp. 7, 41.

24. Graña, *Bohemian versus Bourgeois,* p. 34; see also Hauser, *The Social History of Art,* 4: 16.

25. Lang, *Music in Western Civilization,* p. 833.

26. Ibid., p. 836.

27. Balzac quoted in Levin, *The Gates of Horn,* p. 153; Sainte-Beuve quoted in Leroy, *Histoire des idées sociales en France,* 2: 196.

28. Chateaubriand, *Memoirs,* p. 247.

ty, but instead, *"Bringing in money* is the decisive reason for everything in this little town . . . beauty attracts visitors, whose money makes the innkeepers rich [and] . . . increases the revenue of the town."[29] To so many writers and artists of Tocqueville's generation, the bourgeoisie's obsession with wealth created a world in which everything had its price—art became a commodity, courage and death became marketable, principles transformed themselves into interests, and the beauty of nature became a commercial advantage.

Producing Things at the Expense of Men and Women

The century seemed petty and the individuals small, precisely because the bourgeoisie strained to produce remarkable things instead of creating remarkable men. Sismondi, for example, resented "more braid, more pins, more threads and tissues of silk and of cotton . . . but at what an odious price they have been purchased, it is by the moral sacrifice of so many thousands of men."[30] And in England Ruskin wrote: "The great cry that rises from all our manufacturing cities, louder than their furnace blast is all in very deed for this—that we manufacture everything there except men; we blanch cotton, and strengthen steel . . . but to brighten, to strengthen, to refine or to form a single living spirit, never enters into our estimate of advantages."[31] In this view, the entire bourgeois system supported itself on the practice of using men and women to make things.

Ceaselessly, this generation objected that people were becoming insignificant morsels in a process that digested them. While Baudelaire feared men and women were becoming "marionettes," Chateaubriand grieved they would become "busy bees."[32] Again, Emma Bovary represented her time. In rebelling against the routine and mediocrity of her very bourgeois provincial town, she dreamed of an exciting age of romance, daring, and intelligence, simultaneously refusing to resign herself to the suffocation of her surroundings. Love and fantasy failed her (and by implication Flaubert suggested they would fail us as well) as a means of escape. Ultimately she succumbed. "The upshot of all Emma's yearnings for a larger and more glamorous life is that her poor little daughter, left an orphan by Emma's suicide and the death of her father, is sent to work in a cotton

29. Stendhal, *Scarlet and Black*, pp. 28–29.
30. Quoted in Leroy, *Histoire des idées sociales en France*, 2: 303.
31. Quoted in Williams, *Culture and Society*, p. 141.
32. Baudelaire, *Flowers of Evil*, p. 89; Menczer, ed., *Catholic Political Thought*, p. 101.

mill."[33] The society engendered by the productive forces of the bourgeois economy showed itself to be more powerful than this brave woman's dreams and plans. As Vigny's John Bell, the prototypical bourgeois, claimed, "The earth is mine, because I have bought it; the houses, because I have built them; the inhabitants because I lodge them; and their work because I pay for it."[34] Just as Balzac's gentle Eugénie Grandet ultimately could not resist the miserly practices of her father, and in the end adopted her father's ruthless habits of usury, so, the writers of this generation suggested, bourgeois society was irresistibly remolding the world, rendering individual men and women insignificant. "The earth is mine," proclaimed John Bell.

The Consequences of Self-Interest

Bourgeois values also nourished the privatization of life, precisely because the accumulation of wealth, unlike so many other pleasures, is invariably a private pleasure that isolates people from each other. Such privatization, in turn, inclined individuals to consider only their self-interest, their private and individualistic consumption of goods and pleasures. Indeed, Balzac delineated a distinct correlation between the new approval of self-interested actions and the demise of a sense of public duty and civic virtue.[35] Paul Valéry's claim that "comfort isolates" reflected this point accurately. People who concentrate on accumulating and enjoying possessions will gratify themselves in a private existence and eventually will sever themselves from community problems and political participation.

The French men and women of this generation denounced selfishness and egoism, two words surfacing repeatedly in indictments of bourgeois society. Vigny claimed, "it would seem that selfishness has swamped everything"; Stendhal's Julien Sorel said, "each man for himself in this desert of egoism men call life"; and Delacroix lamented "selfishness replacing all the virtues which were regarded as the safeguards of society."[36] Self-interest, they maintained, undermined happiness. Not only did men use each other (recall that Rastignac was urged to use "men and women only as horses" for his coach), but strong friendships disintegrated as men were isolated by material

33. Wilson, *The Triple Thinkers*, p. 77.
34. Quoted in Bird, *Alfred de Vigny's Chatterton*, p. 106.
35. Lukács, *Studies in European Realism*, p. 25.
36. Vigny, *The Military Necessity*, p. 204; Stendhal, *Scarlet and Black*, p. 334; Delacroix, *Journal*, p. 168.

interests, private homes, and walls and hedges. Stendhal's M. de Rênal, in a moment of desperation, said: "What unhappiness can be
compared to mine? Or what loneliness either? he cried in his rage.
Can it be, this truly pitiable man said to himself, that in my misfortune
I haven't one friend I can ask for advice?"[37] Similarly, George Sand
contended that egoism leads to unhappiness. "Egoism carries with it
its own terrible punishment. As soon as our heart grows cold toward
others, the hearts of others grow cold toward us."[38] In the new bourgeois society, this generation of writers argued, each person's primary
friend and companion will increasingly become, as with M. Grandet,
his gold and his goods.

Tocqueville's generation argued that, by condoning and often extolling a society composed of self-interested individuals, the new commercial society contributed to decadence by destroying genuine emotions. Love and affection, Balzac claimed, were becoming commodities. The men in bourgeois society, calculating in their quest for profit, repressed all feelings that appeared to thwart the "rational" pursuit
of self-interest. While the Englishman Southey declared, "in came
calculation, and out went feeling," Chateaubriand asked, "is not a
whole chain of private feelings in danger of perishing?"[39] Stendhal's
Lucien scoffed that the Ministers of his time "have never known a
moment of spontaneity," and he experienced only disgust when he
discovered the Minister for whom he worked "beside himself with joy
at having made a few thousand francs."[40] When accumulating wealth
displaces all other emotions and becomes an obsessive concern, Stendhal argued, people become "serious-minded" and calculating, entirely unaware of a panorama of emotions inside them. As Simone de
Beauvoir said of Stendhal, "Money, honors, rank, power seemed to
him the most melancholy of idols; the vast majority of men sell themselves for profit; the pedant, the man of consequence, the bourgeois,
the husband—all smother within them every spark of life and
truth."[41] When Balzac pictured his miser Grandet as economizing in
everything, even movement, the reader was struck by a powerful
image of a man confining himself in space, suppressing movement
and spontaneity, or in other words, constricting all sudden and un-

37. Stendhal, *Scarlet and Black*, p. 140.
38. Quoted in Giraud, *L'École romantique française*, p. 145.
39. Southey quoted in Williams, *Culture and Society*, p. 25; Chateaubriand quoted
in Menczer, ed., *Catholic Political Thought*, pp. 101–2.
40. Stendhal, *Lucien Leuwen*, 2: 4, 50.
41. De Beauvoir, "Stendhal or the Romantic of Reality," in Brombert, ed., *Stendhal*, p. 149.

calculated emotions.[42] In regard to bureaucrats, Michelet said: "The wisest work to make themselves forgotten; they avoid living and thinking, pretending to be non-existent, and they play this game so well that at length they do not need to pretend; they truly become what they wish to appear."[43]

The Obsession with Wealth

As people retire into a private existence, as the thirst for accumulating more goods intensifies, they become restless because their very conviction that more possessions will generate greater contentment actually transports them farther from their real needs. They assume their needs center around money and increased private enjoyment, but in fact, so the writers of this generation argued, men and women need friendship and a sense of community. This argument was the foundation for Fourier's entire system; men and women have certain irreducible "passions" or needs that remain unacknowledged in present society, needs that could be fulfilled only in Fourier's new communities.[44] Similarly, Delacroix argued that people refuse to recognize that capitalist society, while satisfying material needs through industrialization, invariably fails to fulfill human needs.

> Man makes progress in all directions: he takes command over matter, as is incontestably shown, but he does not learn how to command himself. Build your railroads and your telegraph lines, cross land and seas in the twinkling of an eye, but let us see you direct the passions as you direct gas balloons! . . . The desire for a happiness which is impossible because it would be obtained without regard to the peace of the soul always manages to place itself beside each new scientific conquest, and seems to render more distant the chimera of that happiness of the senses which people always have in mind.[45]

In addition, this generation argued that bourgeois society threatened freedom, precisely because of its emphasis on private possessions. Although in our day freedom carries such an economic connotation that it is nearly equivalent with political security and the ability to pursue economic self-interest unhindered, in the period of French history we are discussing, this economic view of freedom was

42. Balzac, *Père Goriot* and *Eugénie Grandet,* p. 302.
43. Michelet, *Le Peuple,* p. 106.
44. Charles Fourier, *Design for Utopia,* trans. Julia Franklin (New York, 1971), pp. 65–69.
45. Delacroix, *Journal,* p. 315.

just germinating. A writer such as Guizot might suggest that men and women cling to freedom only because of the wealth that accompanies it; nonetheless, we discover a much older notion, juxtaposed to Guizot's view, dating at least to Plato and adopted by a multitude of French writers, that one can become enslaved to the consumption of goods and pleasures. Even the bourgeoisie of the first decade of the nineteenth century manifested few of the characteristics of their counterparts a few decades later; they too resisted an enslavement to things.

> To this group [i.e., a patrician bourgeoisie situated just below the nobility in the class hierarchy], as to the middle class in general, the amassing of riches had not yet come to be an end in itself. Wealth was considered only as a means of assuring a man leisure to enjoy his family and friends. Such a merchant in the early 19th century, regarding his customers as a landed proprietor might have regarded a feudal fief, considered it beneath his dignity to advertise, to try to get trade away from another merchant, or to attempt to extend his output indefinitely. His ideal of life was an assured income, the possibility of an early retirement from business, and the acquisition of an estate in the country.[46]

Stendhal expressed this aristocratic attitude toward money: "The intelligent man should apply himself to acquiring what is strictly necessary, . . . but if, having achieved that degree of security, he wastes his time in increasing his fortune, the man's a scoundrel."[47] Although this aristocratic disdain for wealth appears somewhat irritating and hypocritical—those enjoying wealth sneering at those trying to acquire it—by and large it was a sincere conviction maintaining that one does not attain freedom by chasing wealth. The somewhat radical Michelet shared this very aristocratic view: "I do not hesitate to affirm that for the man of honor the situation of the most dependence is free in comparison with [the merchant]."[48] Similarly, Rousseau wrote: "The money which a man possesses is the instrument of freedom; that which we eagerly pursue is the instrument of slavery."[49] A free man cannot become obsessed with the accumulation of wealth, according to this argument, because he must busy himself with enjoying friends, conversation, intellectual endeavors, public duties, and the arts. Montesquieu uncovered the roots of this conviction in ancient Greek society. "In fine, every kind of low commerce was infamous

46. Frederick B. Artz, *Reaction and Revolution, 1814–1832* (New York, 1934), p. 24; see also Stearns, *Paths to Authority*, p. 115.

47. Quoted by Baudelaire in *Selected Writings on Art and Artists*, p. 388.

48. Michelet, *Le Peuple*, p. 93.

49. Jean-Jacques Rousseau, *Confessions*, no trans. given (New York, n.d.), p. 37.

among the Greeks, as it obliged a citizen to serve and wait on a slave, on a lodger, or on a stranger. This was a notion that clashed with the spirit of Greek liberty."[50]

The arch-conservative Bonald, greatly influenced by ancient Greek thought, welcomed and echoed this view. A people that does not limit commerce to what is "absolutely indispensable," said Bonald, "can dazzle by the glitter of its enterprises and the grandeur of its successes, . . . but it is an entirely material people, and it will sooner or later be subjugated by a moral people."[51] While concentrating on the accumulation of wealth, Bonald contended, people will neglect moral and intellectual improvement and begin to assume that life's purpose is no higher than self-interested enjoyment, ignoring the proper end of life, which is the attempt to actualize one's many potentials. "Freedom for a being is the power to attain one's end, to reach one's perfection."[52] Bonald belittled the suggestion that one could define freedom in economic terms or indeed that one could achieve freedom in a commercial, middle-class society. Industry is the "most dependent of the professions." Although liberals might attribute the spirit of liberty to the new commercial age, in fact, "all merchants, even the richest, pawn everyday, at every hour, their personal liberty" by remaining personally dependent on customers, markets, and so forth.[53] Similarly, the reactionary Veuillot stated to Lamartine, "Could it be that you really don't know that 'to be free' really means to despise gold? . . . You produce your books in the same commercial fashion as you produce your vegetables and your wine!"[54]

This argument, shared by conservatives such as Chateaubriand, Balzac, and Delacroix along with radicals such as Fourier, Michelet, and Lamennais, rests on Aristotle's teleological premises. Men and women have a proper function or end to attain, an end toward which they tend by nature and toward which they ought to tend. In fulfilling this end, men and women will actualize their potentials to be creative, productive, and intelligent actors, not passive consumers and spectators. Free societies develop a healthy culture that offers the encouragement needed for men and women to cultivate these potentials. But as we have seen, Tocqueville's generation argued that the climate and the soil of bourgeois society nourished petty individuals and smothered any who strove to be great.

50. Baron de Montesquieu, *The Spirit of the Laws*, trans. Thomas Nugent, 2 vols. in one (New York, 1949), Bk. IV, Sect. 8; 1: 38.
51. Bonald, *Oeuvres complètes*, 2: 101–2.
52. Quoted in Henry Moulinié, *De Bonald* (Paris, 1915), p. 340.
53. Bonald, *Oeuvres complètes*, 2: 237.
54. Quoted in Benjamin, *Charles Baudelaire*, p. 32.

A World of Passive Spectators

Certainly Tocqueville's generation also worried that the bourgeoisie would abuse its economic and political power. Balzac's Vautrin, referring to the banker Baron de Nucingen, said "every penny of his fortune is bathed in some family's tears." Vautrin continued by describing the Baron as a "thief on the World Market" who "has grown fat on the fortunes of widows and orphans."[55] Nevertheless, although these writers feared that bourgeois society was or would become oppressive, they feared even more that it was or would become seductive, that principled men and women would become enticed into believing that this new society would indeed bestow freedom and happiness. Thus, the literature of this period depicted a host of characters who were decent, often wonderful, human beings powerless to resist the tantalizing argument that, after acting in their economic self-interest, personal freedom and happiness would descend upon them. In *Cousin Pons*, Balzac described Madame Cibot, Pons's housekeeper, as an upright person with "twenty-six years of scrupulous honesty"; yet, eventually "there hatched out in this woman's heart a serpent—the lust for wealth."[56] Ultimately, Madame Cibot conspired to kill both Pons and her own husband. As Balzac said, bourgeois society is an ocean of mud engulfing all who enter.[57] For the writers of Tocqueville's generation, bourgeois society was seen less as a tyrant's tool and more as a pervasive addiction, disseminating itself slowly and inexorably.

Because this new society bred a composite of isolated individuals, each without support, each grasping for wealth and comforts, it also engendered a submissiveness and servility nourished by a sense of powerlessness and a willingness to serve whoever furnished wealth and comfort. Vigny claimed that his capitalist character John Bell "is very much the egoist, the rude calculator; base with great people, insolent with small."[58] Stendhal's *Lucien Leuwen*, a study of bourgeois society under the July Monarchy, concluded similarly: the world witnesses swarms of honest people reduced to grasping for wealth, begging for favors, docilely serving those who could bestow such rewards. "How impossible to add anything to the current passion for money, the fear of losing one's job, or eagerness to anticipate one's employer's slightest wish."[59] Having no infatuation with money or public acclaim,

55. Balzac, *A Harlot High and Low*, pp. 541, 161–62.
56. Balzac, *Cousin Pons*, pp. 61, 150.
57. Balzac, *Père Goriot* and *Eugénie Grandet*, p. 254.
58. Quoted in Bird, *Alfred de Vigny's Chatterton*, p. 104.
59. Stendhal, *Lucien Leuwen*, 2: 3.

never trembling at the loss of what the powerful people of this world can take away, Lucien remained impervious to the manipulations of his political world.

Rampant powerlessness and submissiveness, these writers feared, would generate an oppression of a new kind, more seductive and less harsh, an oppression in which people proudly proclaimed their individualism while they raced to become alike. Delacroix grieved that cultural variety was disappearing from the earth; Vigny's poem *Les Destinées* likened the human race to a herd of sheep or oxen; and Stendhal contended that men were "confined like an Egyptian mummy inside wrappings always common to all alike."[60] In referring ostensibly to the military, but actually to the entire society, Vigny likened bourgeois society to the "iron mask of the unknown prisoner" that "confers upon all soldiers an aspect of uniformity and reserve."[61] Finally, Chateaubriand speculated that people might become mere puppets. "Presumably the *human species* will grow in stature, but it is to be feared that the individual man may decline, certain eminent faculties of genius be lost, and imagination, poetry, and the arts perish in the cells of a hive-society in which each individual will be nothing more than a bee, a cog in a machine, an atom in organized matter."[62]

Although these writers and artists feared a working-class movement, what Flaubert called the "barracks-like" life of a society envisioned by Babeuf or Cabet, more often they dreaded that French civilization, to paraphrase Baudelaire, would fall asleep on a heap of riches.[63] Their image of China emerged as a model for this oppression through stagnation and bureaucratization. Chateaubriand, for one, worried that bourgeois society was metamorphosing Frenchmen into "Chinamen" who were "whiling away [their] days in a well-being" and "peacefully vegetating amidst all the progress which has been accomplished." Indeed, "it could happen that, as a result of the total deterioration of the human character, the peoples of the world would be content to make do with what they have got: love of gold would take the place of a love of their independence."[64]

These writers feared that people might content themselves with their own oppressive stagnation. In *The Charterhouse of Parma*, Stendhal depicted a world in which servants embraced their servitude and

60. Delacroix, *Journal*, p. 512; Vigny quoted in Denommé, *Nineteenth Century French Romantic Poets*, p. 87; Stendhal, *Scarlet and Black*, p. 338.

61. Vigny, *The Military Necessity*, p. 18.

62. Quoted in Evans, *Social Romanticism in France*, p. 3.

63. Baudelaire, *Selected Writings on Art and Artists*, p. 123.

64. Menczer, ed., *Catholic Political Thought*, p. 104.

delighted in imitating their masters while ridiculing their fellow servants who wanted independence; a world in which the leading opposition liberal assumed the job of running the hated prison in which
his own opposition was confined; a world in which the prisoners,
confined to a cell only three feet high, composed a *Te Deum* in gratitude for the recovery to health of their gaoler.[65] These writers began
to explore the idea that history might disclose a new type of despotism, a more insidious type in which individuals created a new
servitude under the banner of "freedom," in which people announced their free choice while choosing the very gratifications that
pleased their masters. People were becoming compressed, as in the
cell three feet high, to a size beneath human dignity. It is no wonder
that Géricault and Delacroix loved to paint the ferocity of wild, un-
tamed animals, animals who hungered for independence and the
chance to unleash their force on their captors; it is no wonder that war
and crime occupied the imaginations of so many of this generation.
Frightened of an emerging world of timid spectators eager to sell
themselves for the wealth and acclaim of their masters, these writers
longed for a past, noble ferocity.

TOCQUEVILLE'S DISTASTE FOR BOURGEOIS SOCIETY

The Obsession with Wealth

Tocqueville was by birth an aristocrat, his lineage dating at least to
the fifteenth century, and he always felt more at ease in the presence
of aristocratic men. It is therefore not surprising that he, too, manifested an aristocratic disdain toward wealth. For an aristocracy (and
here one must read "the ancient French aristocracy"), "the comforts
of life are not . . . the end of life, but simply a way of living."[66] Wealth
should be merely an instrument to carve out sufficient leisure time in
which to live the good life of cultivating one's mind, the only life
proper to a man of dignity. By contrast, in the new bourgeois society,
"the desire of acquiring the comforts of the world haunts the imagination of the poor, and the dread of losing them that of the rich,"
and this "passion for well-being is essentially a passion of the middle
classes."[67] Like Stendhal and Bonald, Tocqueville worried that wealth

65. Stendhal, *The Charterhouse of Parma*, pp. 31, 315, 374–75.
66. Tocqueville, *Democracy*, 2: 136.
67. Ibid., p. 137. Lamberti also describes Tocqueville's dislike of the middle classes. *Tocqueville et les deux démocraties*, pp. 48–51, 194–98. Jardin shows that although
Tocqueville repudiated legitimism, he chose old monarchists as his friends, not members of the new middle class. *Alexis de Tocqueville*, pp. 359–67.

would be regarded as an end in itself, not merely as a means to the good life. Tocqueville's letters reveal clearly that he considered a life devoted to pursuing wealth to be demeaning and perhaps dishonorable. In his *Memoir* about Tocqueville, Beaumont reported what we can easily infer: While "sensible to its value as a means of action in this world, Tocqueville considered money as of secondary interest. He did not admit the possibility of risking for it honor and happiness."[68]

A brief story illustrates this clearly. When Beaumont's income appeared to be diminishing, Tocqueville haltingly and painfully suggested that, just for a couple of years, Beaumont should enter the financial world long enough to accumulate sufficient resources in order to continue his present way of life. Realizing that Beaumont would regard this world of business as distasteful, Tocqueville assured him that it would be temporary. "Surely I would not want, even from the point of view of enlightened self-interest for your children, to see you devote your life to increasing your fortune." Beaumont, as much an aristocrat as Tocqueville, responded that he had an "extreme," if not "insurmountable," repugnance for the world of business and commerce, and he preferred the way of life that he and Tocqueville had chosen.[69]

Like so many writers and artists of his generation, Tocqueville recognized how seductive this bourgeois life of small pleasures and self-interested action can be; men and women of integrity and intelligence were easily enticed by its promises. Tocqueville despaired that the French people would content themselves with making railroads, finding coal, and buying calico.[70] Complaining that the people of his time were indifferent to all but *bourse ou toilette,* Tocqueville scoffed that the predominant passion of his age was the railroad.[71] And in the United States, which in so many ways depicted a future that Tocqueville thought France could expect, "most of their passions either end in the love of riches or proceed from it."[72] In his social novel titled *Marie,* Tocqueville's friend Beaumont said that "love is not understood" in the United States, because people pursue only money; indeed, for the American, the "first sound in his ears is the chink of money."[73]

68. See Tocqueville, *Memoir,* 1: 45.

69. Tocqueville, *Oeuvres* (M), vol. 8, pt. 3, *Correspondance . . . Beaumont,* pp. 100, 105–6.

70. Ibid., p. 283.

71. Tocqueville, *Oeuvres* (M), vol. 11, *Correspondance . . . Royer-Collard . . . Ampère,* p. 371.

72. Tocqueville, *Democracy,* 2: 239.

73. Gustave de Beaumont, *Marie, or Slavery in the United States,* trans. Barbara Chapman (Stanford, 1958), pp. 21–22, 216.

Tocqueville thought that, as time passed, the craving for money so characteristic of the bourgeoisie would engender a servility feared by so many of his generation. In his *Old Regime*, Tocqueville wrote that "Eighteenth-century man had little of that craving for material well-being which leads the way to servitude," clearly implying a contrast with his own century. Certainly the nineteenth-century obsession with wealth could be accompanied by many "private virtues" such as love of family and "respect for religion," but Tocqueville argued that it was still tenacious, insidious, and "morally debilitating."[74] Having convinced people that a primary goal in life is the accumulation of comfort and wealth, those in charge of a political order gain a certain power over people, gradually rendering the population passive and eventually submissive. If this craving for possessions increases in the future, the men and women of bourgeois society will lose all taste for political participation, because they will immerse themselves in private preoccupation while abandoning public concerns.

> The time will come when men are carried away and lose all self-restraint at the sight of the new possessions they are about to obtain. . . . It is not necessary to do violence to such a people in order to strip them of the right they enjoy; they themselves willingly loosen their hold. The discharge of political duties appears to them to be a troublesome impediment which diverts them from their occupations and business. If they are required to elect representatives, to support the government by personal service, to meet on public business, they think they have no time, they cannot waste their precious hours in useless engagements; such idle amusements are unsuited to serious men who are engaged with the more important interests of life. These people think they are following the principle of self-interest, but the idea they entertain of that principle is a very crude one; and the better they look after what they call their own business, they neglect their chief business, which is to remain their own masters.[75]

The Eclipse of Public Life

Eventually retaining only the capacity to enjoy things in private, men and women lose the capacity to act in public; frivolity and petty enjoyments weaken all taste either for heroic action or for grand historical and national purpose. "The great majority of men of my own age merely want to get on with their small affairs."[76] In 1834, after spending six weeks in the country with people who contented

74. Tocqueville, *The Old Regime*, p. 118.
75. Tocqueville, *Democracy*, 2: 149.
76. Tocqueville, *The European Revolution and Correspondence with Gobineau*, p. 189.

themselves with the everyday pleasures of wealth, comfort, and family, Tocqueville wrote to Kergorlay, "I feel very strongly that it would be easier for me to leave for China, to enlist as a soldier, or to gamble my life in I know not what hazardous and poorly conceived venture, than to condemn myself to the life of a potato, like the decent people I have just seen."[77] Two decades later his opinion had not changed; he now showed his distaste for his time by describing France as "ce pays de boeufs et de vendeurs de boeufs."[78] "One of the saddest consequences" of the Second Empire was to hasten the tendency to render the entire nation "*covetous* and *frivolous*," a nation of people either chasing money dishonestly or spending with an "insane" desperation.[79] Tocqueville again felt a great gulf between himself and the ordinary Frenchman of his day, because he consciously associated himself with an ideal, even unreal, past, with men who had dreamed of glory, of freedom, of founding great states, and of making human beings more noble. Thus Tocqueville admired prosperity but still wanted to restore what he called grandeur to France. "I want, above all, to care for my reputation before dreaming of my purse."[80] Or again, "I want, above all, that no one accuse me of possessing one of these small but insatiable ambitions, which swarm about in our time."[81] Or finally, he wrote to a friend that he wished Providence would present him with an opportunity to accomplish "good and grand things," despite any danger, in order to quench an "internal flame . . . that does not know where to find what feeds it."[82]

What is the effect of this bourgeois acquisitive ethic on political activity? Tocqueville argued that the obsession with wealth enervates political freedom, because selfishness and the private pursuit of wealth surrender public space to an increasingly concentrated governmental power. Citizens disengage themselves from the public sphere to the extent that organized interests and government bodies become active. As concern for accumulating wealth pervades the nation, the citizen turns into the spectator, and individuals no longer consider political decision making a joy, an obligation, or a possibility. Indeed, making political decisions becomes the business, quite literally, of a distant governmental body, and politics becomes regarded as either a "game in which each person seeks only to win," or a drama in which the "actors are not even interested in the success of the play,

---

77. Tocqueville, *Selected Letters*, p. 93.
78. Tocqueville, *Oeuvres* (M), vol. 15, pt. 2, *Correspondance . . . Corcelle*, p. 138.
79. Tocqueville, *Oeuvres* (M), vol. 8, pt. 3, *Correspondance . . . Beaumont*, p. 469.
80. Tocqueville, *Oeuvres* (M), vol. 6, pt. 1, *Correspondance anglaise*, p. 160.
81. Tocqueville, *Oeuvres* (M), vol. 8, pt. 1, *Correspondance . . . Beaumont*, p. 388.
82. Tocqueville, *Selected Letters*, p. 105.

but only in that of their particular role."[83] Consequently, each person
is isolated from his or her fellow citizens and from the public, ultimately becoming powerless to act in concert with others. "Individuals,
each one of whom finding that he confronts the Union alone and
isolated, cannot contemplate resistance."[84] Thus, the government, "in
taking men one by one by their interests rather than by their opinions,
in addressing itself to the small side of the human heart rather than to
the grand," follows the path by which "nations prepare themselves for
a master."[85]

Tocqueville disliked the bourgeois ethos because he thought it
would destroy a certain nobility that once existed in politics, reducing
politics to a petty game of self-interest. In his private notebooks
Tocqueville wrote that the United States proved, despite his persistent doubts, that "the middle classes can govern a state." Although
he was not sure the middle classes could provide guidance in times of
difficulty, he thought they were adequate for ordinary affairs. Nevertheless, his contempt for the middle classes emerges. *"In spite of their
petty passions, their incomplete education and their vulgar manners,* they
clearly can provide practical intelligence."[86] Despite this, American
middle-class government was far preferable to the distasteful French
middle-class rule. Whereas in America each citizen "knows when to
sacrifice some of his private interests to save the rest,"[87] in France
under the July Monarchy, self-interest predominated over all other
political motivations. In his *Recollections* Tocqueville maintained that
the bourgeoisie triumphed so completely that it effectively excluded
all those above it and below it from power, eventually using the state
for its own economic purposes. Thus, the middle classes "treated
government like a private business, each member thinking of public
affairs only in so far as they could be turned to his private profit, and
in his petty prosperity easily forgetting the people."[88] Politics must be
more than a process in which groups seek to maximize their own
economic self-interest; politics must also focus on principles and on
opinions of the common good. To Tocqueville, a politics based solely
on interests was unequivocally repugnant.

> I cannot tell you, my dear friend, the disgust I feel in watching the public
> men of our day traffic, according to the smallest interests of the moment,
> in things as serious and sacred to my eyes as principles. . . . They frighten

83. Tocqueville, *Oeuvres* (M), vol. 8, pt. 1, *Correspondance . . . Beaumont,* p. 604.
84. Tocqueville, *Journey to America,* p. 259.
85. Tocqueville, *Oeuvres* (B), vol. 9, *Études économiques, politiques,* pp. 377–78.
86. Tocqueville, *Journey to America,* p. 271. (My emphasis.)
87. Tocqueville, *Democracy,* 2: 131.
88. Tocqueville, *Recollections,* pp. 5–6.

me sometimes and make me ask myself whether there are only interests in this world, and whether what one takes for sentiments and ideas are not in fact interests that are acting and speaking.[89]

The Greatness of Production, the Pettiness of People

Like so many writers of his generation, Tocqueville lamented that his age labored to manufacture things, leaving people to be petty, selfish, and small. "It would seem as if the rulers of our time sought only to use men in order to make things great; I wish that they would try a little more to make great men; that they would set less value on the work and more upon the workman."[90] A free and healthy political order should seek more than the gratification of self-interested individuals; it should seek to nourish principled and intelligent actors. "Do not let this principle be lost sight of, for the great object in our time is to raise the faculties of men, not to complete their prostration."[91] By contrast, the people of his age were small, mere imitators of past greatness; they could not even "conceive . . . of grand things."[92]

For example, France seemed to have forfeited those intellectual talents that characterized the previous centuries, and like Balzac, Delacroix, Chateaubriand, and so many others, Tocqueville felt that civilization, art, and intelligence might pass from the world. In his notes for *Democracy in America,* Tocqueville wrote of "l'industrie littéraire," and echoing so many of his contemporaries, he blamed the commercial classes for the decline in literature. "Democracy not only enables the taste for literature to penetrate into the industrial classes, it also introduces the spirit of industry into literature."[93] In an 1854 letter he wrote, "It seems as if there is no longer anyone in France who knows how to either read or write. I dare to affirm, Madame, that for the last two hundred years, we have not seen in our country so little taste for matters of the mind."[94] Notwithstanding all the immense achievements in industry and science, Tocqueville could see no progress in his time. "If the brilliant talkers and writers of that time were to return to life, I do not believe that gas, or steam, or chloroform, or electric telegraph, would so much astonish them as the dullness of modern society."[95] By the time of the Second Empire,

89. Tocqueville, *Selected Letters,* p. 129.
90. Tocqueville, *Democracy,* 2: 347.
91. Ibid., p. 93.
92. Tocqueville, *Oeuvres* (M), vol. 11, *Correspondance . . . Royer-Collard . . . Ampère,* p. 61.
93. Yale Tocqueville Collection, C.V.f., Paquet No. 4, p. 15.
94. Tocqueville, *Oeuvres* (B), vol. 7, *Nouvelle correspondance,* p. 349.
95. Tocqueville, *Correspondence . . . Senior,* 2: 85.

France had become a land of "dumb conformity"; Pascal or Bossuet would sadly conclude that France was "receding into semi-barbarism."[96]

When Tocqueville visited factories in Manchester, he noted many of the miseries that Engels noted later—the hovels, the damp cellars serving as homes for as many as fifteen people apiece, the streams filthy with factory waste—all of which horrified Tocqueville. "Here is the slave, there the master: there the wealth of some, here the poverty of most."[97] In *Democracy in America* he argued that if a new aristocracy were to arise, it would be an "aristocracy of manufacturers," one of the "harshest that ever existed in the world," a "vulgar and corrupt" aristocracy completely lacking in all "high feelings." However much the poverty of the working classes in Manchester startled Tocqueville, he was shocked more by the degradation of both classes of men, that is, some men consenting to live in splendor by reducing others to the brutish state of filth and starvation. When he declared that the new aristocracy of manufacturers "impoverishes and debases" the workman, he feared the debasement every bit as much as the impoverishment, because the new bourgeois order tended to smother the wonderful human potentials for courage, intelligence, and creativity.

> When a workman is unceasingly and exclusively engaged in the fabrication of one thing, he ultimately does his work with singular dexterity; but at the same time he loses the general faculty of applying his mind to the direction of the work. He every day becomes more adroit and less industrious; so that it may be said of him that in proportion as the workman improves, the man is degraded. What can be expected of a man who has spent twenty years of his life in making heads for pins? And to what can that mighty human intelligence which has so often stirred the world be applied in him except it be to investigate the best method of making pins' heads? . . . in a word, he no longer belongs to himself but to the calling that he has chosen.[98]

The "mighty human intelligence which has so often stirred the world" fetters itself to the process of making things.

Like Chateaubriand, Tocqueville regarded China as the most vivid example of a centralized, bureaucratized society vegetating in its wealth. Tocqueville ridiculed the French physiocrats of the previous century for praising the centralized administration of the Chinese as

96. Tocqueville, *The Old Regime*, p. 115; *Correspondence . . . Senior*, 1: 140.

97. Alexis de Tocqueville, *Journeys to England and Ireland*, ed. J. P. Mayer, trans. George Lawrence and K. P. Mayer (Garden City, N.Y., 1968), pp. 92–96.

98. For this and the preceding quotations in the text, see Tocqueville, *Democracy*, 2: 168–71.

an example of sound government; rather, China was a hateful state that he labeled "Asiatic democracy."[99] "China appears to me to present the most perfect instance of that species of well-being which a highly centralized administration may furnish to its subjects. Travelers assure us that the Chinese have tranquillity without happiness, industry without improvement, stability without strength, and public order without public morality."[100] A similar European stagnation was Tocqueville's greatest fear, and he argued, as we shall see in more depth later, that a new despotism would emerge, if indeed it did emerge, not from wars or revolution but from the hungering for security and private possessive pleasures that accompanies the atomization of bourgeois society. In other words, tranquillity might bring greater dangers than disorder.

> It is believed by some that modern society will be always changing its aspect; for myself, I fear that it will ultimately be too invariably fixed in the same institutions, the same prejudices, the same manners, so that mankind will be stopped and circumscribed; that the mind will swing backwards and forwards forever without begetting fresh ideas; that man will waste his strength in bootless and solitary trifling, and, though in continual motion, that humanity will cease to advance.[101]

By robbing a nation of its vision and its sense of purpose, by replacing grand ambition with petty concerns, bourgeois society might fasten individuals to the present, offering them nothing more than private comforts and security. After inculcating a love of wealth, the new bourgeois ethic circumscribed and compressed people, making them satisfied with their small existence, "till the very men who from time to time upset a throne and trample on a race of kings bend more and more obsequiously to the slightest dictate of a clerk."[102] So that people might resist the "thousand petty selfish passions of the hour," necessarily "governments must apply themselves to restore to men that love of the future with which religion and the state of society no longer inspire them."[103] Tocqueville wrote, "I dread, and I confess it, lest they should at last so entirely give way to a cowardly love of present enjoyment as to lose sight of the interests of their future selves and those of their descendants and prefer to glide along the

---

99. Tocqueville, *The Old Regime*, p. 163; *Correspondence . . . Senior*, 2: 186.
100. Tocqueville, *Democracy*, 1: 94.
101. Ibid., 2: 277–78.
102. Ibid., p. 332.
103. Ibid., pp. 159–60.

easy current of life rather than to make, when it is necessary, a strong and sudden effort to a higher purpose."[104]

Like so many writers of his generation, Tocqueville dreamed of the past and longed for the future, for a "sudden effort to a higher purpose," in order to avoid what he regarded as a paltry and suffocating spectacle of the emerging bourgeois order. "There are moments when I fear becoming mad in the manner of Don Quixote. My mind is completely crammed with a heroism that is hardly of our time, and I fall very flat when I come out of these dreams and find myself face to face with reality."[105] Unlike so many of his generation, however, Tocqueville was pessimistic about the possibility of finding modern heroes.

104. Ibid., p. 277.
105. Tocqueville, *Selected Letters,* p. 125.

5 Heroes and Hiding Places: The Wish to Escape Bourgeois Society

The sensation of powerlessness coupled with a persistent distaste for the new bourgeois society engendered an intense yearning either for some escape from this society or for some force that could transform it dramatically. This yearning revealed itself in part in the eagerness to believe in the hero, the powerful individual who vanquished his own insignificance only to assist others who were powerless. The French adoration of Napoleon, an obscure lieutenant who rose to dominate Europe, reflected this eagerness. As Stendhal said of Napoleon, "he was our sole religion."[1]

So many characters in French Romantic literature reflect the sensation of powerlessness because they are people, such as René or Chatterton, who have lost all control over their worlds. Nevertheless, in this literature the exceptions to this powerlessness have remained most memorable: Balzac's Vautrin fascinates readers because he is a man of giant stature who wars with society, sometimes proving larger than the events and institutions encircling him. As Lucien, one of his accomplices, said, "Men like you should dwell in caves and never come out. You made me live with your giant's life."[2] Once more, however, Hugo best tapped this pervasive and underlying wish for a hero. His Jean Valjean was a man who, although abused by society, remained so terribly decent, a man persistently in danger who nevertheless consistently rescued those who were isolated, weak, and

1. Quoted in Levin, *The Gates of Horn*, p. 86.
2. Balzac, *A Harlot High and Low*, pp. 398–99.

threatened by the impersonal might of society. Pursued by society, he was of such stature and such strength that he triumphed, even groping through the muck and filth of Parisian sewers to save those he loved. When the gentle child Cosette was mistreated, Jean Valjean arrived to save her. "Cosette was no longer afraid . . . she was no longer alone; she had somebody to look to."[3] The classical French theater had its heroes, but the society from which they rose did not pursue them, nor did they direct their efforts toward the powerlessness of individual persons.

As Tocqueville argued, however, when each person feels powerless, it is difficult to convince anyone that even the strongest individual could overcome the societal powers that dominate each like a "powerful stranger." As a consequence, the men and women of nineteenth-century France turned elsewhere to seek their heroes, heroes whom they hoped could extract them from what they regarded as a suffocating age. They turned (1) to a natural progression of history that would lead to a better age and (2) to an extraordinary faith in the laboring classes.

HEROES

Salvation through Historical Progress

Although most French writers in this generation had only a superficial knowledge of Goethe and Hegel, and although few by the time of Tocqueville's death had heard of Marx or Darwin, nevertheless most French writers of this era still viewed history as linear, as a sequence of distinct, nonrecurring events. To do this, they drew upon a French tradition that stretched from Bossuet to Guizot and included such well-known prophets of progress as Turgot and Condorcet. Tocqueville's generation generally pictured history as progressing toward some goal, some superior state of society, or, as Hugo said, *l'ascension à la lumière.*[4] "The people," said Hugo, "rough-hewn by the 18th century, shall be completed by the 19th," and "the 20th century shall be happy."[5] Even in the popular songs of Béranger, the notion of historical progress appeared.[6]

De Staël avowed that the notion of historical progress was an essential component in her political thinking. "In what discouragement

3. Hugo, *Les Misérables*, 1: 431.
4. Quoted in Giraud, *L'École romantique française*, p. 50.
5. Hugo, *Les Misérables*, 2: 280, 475.
6. Clement, *Romanticism in France*, p. 262.

would the spirit fall, if it ceased to hope that each day adds to the body of the enlightenment."[7] Announcing that the Golden Age would be blossoming in the future, Saint-Simon warned the industrialists to support his program, to "obey history or be crushed by it," because "a day will come when I shall make a paradise of the earth."[8] Even de Maistre claimed that the unfolding of history taught men both political lessons and God's will.[9] Finally, the great liberal historian Guizot seasoned Bossuet's providential theory of history with a dash of class analysis, arguing that men and women were completing a "plan of Providence" that they did not even understand.[10]

Baudelaire was one of this generation's few dissenters. He detested the doctrine of historical progress because it summoned history to be a hero. History was magically to perform the tasks of men and women, and men and women could thus be excused for relaxing in their passivity. The mysterious force of history became the active, automatic hero and the obedient servant, engineering the construction of a new order or a Golden Age. "Faith in progress," said Baudelaire, "is a doctrine for the lazy."[11] Indeed, one finds evidence to support Baudelaire's cynicism. History does appear to be a new faith in this era, a force for good that would by itself bravely triumph over ignorance and oppression. Long before Hegel's "Cunning of Reason," Turgot and Condorcet argued that the irrational deeds of men acted invisibly to complete God's plan. Said Turgot, "Their passions, their very rages, have led them without knowing where they were going."[12] Condorcet added that wars and revolutions unconsciously furthered some divine plan for progress. "The very passions of men, their interests falsely understood, lead them to spread enlightenment, liberty, happiness, to do good despite themselves."[13] When Saint-Simon claimed "obey history or be crushed by it," some abstract entity called history, not men and women active in the world, constituted the irresistible force to be reckoned with. Guizot, like so many of his generation, simply rested more easily in the embrace of a faith when he said, "For my own part, I am convinced that there is, in reality, a

7. Quoted in Leroy, *Histoire des idées sociales en France*, 2: 171.

8. Quoted in Manuel, *The New World of Henri Saint-Simon*, pp. 67, 70.

9. Bayle, *Les Idées politiques de Joseph de Maistre*, pp. 23, 60.

10. François Pierre Guillaume Guizot, *The History of Civilization in Europe*, trans. William Hazlitt (New York, n.d.), p. 237; see also Stanley Mellon, *The Political Uses of History* (Stanford, 1958).

11. Quoted in F.W.J. Hemmings, *Culture and Society in France, 1848–1898* (New York, 1971), p. 39; see also Baudelaire, *Selected Writings on Art and Artists*, p. 121.

12. Quoted in Manuel, *The Prophets of Paris*, p. 47.

13. Quoted in ibid., p. 73.

general destiny of humanity."[14] Baudelaire was correct: history became a chimerical errand boy sent to perform the heroic task of which men and women felt incapable.

Tocqueville exhibited an ambivalence toward this notion of historical progress. In one letter to Beaumont, for example, he wrote that "after all, rational equality is the only state natural to man, since nations get there from such various starting points and following such different roads."[15] On other occasions, he embraced the notion that Providence acts through history, as when he announced that equality was a "providential fact."[16] Similarly, one finds hints that he never entirely escaped an argument such as Bossuet's that we find God's purpose in history. "I cannot believe," he wrote Kergorlay, "that God has for several centuries been pushing two or three hundred million men toward equality of conditions in order to make them wind up under the despotism of Tiberius and Claudius."[17] In his notebooks, he once described people, institutions, and events as "passive instruments in the hands of God."[18]

In general, however, Tocqueville avoided all arguments based on assumptions about progress or God's role in history. Historical theories that purport to demonstrate some necessary or determined goal, whether these theories emerge from de Maistre or Saint-Simon or Gobineau, inform people in an insidious and subtle fashion that they are not responsible for the successes and failures of history. Certainly Tocqueville regarded the freedom to direct history as limited; but within these limits, history was open to human creativity and subject to human action. Anxious to give historical responsibility to the men and women making decisions in history, Tocqueville argued that the path of history could ascend either to the doorstep of freedom or to that of despotism, either to "a democracy without poetry or elevation indeed, but with order and morality," or to "a yoke heavier than any that has galled mankind since the fall of the Roman Empire."[19] The faith that men and women could become passengers as history rode by itself into a Golden Age and the widespread resignation to Gobineau's theory of inevitable European decline were opposite sides of the same coin, and the entire coin was forged from the sensations of

14. Guizot, *The History of Civilization in Europe*, p. 6.
15. Tocqueville, *Journeys to England and Ireland*, p. 9.
16. Tocqueville, *Democracy*, 1: ix.
17. Tocqueville, *Oeuvres* (M), vol. 13, pt. 1, *Correspondance . . . Kergorlay*, p. 373.
18. Yale Tocqueville Collection, C.V.b., Paquet No. 13, p. 27.
19. Tocqueville, *Memoir*, 1: 377. For a discussion of how Tocqueville's theory of history compared with Guizot's, see François Furet, *Interpreting the French Revolution*, trans. Elborg Forster (London, 1981), pp. 135–39.

isolation and powerlessness. Thus, Tocqueville rejected his generation's view of history as hero, the view that history would become the
champion of the age, a carriage transporting men and women into a
better future.

Faith in the Strength and Purity of the Laboring Classes

If the writers of Tocqueville's generation saw the aristocracy as
destined for extinction, and the middle classes obsessed with petty
concerns devoid of high ideals, they uncovered virtue, simplicity, and
courage in the laboring classes, including both the peasantry and the
urban working class. Many of these writers idealized *le peuple.* The
consensus on this point is not as extensive, because for conservatives
and even most liberals of the early nineteenth century, the lower
classes were barely visible. For de Staël, Guizot, Constant, Thiers, and
Cousin, the lower classes had no special virtues other than obedience
to the propertied classes, along with an ability to exert useful labor.[20]
But for many middle-class artists and writers, the ordinary citizen
engaged in day-to-day labor emerged as a new sort of hero. Even by
the time of Géricault, we see not the classical subject matter insisted
upon by David, but anonymous individuals immersed in ordinary
struggles of daily life—for example, Géricault's portraits of the el-
derly and insane.[21] In many of Daumier's watercolors, working men
and women became the predominant subjects—for example, in the
Washerwoman, the *Towman,* and the *Water Carrier*—and wind, weight,
a hill to climb, or a job to perform confronted them as obstacles,
suggesting that survival in the new bourgeois world required heroic
and Sisyphean struggles on the part of the laboring classes. Similarly,
Millet depicted the simple and courageous virtues of the peasant class,
although he had no intention of romanticizing their exhausting labor.
Finally, in regard to Courbet's *Burial at Ornans,* one commentator
declares that "figuratively speaking, one might say that Courbet cast
into the grave the previous history of art," because his subject matter
was not the burial of some classical hero but the burial of an ordinary
man, of everyman.[22] Said Baudelaire, arguing against those painters
who confined themselves to classical subject matter, "There are private
subjects that are much more heroic than these. Scenes of high life and
of the thousands of uprooted lives that haunt the underworld of a

20. Douglas Johnson, *Guizot* (Toronto, 1963), pp. 111–12, 129; Leroy, *Histoire des
idées sociales en France,* 2: 172–73, 178.
21. Egbert, *Social Radicalism and the Arts,* p. 166.
22. Elsen, *Purposes of Art,* p. 280.

great city, criminals and prostitutes . . . are there to show us that we have only to open our eyes to see and know the heroism of our day."[23]

In literature, Lamartine's poetry expressed not the poetic sentiments of some classical hero but the subjective anxieties, aspirations, and fears of the ordinary person. In the works of Hugo and Sue, the crowd composed of lower-class men and women inserted itself into literature, and Hugo openly acknowledged his attempt to describe "obscure heroes, sometimes greater than illustrious heroes."[24] Hugo assumed that working men and women were naturally good, that they became evil only if coerced or enticed by society. In *Les Misérables*, Fantine sold her possessions, her hair, finally her teeth, before being forced into prostitution by desperate necessity.[25] According to a few writers, the people embodied a certain practical knowledge attributed to experience, simplicity, and authenticity. Indeed, for this Romantic generation, some forms of art, such as the folk songs that supposedly emanated from the "folk" or nation, were superb artistic achievements precisely because they emerged spontaneously from the people. Hugo, Lamartine, and Sand hunted for and encouraged working-class poets and writers because the working class possessed inspiration generated by simplistic, natural virtues. Sand wrote to her favorite working-class pupil, the poet Poncy, that if he merely loved his wife with full sincerity, he would find the inspiration necessary for great poetry.[26] Similarly, Comte claimed that the working classes were "a most important source of moral power." Michelet said that "the instinct of the people may be obscure but it is sure" and, as a result, "the people have been wiser than the scholar."[27]

Part of this admiration for the people issued from the recognition that the peasantry and the urban working class harbored a tremendous reservoir of energy that could be released; after all, the people once composed the crowds that toppled the Old Regime and the army that marched the width of Europe. Relatively uncorrupted by the new commercial society and guardians of a supposedly limitless power, the laboring classes found themselves holding the obligation of implementing history's plan. The people, exhausted laborers by day, at night were supposed to shoulder the heroic task of transporting all

23. Baudelaire, *Selected Writings on Art and Artists*, p. 106.

24. Hugo, *Les Misérables*, 1: 695; Walter Benjamin, *Illuminations*, ed. Hannah Arendt, trans. Harry Zohn (New York, 1969), p. 166.

25. Hugo, *Les Misérables*, 1: 188–90.

26. George, *The Development of French Romanticism*, pp. 100–101.

27. Auguste Comte, *A General View of Positivism*, trans. J. H. Bridges (Stanford, Calif., n.d.), pp. 237–40; Michelet quoted in Soltau, *French Political Thought in the 19th Century*, pp. 112, 116.

these middle-class writers to a new and virtuous society. One by one, Saint-Simon, Fourier, Lamennais, Comte, and many others turned to the laboring classes to discover a force that would render their ideas effective (which is *not* to say that these writers always envisioned a society distinguished by popular, participatory power). Michelet's *History of the French Revolution* perhaps best captured this faith in the instinctive heroism of the people:

> A thing to be told to everybody, and which it is but too easy to prove, is that the humane and benevolent period of our Revolution had for its actors the very people—everybody. . . . I have also found that those brilliant, powerful speakers, who expressed the thoughts of the masses, are usually but wrongfully considered as the sole actors. The fact is that they rather received than communicated the impulse. The chief actor is the people.[28]

To some writers, the laboring classes had become a collective hero, a force about to construct a new and better future.

How did Tocqueville regard this glorification of the natural virtues, wisdom, and strength of the people? To begin with, he usually evinced a strong sympathy for oppressed peoples; he struggled to free France's colonial slaves (his antislave speeches were banned in the southern United States); he castigated the oppression of the Irish; he was horrified at factory conditions in Manchester; he despised the oppression resulting from India's caste system; and he denounced the legalized slaughter of American Indians. Beyond mere sympathy, however, he admired and respected, if sometimes in a paternalistic manner, the natural goodness of the French laboring classes, particularly the peasantry. In April 1848, Tocqueville wrote: "My principal hope comes from the spectacle presented to me by the people properly so-called. They lack enlightenment, but they have instincts that I find worthy of admiration; one encounters in them . . . the sentiment of order, true love of country, and very great sense in things about which they can judge by themselves. . . ."[29] The French peasant, he felt, exhibited qualities—common sense, healthy political passion, and firm principles—that could be harnessed to regenerate the French political system. "I have always thought, after all, the peasantry were superior to all other classes in France," he said, and added that although "deplorably in want of knowledge and education," with

28. Jules Michelet, *History of the French Revolution*, trans. Charles Cocks, ed. and introduced by Gordon Wright (Chicago, 1967), p. 12.
29. Tocqueville, *Selected Letters*, p. 208.

instruction the peasantry could "make good use of their natural good qualities."[30]

Tocqueville also admired the energy of the people and contended that by offering "material strength," "enthusiasm," and "passion," they were a necessary, if not a sufficient, force in founding a new, enduring, and free political order.[31] Similarly, he agreed with Machiavelli that one might successfully subdue a government, but to defeat an aroused people is virtually impossible.[32] In a world distinguished by the plodding and suffocating existence of the bourgeoisie, the laboring classes alone were capable of great passion and hence great good. His admiration for the strength of the peasantry surfaced carefully in his *Old Regime:* "It was only after [the bourgeois] had put arms in the [peasants'] hands that he realized he had kindled passions such as he had never dreamed of, passions which he could neither restrain nor guide, and of which, after being their promoter, he was to be the victim."[33] One year before his death, Tocqueville wrote Beaumont that perhaps a new revolution, pushed by the laboring classes but guided of course by the enlightened classes, could restore liberty to France.[34] Indeed, his theory of revolution always included an alliance between an enlightened aristocracy and an energetic people; the middle classes, who were wedded to the present, were least capable of making a heroic effort to bring about a better future.

Thus, one the one hand Tocqueville, engulfed in a sense of powerlessness and imbued with a feeling of disgust, also yearned to harness the energy of the lower classes to bring a new, more moral, political order. Yet his own analysis of bourgeois society seemed to crush this faith in the people as hero. The people, in fact, were as susceptible as all other classes to the corrupting influences of the bourgeoisie. Indeed, why would so many thinkers believe that some mystical purity and instinctive spontaneity would protect the laboring classes from the acquisitive ethic of the bourgeoisie? Tocqueville, in his blacker moments, might well have agreed with Flaubert's description of democracy as an attempt to "elevate the proletariat to the level of stupidity of the bourgeoisie."[35] Although the passions for consum-

30. Tocqueville, *Correspondence . . . Senior,* 2: 126.
31. Drescher, ed., *Tocqueville and Beaumont on Social Reform,* pp. 198–99.
32. Tocqueville, *Oeuvres* (M), vol. 6, pt. 1, *Correspondance anglaise,* p. 236.
33. Tocqueville, *The Old Regime,* p. 136.
34. Tocqueville, *Oeuvres* (M), vol. 8, pt. 3, *Correspondance . . . Beaumont,* p. 544.
35. Quoted in Levin, *The Gates of Horn,* p. 287.

ing wealth and pleasures were inveterate traits of the bourgeoisie, they spread to all classes. None could claim immunity. "The passion for physical comforts is essentially a passion of the middle classes; with those classes it grows and spreads, with them it is preponderant. From them it mounts into the higher orders of society and descends into the mass of the people."[36] Despite his admiration for the energy and common sense of the laboring classes, Tocqueville saw these classes as succumbing to the same ethic of selfishness that captured every other class; consequently, he could not regard the people as a hero capable of bringing about a world of natural goodness, devoid of self-interest.

WAYS TO ESCAPE FROM BOURGEOIS SOCIETY

The Private World

If some of the writers of Tocqueville's generation longed to transform their age by finding new heroes, most busied themselves with ways to escape from and protect themselves against bourgeois society; if the public world seemed threatening or suffocating, the private world seemed to be a possible place of charm and refuge. This explains why writers of this period could perceive the prison as a means of escape. It is a paradoxical claim easily resolved, because the prison became a metaphor for a safe, private place isolated from a hostile world. After arriving in a village and being refused all assistance or lodging, Jean Valjean sought refuge in the city jail, only to be denied even this haven.[37] Balzac's Vautrin scrutinized his prison cell to make certain that he could not be observed, and then he sighed, "I am safe."[38] As champion of liberal individualism, Stendhal manifested this metaphorical view of prison most clearly, because both Julien and Fabrice discovered happiness, freedom, and self-knowledge within prison walls. While Parma as a whole was a "city of prisoners" Fabrice was free inside the prison and, when released, suffered "despair of being out of prison."[39] Stendhal regarded the bourgeois world to be a suffocating prison, and hence, by a clever but dubious reversal, the prison cell could offer a means of escape. "The Stendhalian prison,"

36. Tocqueville, *Democracy*, 2: 137–38.
37. Hugo, *Les Misérables*, 1: 65; see also Victor Brombert, "The Happy Prison," in David Thorburn and Geoffrey Hartman, eds., *Romanticism* (Ithaca, 1973).
38. Quoted in Brombert, "The Happy Prison," in Thorburn and Hartman, eds., *Romanticism*, p. 64.
39. Stendhal, *The Charterhouse of Parma*, pp. 463, 386.

says one commentator, "assumes a protective and dynamic role. It liberates one from the captivity of social existence." Julien Sorel's only complaint was that he could not lock the door of his prison cell from within, thus securing himself further from a threatening world.[40]

Even those who most berated the privatization of life and the resulting isolation of individuals from each other ironically began to regard such social fragmentation as inevitable, ultimately suggesting that a certain kind of private life might offer hope, escape, or fulfillment. These writers regarded the public world of serious political debate as either bankrupt or doomed to disappear. If one could at best be an observer in the game of politics, one might still have the opportunity to make some decisions in private life. As Flaubert said, "Oh, if I could only fly to a country where one would see no more uniforms, hear no drums and talk about no massacres, where one was not obliged to be a citizen! But the earth is no longer habitable for poor mandarins."[41] Even political reformers abandoned the public world, and private and often economic decision making became primary. "The social revolution is seriously compromised," Proudhon contended, "if it comes through a political revolution."[42] "My theory of society," Fourier added, "is not concerned with any religious, political, or administrative reform, but solely with industrial reform. . . . Man's goal is not the attainment of illusory juridical rights but the flowering of the passions."[43] Finally, Saint-Simon announced that "henceforth economic life constitutes the whole of social life," and politics will be merely "the science of production."[44]

Love, the preeminently private pursuit, emerged for some as the ultimate consolation for being confined to an isolated and private existence. Of his character Lucien, Stendhal said, "he had found only one remedy for the ridiculous affliction, so rare in our age, of taking things seriously. It was to be shut up in a little room along with Madame de Chasteller."[45] By uniting two isolated individuals in an intimate, private world, love cures loneliness and despair while mitigating the harshness of society. When near death, Jean Valjean told Cosette and Marius, "love each other dearly always. There is scarcely anything else in the world but that—to love one another."[46] Arguing

40. Brombert, *Stendhal: Fiction and the Themes of Freedom*, pp. 172–73.
41. Quoted in Levin, *The Gates of Horn*, p. 288.
42. Quoted in Woodcock, *Pierre-Joseph Proudhon*, pp. 75, 171.
43. Quoted in Manuel, *The Prophets of Paris*, pp. 205, 220.
44. Quoted in Durkheim, *Socialism and Saint-Simon*, pp. 137–39.
45. Stendhal, *Lucien Leuwen*, 2: 344.
46. Hugo, *Les Misérables*, 2: 747.

that society, by severing old ties and separating individuals from each other, compels people to join together out of despair, Balzac said, "society is thus ceaselessly forging anew the bonds between two friends or two lovers."[47] Celio, a character in Musset's play *Marianne*, speculated, "Perhaps it's the effect of falling in love for the first time; perhaps this vast desert we live in suddenly becomes so terrifying that it seems unbearable without this new, unique, infinite happiness, that is revealed by one's heart."[48] Goethe's Werther, a hero for this Romantic generation, exclaimed, "Alas! the void—the fearful void within me! Sometimes I think if I could once—only once—press her to my heart, this void would be filled."[49] In sum, love became a panacea for society's ills, the private escape from a boring, threatening, or stultifying world. Love permitted people to avoid anxiety, triumph over loneliness, endure hardship, escape the unbearable, enliven what was boring, enrich a life that was petty—all accomplished by retiring into a private world, by divorcing oneself from public concern. Musset claimed, "love is everything," and Werther, referring to two lovers who had simply kissed, declared, "They lost sight of everything. The world vanished before them."[50]

In this Romantic generation that surrounded Tocqueville, love came to be regarded as a mystical power that strengthened and enlivened individuals, communities, and even nations. Saint-Simon, Fourier, and Lamennais all embraced love as a political force, as a cohesive bond which would unite a new society. In his Religion of Humanity, Comte proclaimed the "final systematization of the whole of existence around its true universal center: love," and Lamennais said flatly, "God is love."[51] Those in love, as Rougemont said, yearn to be "defeated, to lose all self-control, to be beside [themselves] and in ecstasy," indeed to deliver themselves happily to love.[52] Thus, while love was a force to vivify and inspire it was also something mysterious to which one could surrender, a force that seemed to redeem one's powerlessness. Musset exemplified this when he said: "Whatever she would have me do / She may demand./ My life itself I'd yield up too / At her command."[53]

47. Balzac, *Cousin Pons*, p. 68.

48. Alfred de Musset, *Seven Plays*, trans. Peter Meyer (New York, 1962), p. 15.

49. Goethe, *The Sorrows of Young Werther*, p. 92.

50. Musset quoted in Denommé, *Nineteenth Century French Romantic Poets*, p. 134; Goethe, *The Sorrows of Young Werther*, p. 129.

51. Comte quoted in Manuel, *The Prophets of Paris*, pp. 292, 214; F. Lamennais, *Paroles d'un croyant* et *Essai sur l'indifférence en matière de religion* (Paris, 1912), p. 67.

52. Denis de Rougemont, *Love in the Western World*, trans. Montgomery Belgion, rev. ed. (New York, 1974), pp. 282, 16, 46–48.

53. Quoted in Conder, ed., *A Treasury of French Poetry*, p. 216.

Hypocrisy, Masks, and Emotions

Despite finding safety in a private world, the writers of Tocqueville's generation found dangers as well, because they argued that
bourgeois society fostered hypocrites trying ambitiously to forge
ahead in the world; men and women were out of touch with their own
emotions and were simply playing roles designated for them by a
society that rewarded them for their performances. He is "not a great
nobleman," Stendhal said of one character, "but only patterned after
a great nobleman."[54] Similarly, Stendhal's character Lucien described
a provincial nobleman as "an exact replica, in clothes and manners, of
a provincial actor in the role of the *noble father*," and the prince of
Stendhal's Parma, instead of being himself, tried to duplicate Louis
XIV's speech, Joseph II's pose of leaning on a table.[55] Very few people,
outside of the honest laboring classes, of course, were regarded as
sincere, for all were acting out roles. Balzac spoke of the "million
actors who play their parts on the great stage of Paris," and his character Vautrin, in composing his revenge, whispered to Lucien, "I am
the author, you will be the play."[56] Delacroix noted in his *Journal* that,
with three different friends he was three different people, and Nerval
claimed that "in everyone is a spectator and an actor, one who speaks
and one who answers."[57] In one of Musset's plays, a character remarked, "In this world, when people speak to you, it's only a question
of knowing whom they're addressing, the real or conventional, the
person or the part."[58] Finally, in a haunting image, Baudelaire likened each person in society to "some paid dancer, fainting at her
duty, / Still with her vacant smile."[59]

The idea that the men and women of bourgeois society were inau-
thentic emerged in the metaphor of the mask, a metaphor that Rousseau had used frequently. "The man of the world almost always wears
a mask. He is scarcely ever himself and is almost a stranger to himself. . . . Not what he is, but what he seems, is all he cares for."[60]
Again, "I perceive only the mere apparitions of men. . . . Hitherto I
have seen a great number of masks: when shall I behold the faces of
mankind?"[61] Delacroix wrote, "Haven't people often taken me for a

54. Stendhal, *Lucien Leuwen*, 2: 116–17.
55. Ibid., 1: 125; Stendhal, *The Charterhouse of Parma*, p. 120.
56. Balzac, *Cousin Pons*, p. 19; Balzac, *A Harlot High and Low*, p. 93.
57. Delacroix, *Journal*, p. 52; Nerval, *Selected Writings*, p. 139.
58. Musset, *A Diversion*, in *Seven Plays*, p. 172.
59. Baudelaire, *Flowers of Evil*, p. 45.
60. Jean-Jacques Rousseau, *Émile*, trans. Barbara Foxley (London, 1911), p. 191.
61. Rousseau, *Eloisa*, 2: 33.

man of firm will? The mask is everything," and Fourier likened society to a gathering in which each hid behind his mask. "Nothing is more common than a gathering of pretended friends, each a mass of egoism, with nothing of friendship but its mask, no real motive but interest."[62] Balzac's Vautrin, the avowed enemy of society, entered the social world only when armed with real masks, pseudonyms, and disguises, including the actual mutilation of his face to conceal his identity.

Although it thwarts authenticity, the mask can also protect if it is assumed consciously. When Stendhal said, "I wear a mask with pleasure, I would change my name with joy," and when he wrote, "Look at life as though it were a masked ball," he expressed his delight in the mask because it secured his private existence in what he regarded as a suffocating world.[63] Stendhal himself used one hundred pseudonyms, signifying his conviction that, as Brombert says, "hypocrisy is the only way of keeping one's independence in a hostile world."[64] One of Stendhal's characters lamented that one is "surrounded by coarse creatures to whom one must always lie in order not to be the victim of the brute force they have at their command."[65]

Brute force was not the real issue. The mask, if used consciously, protected one from the subtle and insidious psychological coercions of society. This entire argument relates to Rousseau's claim that "the first impulses of nature are always right" and that "customs consist in control, constraint, compulsion."[66] For the vast majority of people in this new commercial world, the roles they played, and the costumes they wore that were appropriate to those roles, suggested their susceptibility to the constraining customs of a suffocating society. For a select few, the mask supposedly protected a private world and the private emotions of that world—love, fear, aspirations, apprehensions.

This protection of the emotions was exceedingly important to a Romantic generation that had strong reservations about excessive reliance on reason. Of course, no definition of reason ever suffices fully, but Tocqueville's generation identified reason with the questioning of Descartes, the science of Newton, and the calculations of the merchant. Chateaubriand declared that reason undermined imagination

---

62. Delacroix, *Journal*, p. 48; Fourier, *Design for Utopia*, p. 157.

63. Quoted in Brombert, *Stendhal: Fiction and the Themes of Freedom*, p. 8; and Jean Starobinski, "Truth in Masquerade," in Brombert, ed., *Stendhal*, p. 120.

64. Quoted in Giraud, "Romantic Realism in *Lucien Leuwen*," in Brombert, ed., *Stendhal*, p. 73.

65. Quoted in ibid., p. 74.

66. Rousseau, *Émile*, pp. 56, 10.

and hence art; Musset said science was fine but mysterious nature taught us something superior; Flaubert argued that reason paralyzed action in the world; Géricault needed a "sacred fire" of emotion to paint well; Fourier suggested an individual was truly authentic not when reasoning but when at play; and even Comte eventually shed his rigid positivism and sought to make "feeling systematically supreme over reason."[67] Thus, the private world of emotions and imagination had to be protected against any new encroachments by this world of calculating businessmen.

For this same reason, writers complained that no true and noble passions could any longer blossom in France. Passion, not reason, was the author of grand deeds, a sentiment familiar to Enlightenment figures such as Diderot, Rousseau, and, in this passage, Helvétius. "It is therefore to strong passions that we owe the invention and wonders of arts; and consequently they are to be considered as the germ productive of genius, and the powerful spring that carries men to great actions."[68] Whereas Saint-Simon reminded his followers just before his death that "to accomplish something great one must have passion," one of Stendhal's characters lamented that "there is no real true passion left in the nineteenth century."[69] Turgot's contention that men and women would become, and would want to become, calmly rational creatures was only a small landmark on a long-passed horizon.

Tocqueville's Response

Tocqueville embraced none of his generation's enthusiasm for escape to a private place. Indeed, the atomization and privatization of society fostered by the new middle-class society generated the exact conditions required for a new despotism. Solitude is a "state against nature," free nations invariably exhibit "public virtues," and only a despotism "immures . . . each in his private life."[70] "Private life in

67. Cited in George Mras, *Eugene Delacroix's Theory of Art* (Princeton, 1966), p. 74; Musset, *Camille and Perdican,* in *Seven Plays,* p. 76; Levin, *The Gates of Horn,* p. 247; Brombert, *The Novels of Flaubert,* pp. 269–70; Lorenz Eitner, ed., *Neoclassicism and Romanticism, 1750–1850* (Englewood Cliffs, N.J., 1970), p. 100; Clement, *Romanticism in France,* pp. 234–35; Comte, *A General View of Positivism,* pp. 63, 15.

68. Claude-Adrien Helvétius, *De L'Esprit, or, Essays on The Mind and Its Several Faculties,* no trans. given, new ed. (London, 1810), p. 231.

69. Saint-Simon quoted in Manuel, *The New World of Henri Saint-Simon,* p. 365; Stendhal, *Scarlet and Black,* p. 304.

70. Tocqueville, *Oeuvres* (B), vol. 9, *Études économiques, politiques,* p. 327; *Memoir,* 2: 299; *The Old Regime,* p. xiii.

Germany evidently has very engaging aspects," he remarked, "but what poor citizens!"[71] Stendhal had it backwards, because the prison cell, Stendhal's metaphor for a free and safe private existence, isolates a man from his fellows, gently exposing him to fear and manipulation by the institution of the prison. In his writings on prisons, Tocqueville suggested that once a prisoner was completely isolated, society could manage "to inculcate in him entirely new sentiments, to change profoundly the nature of his habits, to destroy his instincts."[72] As we will see in a later chapter, the practice of seeking refuge in a private world is, in Tocqueville's opinion, the ethos most suitable to a new despotism. Similarly, Tocqueville would have despised Saint-Simon's claim that politics should become a "science of production." Such a claim conceals the assumptions that a benevolent technocracy can make us happy and that men and women are merely private consumers of goods and pleasures, not public participants in a political world.

In the same way, Tocqueville was never swept away by the passion of romantic love, a passion he regarded as a private preoccupation not conducive to, and perhaps obstructive of, political freedom and political greatness. Like Aristotle, Tocqueville embraced the political virtue of friendship and argued that the highest pleasure in life emerged from individuals acting together to make public decisions. "The intimate life with friends," Beaumont wrote to a like-minded Tocqueville, "the animated life of the Chamber with all its grand interests and even its anxieties seem to me the only good."[73]

Tocqueville did agree that the new commercial society tended to render individuals hypocritical. In aristocratic society, Tocqueville maintained, one's position was more or less settled from birth, and although this might be oppressive, this practice engendered little anxiety. With the collapse of the old aristocratic order, everyone was thrown into the marketplace, and one's success depended upon one's appearance, as Hobbes so astutely pointed out. "The *Value,* or Worth of a man, is as of all other things, his Price; that is to say, so much as would be given for the use of his Power. . . . And as in other things, so in men, not the seller, but the buyer determines the Price."[74] Free to enter the marketplace, that is, free to enter into competition with

---

71. Tocqueville, *Oeuvres* (M), vol. 8, pt. 3, *Correspondance . . . Beaumont,* p. 228.
72. Tocqueville, *Oeuvres* (B), vol. 9, *Études économiques, politiques,* pp. 320–21; see also Boesche, "The Prison: Tocqueville's Model for Despotism."
73. Tocqueville, *Oeuvres* (M), vol. 8, pt. 1, *Correspondance . . . Beaumont,* p. 502.
74. Thomas Hobbes, *Leviathan,* Part I, Chapter 10.

fellow citizens, the individual suffers anxiety arising from multiple desires and limited possibilities.

> The same equality that allows every citizen to conceive these lofty hopes renders all the citizens less able to realize them; it circumscribes their powers on every side, while it gives freer scope to their desires. . . . They have swept away the privileges of some of their fellow creatures which stood in their way, but they have opened the door to universal competition.[75]

Thus, as Rousseau had said, individuals strain to appear what they are not, to act out the person they would like to be, to raise their value in the marketplace. "In the confusion of all ranks everyone hopes to appear what he is not."[76] In the new commercial society, private feelings had been given a new freedom and in some cases—as between father and son—were more sincere.[77] But in the larger society, hypocrisy and insincerity were the rule; "scarcely any exhibit their true feelings, but merely those which they think useful or popular."[78] Or, echoing Rousseau, he said in his unpublished notes, "I have only a single advantage over the majority of my contemporaries; I dare to say all that I think."[79]

Tocqueville was too much influenced by Rousseau not to express concern about the insincerity of the private world; but Tocqueville, political to the end, adapted the category of insincerity or inauthenticity to his analysis of political movements. An authentic political movement corresponds to the needs and circumstances of the moment, whereas a movement that adopts historical roles appropriate to past eras constructs a cage that constricts the movement and ultimately destroys it. The revolutionaries of 1848, Tocqueville claimed, were merely poor imitators of the Jacobins and Girondins of 1793, lacking the genius and appropriate passion that animated those earlier men. He wrote, "The whole time I had the feeling that we had staged a play about the French Revolution, rather than that we were continuing it. . . . We tried without success to warm ourselves at the hearth of our fathers' passions; gestures and attitudes as seen on the stage were imitated, but their enthusiasm could not be copied, nor their fury felt."[80] Like Marx, who claimed that the men and women of 1848

75. Tocqueville, *Democracy*, 2: 146.
76. Ibid., p. 53.
77. Ibid., pp. 208, 230.
78. Tocqueville, *Memoir*, 2: 339–40.
79. Yale Tocqueville Collection, C.V.h., Paquet No. 3, Cahier No. 3, p. 98.
80. Tocqueville, *Recollections*, pp. 67–68.

were borrowing the names and "costumes" of 1789 to perform a "parody" of the French Revolution (i.e., Louis Blanc aspiring to be Robespierre and the *Montagne* of 1848 posing as the *Montagne* of 1793), Tocqueville denigrated 1848 as a "vile tragedy played by a provincial troupe."[81] Echoing Marx's claim that "the tradition of all dead generations weighs like a nightmare on the brain of the living," and that an authentic revolution closes its eyes to the past and marvels at the "poetry of the future," Tocqueville wished "that all our history could be burnt, if this is the use that is made of it."[82] Louis Napoleon's court imitated the restored Bourbons and, as Tocqueville told Senior, the court ladies "have taken to trains and little pages. . . . Heaven preserve you from the mistakes which lead to revolutions and from the revolutions which lead to masquerades."[83] Though not as memorable, it was a sentiment quite similar to Marx's famous dictum that history repeats itself, "the first time as tragedy, the second as farce."[84] Tocqueville simply adapted the concern about role-playing and insincerity to an analysis of political movements.

Finally, did Tocqueville absorb his generation's distrust of reason? He acknowledged that most of his ideas sprang from the eighteenth century, and occasionally we see Turgot's or Condorcet's faith in reason. "Reason, like virtue, does not bend at all in different climates, and does not vary with temperaments and the nature of places. It is one, it is inflexible."[85] Nevertheless, having long suffered doubt, Tocqueville argued for the necessity of faith and illusion; faith and hope are two of "the most permanent and invincible instincts of human nature," because "each has a need to nourish some illusion."[86] Furthermore, reason can induce paralysis of action. "Reason has always been for me like a cage that keeps me from acting, but not from gnashing my teeth behind the bars."[87] Because any person requires a noble purpose and passion to ascend beyond the petty interests of the moment, grand action arises not from calculation, but from establishing an "ephemeral conviction."[88]

81. Karl Marx, *The 18th Brumaire of Louis Bonaparte*, no trans. given (New York, 1963), p. 15; Tocqueville, *Recollections*, p. 68.

82. Marx, *The 18th Brumaire of Louis Bonaparte*, pp. 15, 18; Tocqueville, *Correspondence . . . Senior*, 1: 75, 255.

83. Tocqueville, *Correspondence . . . Senior*, 2: 32.

84. Marx, *The 18th Brumaire of Louis Bonaparte*, p. 15.

85. Tocqueville, *Journey to America*, p. 164.

86. Alexis de Tocqueville, *Oeuvres* (B), vol. 8, *Mélanges, fragments*, p. 487; Tocqueville, *Oeuvres* (M), vol. 8, pt. 3, *Correspondance . . . Beaumont*, p. 512.

87. Tocqueville, *Oeuvres* (M), vol. 11, *Correspondance . . . Royer-Collard . . . Ampère*, p. 109.

88. Tocqueville, *Recollections*, p. 106.

In his fondness for releasing passion, Tocqueville agreed with his Romantic generation. Passion, perhaps guided by reason, impels men and women to leap historical obstacles; "some kind of high passion is always needed to revivify the human spirit."[89] Sadly, wearisome bourgeois society dissipates ennobling passion.

> The further away I am from youth, the more regardful, I will say almost respectful, I am of passions. I like them when they are good, and I am not even very certain of detesting them when they are bad. That is strength, and strength, everywhere it is met, appears at its best in the midst of the universal weakness that surrounds us. I see only poltroons who tremble at the least agitation of the human heart and who speak to us only of the perils with which passions threaten us. These are, in my opinion, bad chatterboxes. What we meet least in our day are passions, true and solid passions that bind up and lead life. We no longer know how to want, or love, or hate. Doubt and philanthropy render us incapable of all things, of great evil as well as great good, and we flutter heavily around a multitude of small objects, none of which either attracts us, or strongly repels us, or holds us.[90]

About eight months before his death, Tocqueville wrote: "It requires strong hatreds, ardent loves, great hopes, and powerful convictions to set human intelligence in motion, and, for the moment, people believe strongly in nothing, they love nothing, they hate nothing, and they hope for nothing except to profit at the stock exchange."[91]

In previous chapters we have seen that Tocqueville shared the concerns and anxieties of his generation, but in this chapter we see that, by and large, he did not accept their solutions. He had little or no faith in some magical progression of history, and his conviction about the corrupting powers of the bourgeois ethos far outweighed any confidence he placed in the laboring classes. Thus, he saw no place for heroes. In the same way, he saw no refuge. Fleeing to a private escape, forgetting a troubled world in a fury of love, playing games with masks to protect one's identity—none of these offered any permanent possibilities for escape from the suffocations of society. As we shall see, unlike previous empires that allowed private escapes to individuals who did not threaten political stability, the new despotism will seep into private homes and private lives, ultimately controlling the thoughts and behavior of individuals who believe themselves securely free.

89. Tocqueville, *The European Revolution and Correspondence with Gobineau*, p. 150.
90. Tocqueville, *Selected Letters*, pp. 152–53.
91. Ibid, p. 376.

In his unpublished notes, Tocqueville wrote that "one can no longer have anything but a despotism or a republic."[92] He saw one chance to escape the new despotism—by harnessing the political passion so much admired by the Romantics and by using this passion to bring genuine democratic freedom to the liberal institutions and laws emerging in the new representative governments of Europe and North America. We turn now to see what Tocqueville meant by this much-used word *freedom.*

92. Yale Tocqueville Collection, C.V.h., Paquet No. 3, Cahier No. 3, p. 21.

PART TWO

Freedom: Tocqueville's Hope

6 Freedom as Decentralization and Participation

In winding our way down and into Tocqueville's conception of freedom, in striving to reconstruct his image of freedom in an urban and industrial world, we must first recognize that Tocqueville clung to freedom as an imperative that was impossible to justify by its secondary benefits. However useful freedom generally may be to economic prosperity and human happiness, Tocqueville thought one could not in this way demonstrate freedom to be a moral imperative, for its worth would then depend on, and vary with, its usefulness. In his words: "Those who prize freedom only for the material benefits it offers have never kept it long. What has made so many men, since untold ages, stake their all on liberty, is its intrinsic glamour, a fascination it has in itself, apart from all 'practical' considerations. . . . The man who asks of freedom anything other than itself is born to be a slave."[1] Pascal suggested that people are drawn to God, not by logical proofs but by the heart,[2] and Tocqueville argued similarly about the attraction of freedom. "There is an instinctive tendency [toward freedom], irresistible and hardly conscious, born out of the mysterious sources of all great human passions."[3] Freedom nourishes life like art or good health, never necessary for mere existence but essential for some better existence that Nature or God designated individuals to

---

1. Tocqueville, *The Old Regime*, pp. 168–69.

2. Jean Mesnard, *Pascal: His Life and Works*, trans. G. S. Fraser (London, 1952), pp. 157–66.

3. Tocqueville, *The European Revolution and Correspondence with Gobineau*, pp. 167–68.

have. It is the prime sustenance that produces a flowering of human potential, or, in Aristotelian language, enables human beings to fulfill their function and attain their proper end. Like Mill, who argued that those who have knowledge of both will always choose Socrates' dissatisfaction over a pig's satisfaction, Tocqueville regarded freedom as the goal individuals would choose if they were *free* to choose—ultimately the most vicious political circle.

For Montesquieu,

> There is no word that admits of more various significations and has made more varied impressions on the human mind, than that of liberty. Some have taken it as a means of deposing a person on whom they had conferred a tyrannical authority; others for the power of choosing a superior whom they are obliged to obey; others for the right of bearing arms, and of being thereby enabled to use violence; others, in fine, for the privilege of being governed by a native of their own country, or by their own laws. A certain nation for a long time thought liberty consisted in the privilege of wearing a long beard. Some have annexed this name to one form of government exclusive of others; those who had a republican taste applied it to this species of polity; those who liked a monarchical state gave it to monarchy. Thus they have all applied the name of liberty to the government most suitable to their own customs and inclinations.[4]

Like Montesquieu, Tocqueville argued that freedom can flourish under any of the classical forms of government: monarchy, aristocracy, or democracy. "I have only one passion, the love of liberty and human dignity. All forms of government are in my eyes only more or less perfect ways of satisfying this holy and legitimate passion of man."[5] If he were to maintain that only democracies or republics can be free, he would be tacitly condemning his ancestors along with much of the French past, a condemnation he emphatically refused to make. As he said, "freedom has appeared in the world at different times and under various forms; it has not been exclusively bound to any social condition, and it is not confined to democracies."[6] The character of freedom does not change, but its quality and extent might. Thus, whoever ventures to explain Tocqueville's conception of freedom must grapple with phrases such as "democratic monarchy," "feudal liberty," and "bourgeois aristocracy"[7]—all of which should alert the modern reader

4. Montesquieu, *The Spirit of the Laws*, XI, 2, 1: 149.
5. Tocqueville, *Selected Letters*, p. 115.
6. Tocqueville, *Democracy*, 2: 100.
7. Tocqueville, *The European Revolution and Correspondence with Gobineau*, pp. 102, 169; Tocqueville, "M. Cherbuliez' *On Democracy in Switzerland*," in *Democracy in America*, ed. J. P. Mayer, trans. George Lawrence (Garden City, N.Y., 1969), p. 737.

to try to see Tocqueville's notion of freedom through Tocqueville's eyes.

FREEDOM AS MASTERY

In lamenting that "the human race, for good or for ill, is now its own master,"[8] Chateaubriand provided an entrance into the web of components that constitutes Tocqueville's conception of freedom. He was suggesting that, bereft of all the once-accepted traditions, religious beliefs, and social ties of past ages, men and women had been set adrift in the nineteenth century to perish or to flourish by their own efforts. To avoid decadence, to become free, people must masterfully control both themselves and their political world. Tocqueville's notion of freedom interlocks nicely with this idea of mastery, a word of course with a hint of feudalism about it. A free man masters and orders himself and his world, much as a master controls both his estate and his servants. Having destroyed all possible bridges extending back to the freedom embedded in aristocratic hierarchy, all—through some structure of democracy—must now become masters. Juxtaposed to this wish for mastery, however, looms Tocqueville's reluctant recognition, outlined in chapter 3, that a sense of powerlessness everywhere gripped the men and women of his age, a "powerlessness of both men and governments" to control events.[9] Inhabiting a world spinning beyond their control and perceiving the political world as a "powerful stranger," the French "cower" before "the pettiest officer." They busy themselves with their private affairs, and thus "neglect their chief business, which is to remain their own masters."[10]

The United States offered the early nineteenth-century exception to this pervasive sense of powerlessness. After witnessing the mastery of one's political life resulting from the direct democracy of America's townships, Tocqueville admired the power that citizens can wield in directing their political world. Americans rushed forward into the future, he said, ousting old opinions that had shaped the social world without being questioned, lowering economic barriers that had "imprisoned society," and altering political institutions to suit newly perceived common needs. "Under their hand, political principles, laws, and human institutions seem malleable, capable of being shaped and

8. Menczer, ed., *Catholic Political Thought*, p. 99.
9. Tocqueville, *Oeuvres* (M), vol. 15, pt. 2, *Correspondance . . . Corcelle*, p. 48.
10. Tocqueville, *Democracy*, 1: 96, 2: 149.

combined at will."[11] Indeed, the men and women of North America
actively and consciously shaped the future, quite unlike Europeans
who passively awaited its arrival, as passengers await a train. "There is
not a country in the world where man more confidently takes charge
of the future, or where he feels with more pride that he can fashion
the universe to please himself."[12]

THE LINK BETWEEN MASTERY AND DEMOCRATIC, DECENTRALIZED PARTICIPATION

Although known in the political world primarily as a member of
the Chamber of Deputies and as Foreign Minister, Tocqueville perhaps most cherished his position as President of the Conseil Général
of La Manche; his participation in local government was, as Beaumont said, the political activity "perhaps nearer to his heart than any
other."[13] He took his turn on a jury, even when it hindered the
writing of *Democracy,* and he shouldered the responsibility of register-
ing the lodgers and servants of the families in his locality as soon as
they became eligible to vote.[14] In Tocqueville's opinion, the establishment of local liberties was, in Europe at least, the gift of the Middle
Ages, an era of dispersed powers each soaked in the medieval *"spirit of
locality."*[15] With the central government checked at every point by
formal groups or intermediate associations—classes, guilds, villages
with special grants and privileges, geographical areas with formal
rights against the Crown, extended families, provincial institutions,
trade corporations, the powers of clergy and parish—what Tocqueville called democratic despotism was impossible, precisely because
society boasted multiple aggregations of power capable of obstinate
resistance. Although Tocqueville by no means glorified feudal
times—times in which "arbitrary power, violence, and great freedom
all existed"—he did share the enthusiasm of Bodin and Montesquieu
for the medieval monarchy that, in theory, assured local freedom.[16] It
was a questionable picture of French politics in the Middle Ages pop-

---

11. Ibid., 1: 45.
12. Tocqueville, *Journey to America,* p. 186.
13. Quoted in Tocqueville, *Memoir,* 1: 68–75.
14. Tocqueville, *Oeuvres* (M), vol. 8, pt. 1, *Correspondance . . . Beaumont,* p. 274;
Tocqueville, *Correspondence . . . Senior,* 1: 100–101.
15. Tocqueville, *Oeuvres* (M), vol. 5, pt. 2, *Voyages en Angleterre, Irlande, Suisse et
Algérie,* p. 222; *Journeys to England and Ireland,* p. 197.
16. Tocqueville, *The European Revolution and Correspondence with Gobineau,* pp. 45–
46; Montesquieu, *The Spirit of the Laws,* XI, 8, 1: 163. Even Bodin, often dismissed as an
apologist for absolute power, suggested that once guilds, associations, and communities

ularized by Guizot, Barante, Thierry, and other historians under the French Restoration.[17]

The Middle Ages offered Tocqueville a welcome example of class cooperation in the pursuit of political ends, and he admired the close and daily contact of the nobility with common citizens, something he thought formed a sharp contrast to the isolation of citizens from one another that haunted the nineteenth century (as we saw in chapter 2). Indeed, Tocqueville claimed the medieval community was frequently a form of direct democracy, that municipal officials were elected by the "entire population of the town," and, with his profound French pride, he announced similarities between the townships of New England and the medieval communes of France. "In short, the French and American systems resembled each other—insofar as a dead creature can be said to resemble one that is very much alive. . . . Transported overseas from feudal Europe and free to develop in total independence, the rural parish of the Middle Ages became the township of New England."[18] By the eighteenth century, almost all Tocqueville's beloved municipalities had lost their independence to monarchical intrusion, and the Intendant, the middle-class representative of royal power, carefully watched and circumscribed the decisions of localities. Once eager to deliberate in common so as to master their own affairs, the French municipalities had to humiliate themselves by pleading for permission to build a church or plan a festival. "On studying the records I found that it took a year at least for a parish to get permission to repair a church steeple or the priest's house."[19] Tocqueville revealed all too clearly both an anger at French monarchs, especially Louis xiv, and a touch of nostalgia for a previous aristocratic age. Nevertheless, despite this admiration of the past, Tocqueville persisted in arguing that a return to the kind of freedom found in feudal times was impossible. "Thus the question is not how to reconstruct aristocratic society, but how to make liberty proceed out of that democratic state of society in which God has placed us."[20]

---

lost the right to deliberate and decide in common, freedom had disappeared. Jean Bodin, *Six Books of the Commonwealth*, trans. and abridged by M. J. Tooley (New York, 1967), III, 7, pp. 99–107.

17. See, for example, Guizot, *History of Civilization in Europe*, p. 151.

18. Tocqueville, *The Old Regime*, pp. 48, 85, 44.

19. Ibid., pp. 62, 47, 45. In his analysis, Tocqueville consistently understated the importance of foreign wars in centralizing the French monarchy, and he underestimated the role of the aristocracy in the local government of the Old Regime. See Richard Herr, *Tocqueville and the Old Regime* (Princeton, 1962), pp. 120–25; also Georges Lefebvre, *The Coming of the French Revolution*, trans. R. R. Palmer (Princeton, 1947), pp. 7–20, 131–41.

20. Tocqueville, *Democracy*, 2: 340.

Democratic freedom necessitates even more extensive decentralization and direct participation. In private notebooks written toward the end of his life, Tocqueville wrote that the word *democracy* must be "clearly defined" to avoid interminable confusion. "But *democratic government, democratic monarchy* can mean only one thing in the true sense of these words: a government where the people more or less participate in their government."[21] Unfortunately, Tocqueville used the word *democracy* with many different meanings, and he spent a great part of his life intermixing the words *democracy* and *equality*, using the latter word in a host of different ways, thus compounding the interminable confusion he deplored. Nonetheless, if the word *democracy* did not always, for Tocqueville, imply freedom, he did consistently insist that freedom requires decentralization and decentralization requires participation. In the United States, democracy fostered freedom precisely because of widespread municipal participation, a participation whose importance easily exceeded that of national liberties, for "America created municipal liberty before it created public liberty."[22] In the New England township, a general assembly of citizens discussed common affairs and debated in ways that reminded Tocqueville of the Athenian marketplace. They made it clear that the town's chosen officers, the selectmen, had to consult the assembled citizens before embarking upon new endeavors. Decentralization clearly resides at the heart of his thesis that freedom entails mastery of one's world. "The people reign in the American political world as the Deity does in the universe. They are the cause and the aim of all things."[23]

Men and women learn to master their world cooperatively only through political participation. Even though Tocqueville once said that political philosophers should originate laws, leaving individuals with political experience to institute them, he generally manifested a resolute mistrust of the picture of politics given by books. The eighteenth-century philosophes, while passionately concerned with political reform, lacked all political experience, but, even worse, so did their audience. Tocqueville argued that the least political experience, the smallest habit of occasional political participation, would have made the French people wary of clinging to the faith that political change could follow the ideas of the philosophes.[24] Authentic ideas,

21. Tocqueville, *The European Revolution and Correspondence with Gobineau*, p. 102.
22. Tocqueville, *Journey to America*, p. 183.
23. Tocqueville, *Democracy*, 1: 60, 42, 65.
24. Tocqueville, *The Old Regime*, pp. 140–41. Tocqueville probably underestimated the extent to which the philosophes either held public office or influenced those who did.

ideas that insightfully confront the needs and possibilities of one's time, surface in political participation. "True information is mainly derived from experience; and if the Americans had not been gradually accustomed to govern themselves, their book-learning would not help them."[25]

Tocqueville confided to Beaumont that living as a free man is an "art,"[26] but it is an art perfected only while living as a free man, ultimately a strikingly circular problem that befalls all efforts toward political regeneration. "Liberty alone can teach us to be free."[27] If the ability to be free unfolds only while one acts in a free community, then how does one cultivate this ability? Tocqueville confronted this problem when he talked about slavery. Surely slavery induced a thousand vices and a thousand habits inimical to genuine political freedom and, as the proponents of slavery declared, to free a slave is to free someone incapable of citizenship. Although Tocqueville agreed, he insisted that this could never be an excuse for perpetuating slavery. Freedom may involve pain and difficulty, but freedom is the only way in which the capacities of the slave will be developed. "The period which follows the abolition of slavery has therefore always been a time of uneasiness and social difficulty. This is an inevitable evil; we must resolve to meet it or make slavery eternal."[28] Similarly, a people not enslaved but still unaccustomed to the habits of participatory freedom can learn those habits only with the introduction of free institutions that encourage individual participation. A free society forces men and women to rely on themselves in mastering their world, just as the American Indian in the forest and the orphaned child who scrapes to survive in the streets develop the skills of self-reliance out of necessity.[29] Of the 1848 French National Assembly, composed of intelligent men long denied any occasion for political action, Tocqueville said, "I am sure that nine hundred English or American peasants chosen at random would have had much more the look of a great political body."[30]

The benefits of participation are immense. The United States of 1831 was Tocqueville's example of the ways in which people learn freedom and learn about political affairs, just as one learns a lan-

---

25. Tocqueville, *Democracy*, 1: 329.
26. Tocqueville, *Oeuvres* (M), vol. 8, pt. 1, *Correspondance . . . Beaumont*, p. 411.
27. Drescher, ed., *Tocqueville and Beaumont on Social Reform*, p. 130.
28. Ibid., p. 102.
29. Tocqueville, *Journey to America*, p. 254; Alexis de Toqueville [sic] and Gustave de Beaumont, *On the Penitentiary System in the United States and Its Application in France*, trans. Francis Lieber (New York, 1970), p. 116.
30. Tocqueville, *Recollections*, p. 127.

guage—by using it. "The American people, taken in mass, is not only the most enlightened in the world, but, what I rank as much more important than that advantage, *it is the people whose practical political education is the most advanced.*"[31] One learns, through participation, about the entire operation of the political system. The jury, for example, "is a school where the people come to learn their rights," and municipal institutions enable Americans "to know the laws by participating in the act of legislation." "Municipal institutions constitute the strength of free nations. Town meetings are to liberty what primary schools are to science; they bring it within the people's reach, they teach men how to use and how to enjoy it. A nation may establish a free government, but without municipal institutions it cannot have the spirit of liberty."[32] Not only does participation teach one how the political system functions, but it teaches men and women of their own interdependence while inculcating a concern for public affairs. Indeed, the obligation to participate in decision making and in institutions like the jury "rubs off that private selfishness which is the rust of society." Eventually the habits of free individuals created by public action resonate through the entire political culture, invigorating each component, down to the games of children where elections and trial by jury become commonplace.[33]

More important, even though participation teaches us of our obligations toward others and of our interdependence, it also produces an inner strength and confidence in personal independence. "To be free one must have the capacity to plan and persevere in a difficult undertaking, and be accustomed to act on one's own."[34] But this individual confidence flowers only in cooperative, participatory struggles to master the decision making of one's world. Democratic freedom demands that one rely on oneself, one's efforts, and one's neighbors in order to accomplish anything. Tocqueville marveled at the American's ability to associate with others to build a school, hospital, or church, assuming that such activities are the business either of local government or of private associations and not of distant national officials. In the absence of a strong and intrusive government, "each man learns to think and to act for himself without counting on the support of any outside power. . . ."[35]

31. Tocqueville, *Journey to America,* p. 246.
32. Ibid., p. 304; *Democracy,* 1: 330, 63.
33. Tocqueville, *Democracy,* 1: 295, 330.
34. Tocqueville, *Journeys to England and Ireland,* p. 106.
35. Tocqueville, *Journey to America,* p. 39.

THE STERILITY OF CENTRALIZATION

Beyond imparting the habits of freedom, decentralization exposes the innate sterility of centralized government that "preponderates, acts, regulates, controls, undertakes everything, provides for everything, knows far more about the subject's business than he does himself—is, in short, incessantly active and sterile."[36] The sterility of centralization arises from the indifference that such government eagerly encourages in citizens who might otherwise engage themselves in public affairs. Although communities in the United States distributed power with some rough measure of equality and attempted to encourage participation, in France most subjects (hardly citizens, in Tocqueville's eyes, and more like spectators) gazed upon the public world as if it were an uninteresting stage production in which only a few were graced with the right to act. Europe could boast only of the spectacle of nations composed of "settlers, indifferent to the fate" of public affairs, leaving judgments about schools, churches, local finances, community affairs, and national decisions to "a powerful stranger whom he calls the government."[37]

By contrast, in decentralized governments thousands of citizens, rather than dozens of functionaries, throw themselves into constructing their world. Tocqueville noted favorably an American who suggested that the financing of local projects by centralized government fosters apathy, whereas decentralized financing engenders more widespread participation. Communities that rely on the national government to finance education remain "indifferent about their schools," but when using their own money, "they take a great interest."[38] Thus, decentralized activity is direct and forceful, because communities know their immediate needs, a conviction that one sees in Tocqueville's quotation of his friend Francis Lieber. Lieber argued that the very idea

36. Tocqueville, *The Old Regime*, p. 253. Tocqueville distinguished between a centralized government, which speaks for the nation and deals with general laws and principles, and a centralized administration, which enables the tentacles of the central government to meddle in local affairs; he approved of the former and disapproved of the latter. (*Democracy*, 1: 89–92.) For our purposes, we shall ignore his distinction, because (1) after *Democracy*, he rarely made the same distinction and usually ignored it himself, using merely the word *centralization*, and (2) in practice, as Tocqueville's own analysis demonstrated, it is hard to see how a centralized government would not invariably give birth to a centralized administration. Furet's excellent study of Tocqueville's *Old Regime* supports this view. (*Interpreting the French Revolution*, pp. 144–49, 159.) For a fine discussion of Tocqueville's idea of centralization, see Schleifer, *The Making of Tocqueville's "Democracy in America,"* ch. 10.

37. Tocqueville, *Democracy*, 1: 96.

38. Tocqueville, *Journey to America*, pp. 227–28.

of appealing to distant government to solve local concerns "does not come into anybody's head," that a republic is not a set of institutions but a set of habits and thus, in America, "the people have something of the republic in the marrow of their bones." Both Tocqueville and Lieber admired not administrative efficiency but popular effort and enthusiasm. "The republic is everywhere, in the streets as much as in Congress. If there is something blocking the public way, the neighbors on the spot form a body to discuss it; they appoint a commission and put the trouble to rights by their collective effort sensibly directed."[39]

Tocqueville most admired the energy that bursts forth from a multiplicity of actions, an energy he described as the "blind but energetic passions of locality."[40]

> No sooner do you set foot upon American ground than you are stunned by a kind of tumult; a confused clamor is heard on every side, and a thousand simultaneous voices demand the satisfaction of their social wants. Everything is in motion around you; here the people of one quarter of a town are met to decide upon the building of a church; there the election of a representative is going on; a little farther, the delegates of a district are hastening to the town in order to consult upon some local improvements; in another place, the laborers of a village quit their plows to deliberate upon the project of a road or a public school.[41]

To Tocqueville's immense astonishment and pleasure, Americans seemed to have the habit of participation and to take great pleasure in that habit. "If an American were condemned to confine his activity to his own affairs, he would be robbed of one half of his existence; he would feel an immense void in the life which he is accustomed to lead, and his wretchedness would be unbearable."[42] In the midst of the energy and clamor of participatory democracy, Americans learned to embrace a life of tumultuous change. They not only adjusted themselves to a world of change, but the individual citizen "feels the need of it, he loves it, for instability instead of causing disasters for him, seems only to bring forth wonders around him."[43]

In his suggestion that popular energy, once released, can perform wonders, Tocqueville revealed a populist thread in his thinking. "Political liberty is a difficult food to digest. It is only extremely robust

---

39. Ibid., p. 43.
40. Tocqueville, *Oeuvres* (M), vol. 5, pt. 2, *Voyages en Angleterre, Irlande, Suisse et Algérie*, p. 184.
41. Tocqueville, *Democracy*, 1: 259.
42. Ibid., p. 260.
43. Tocqueville, *Journey to America*, p. 187.

constitutions that can take it. But when it has been digested, albeit with pain, it gives the whole body . . . an energy which surprises even those who expected the most from it."[44] At least twice Tocqueville quoted Montesquieu's well-known claim that "the soil is productive less by reason of its natural fertility than because the people tilling it are free,"[45] arguing that purposeful energy can fertilize the most mediocre land. Energy vanquishes sterility. In a similar way, Tocqueville disputed with those who contended that centralized government acts more efficiently than decentralized government. Centralization may indeed be efficient in the routine of government, providing order and stability with a certain amount of skill, but it nonetheless induces apathy and "perpetuates a drowsy regularity in the conduct of affairs which the heads of the administration are wont to call good order and public tranquillity."[46] Even though Tocqueville conceded that centralization exhibits consistency in policy, perseverance in its tasks, and accuracy in the details of administration, he stressed that decentralized participation may do "fewer things well, but it does a greater number of things. . . . Democracy does not give the people the most skillful government, but it produces what the ablest governments are frequently unable to create: namely, an all-pervading and restless activity, a superabundant force, and an energy which is inseparable from it and which may, however unfavourable circumstances may be, produce wonders."[47] An engineer can give reluctant carpenters instructions for a perfect house, but neighbors willfully acting in concert can build a dozen very good houses in the same amount of time.

ASSOCIATIONS

This discussion of decentralization enables us to understand Tocqueville's love of associations. If one hunts assiduously, one can uncover evidence to support the pluralist interpretation of Tocqueville's idea of associations. According to this interpretation, associations—that is, groups representing individuals with a common interest—constitute a buffer between the individual and the state. In

44. Ibid., pp. 182–83. Rousseau used this identical metaphor of freedom as a difficult food to digest. See Jean-Jacques Rousseau, *The Government of Poland*, trans. Willmoore Kendall (New York, 1972), pp. 29–30.

45. Tocqueville, *The Old Regime*, p. 123; Tocqueville, *Oeuvres* (B), vol. 7, *Nouvelle correspondance*, p. 304.

46. Tocqueville, *Democracy*, 1: 94.

47. Ibid., pp. 261–62.

addition, the very action of these groups pursuing narrow group interests brings about a "functional representation," because the resulting balance of these competing interests approximately reflects the general good.[48] Through lobbying, compromise, disseminating information, and elections, associations become the "mechanisms for creating and maintaining the consensus necessary for a democratic society."[49] In fact, Tocqueville did argue that associations served as intermediary powers between the individual and the state, powers that he hoped could replace the traditional groups of aristocratic society. "An association for political, commercial, or manufacturing purposes, or even for those of science and literature . . . by defending its own rights against the encroachments of the government, saves the common liberties of the country."[50] Moreover, he did say that an association seeks to persuade the majority to yield to its interests and to adhere to its ideas, always using legal mechanisms and the legislative process. "They always entertain hopes of drawing over the majority to their own side."[51]

Yet to proceed no further in one's discussion of Tocqueville's concept of associations is to wring the life out of his word until, although the word remains, the original meaning disappears, like a magician who, having put one person in a trunk, opens it later to display a stranger. One can see this in the pluralist's exclusive use of the noun *association*, disregarding Tocqueville's just as frequent use of the verb *s'associer*. Like the very associations described by pluralist interpretations of Tocqueville, the noun towers above us as a thing already built, as a reified entity beyond our command.[52] When Tocqueville used the verb *s'associer*, he conveyed immediately the sense of purposeful action and energy that dwells at the heart of his idea of associations.

French writers praised associations first and primarily for overcoming individual isolation by actively uniting individuals in cooperative efforts, and they consciously likened these new organizations to the intermediate associations, groups poised between king and subjects, that had been so cherished by Bodin and Montesquieu. Once more Tocqueville's generation journeyed back to the Middle Ages, for the medieval use of the word *s'associer* conveyed a sense of friends acting together, a sense that Bodin still imparted when he used the

48. Bendix, *Nation-Building and Citizenship*, pp. 91–101.
49. Lipset, *Political Man*, p. 7.
50. Tocqueville, *Democracy*, 2: 342.
51. Ibid., 1: 203.
52. Bendix even argues that associations are "impersonal" and founded merely on a "coalescence of interests" for "private ends." (*Nation-Building and Citizenship*, pp. 171, 168, 60.)

word. Friendship, Bodin declared, is the "tie of human associations"; if an association is ruled hierarchically, "it is not properly speaking a guild, but a form of family, like the colleges of young scholars where none of the bursars have [*sic*] a deliberative voice."[53] Rousseau used the word *association* to describe both the union of dispersed "savages" and his participatory community; the Saint-Simonians declared the final goal of the world to be "universal association"; Fourier posited the association as the answer to isolated, self-interested individuals; and Michelet claimed that an authentic association must overcome individualism and egoism.[54] The very language Tocqueville used to describe an association sometimes had the unmistakable imprint of Rousseau. "When men associate [*s'associent*] for whatever purpose, each alienates a certain portion of his freedom to act and to think, a freedom of which the association makes use."[55] By Tocqueville's time, the word *association* was dripping with a connotation that has since evaporated. Tocqueville could not escape this connotation, nor did he try. It was one of his solutions to the problems of isolation, privatization, the fragmentation of society, and powerlessness—problems that we have seen were concerns of his generation. Linked to each other only by self-interest, workers and owners, Tocqueville claimed, have "frequent relations, but no real association."[56] An association, he maintained, is a cooperative effort directed toward accomplishing things "unattainable by isolated effort."[57]

Rather than perceiving an association as the representative of the interests of passive citizens, Tocqueville called the "art of association" the "mother of action." All individuals, not just a few, must become active, for all will in the end "become powerless if they do not learn voluntarily to help one another."[58] In an imaginary political landscape dominated by Tocquevillian associations, people do not merely beckon to established powers to grant their interests, but they actively carry out their intentions. "The power of the association has reached its highest degree in America. . . . It is never by recourse to a higher authority that one seeks success, but by an appeal to individual powers

53. Jean Bodin, *Method for the Easy Comprehension of History*, ed. and trans. Beatrice Reynolds (New York, 1969), p. 213; Bodin, *Six Books of the Commonwealth*, III, 7, p. 100.

54. Jean-Jacques Rousseau, *The Social Contract* and *Discourses*, trans. G.D.H. Cole (New York, 1950), *The Social Contract*, Bk. III, Ch. 17; Iggers, ed., *The Doctrine of Saint-Simon*, p. 58; Fourier, *Design for Utopia*, p. 88; Michelet, *Le Peuple*, p. 221.

55. Yale Tocqueville Collection, C.V.j., Paquet No. 2, Cahier No. 1, p. 4. Compare with Rousseau, *The Social Contract*, I, 6.

56. Tocqueville, *Democracy*, 2: 171.

57. Tocqueville, *Journeys to England and Ireland*, p. 75.

58. Tocqueville, *Democracy*, 2: 125, 115.

working in concert."[59] Indeed, Tocqueville only despised those associations in Europe that were rigidly hierarchical while admiring those in the United States that have "established a government."

> The members of [European] associations respond to a watchword, like soldiers on duty; they profess the doctrine of passive obedience; say, rather, that in uniting together they at once abjure the exercise of their own judgment and free will. . . . He who in given cases consents to obey his fellows with servility and who submits his will and even his thoughts to their control, how can he pretend that he wishes to be free?[60]

If members of associations cannot meet directly, they may have to govern themselves through representatives, uniting in "electoral bodies" and selecting "delegates to represent them in a central assembly."[61]

Associations pursue mainly, although not exclusively, public ends; that is, they pursue their ideas of the public good and not simply private interests. Again Bodin provides a reference. When heads of families associate, Bodin said, their purpose becomes a public one, and they must concern themselves with the commonwealth first, their private interests second. "When the head of the family leaves the household . . . he ceases to be lord and master, and becomes an equal and associate with the rest. He sets aside his private concerns to attend to public affairs."[62] Similarly, Tocqueville enthusiastically praised those efforts made in the United States for the common good. "In no country in the world do the citizens make such exertions for the common weal."[63] When he discussed associations, he emphasized not those that lobbied for material self-interest but those that cooperatively acted for the common good, which explains why he regarded "townships, cities, and counties" as premier, perhaps even prototypical, associations. The following passage reveals the predominantly public nature of the associations Tocqueville had in mind:

> Americans of all ages, all conditions, and all dispositions constantly form associations. They have not only commercial and manufacturing companies, in which all take part, but associations of a thousand other kinds, religious, moral, serious, futile, general or restricted, enormous or diminutive. The Americans make associations to give entertainments, to found seminaries, to build inns, to construct churches, to

59. Tocqueville, *Journey to America,* p. 219.
60. Tocqueville, *Democracy,* 1: 205.
61. Ibid., p. 199.
62. Bodin, *Six Books of the Commonwealth,* I, 6–7, p. 18.
63. Tocqueville, *Democracy,* 1: 95.

diffuse books, to send missionaries to the antipodes; in this manner they found hospitals, prisons, and schools. . . . Wherever at the head of some new undertaking you see the government in France, or a man of rank in England, in the United States you will be sure to find an association.[64]

In sum, the idea of associations is not a pluralist defense of a politics of self-interest but in important ways a critique of interest-group politics.

TOCQUEVILLE'S PESSIMISM: THE INEVITABILITY OF CENTRALIZATION

Unfortunately, with the disappearance of the old aristocratic institutions and with the historical movement toward equality, centralization seemed irreversible—what Tocqueville called a truly "democratic instinct," counterposed to the inherent tendency for decentralization in the dispersed, aristocratic society of the Middle Ages. "A democratic people tends toward centralization, as it were, by instinct. It arrives at provincial institutions only by reflection."[65] Stripped of the web of ties, groups, and privileges that once protected individuals in aristocratic society, people found no buffer between them and the state. "After the destruction of classes, corporations and castes, [the state] appeared as the necessary and natural heir to all the secondary powers. There was nothing so large that it could not overtake, nothing so small that it could not touch. The idea of centralization and that of the sovereignty of the people were born on the same day."[66] Indeed, "whenever a nation destroys its aristocracy, it almost automatically tends toward a centralization of power."[67] Wrenched from the guilds, families, communities, and classes that once surrounded them, individuals confronted a new bourgeois world both proud of their independence and naked in their powerlessness. Their hopeful gaze fell to the government, no longer to a local group that might offer assistance. Even though the individual's independence "fills him with self-reliance and

64. Ibid., p. 198; 2: 114.
65. Tocqueville, *Memoir*, 1: 234 (from "France before the Revolution").
66. Tocqueville, *Oeuvres* (B), vol. 9, *Études économiques, politiques*, p. 14; see also *Democracy*, 1: 11. For Tocqueville, the most important, but probably most elusive, goal of the modern legislator is to place the greatest possible number of intermediaries, modern variants of Montesquieu's intermediate associations, between the individual and the state. (Yale Tocqueville Collection, C.V.b., Paquet No. 13, p. 21.)
67. Tocqueville, *The Old Regime*, p. 60.

pride among his equals," he finds himself isolated and cannot turn to a group since all have been rendered "impotent." "In this predicament he naturally turns his eyes to that imposing power which alone rises above the level of universal depression."[68]

Even when people are in principle hostile to centralization, necessity will slowly suffocate their principles, for reasons outlined by Tocqueville's generation in chapter 4. For example, once the love of wealth dominates all other passions in the new bourgeois order, Tocqueville thought people would shout for the government to enforce the order essential to their accumulation of goods and pleasures. "The increasing love of well-being," he argued in *Democracy*, caused "democratic nations to dread all violent disturbances." This in turn "disposes the members of the community constantly to give or to surrender additional rights to the central power," which seemed to be the only body able to protect their possessions. Moreover, the obsessive disposition of the middle classes to think only of their private interests, Tocqueville felt, would tend to hasten centralization. Notwithstanding universally accepted ideas that denounce increasing governmental power, in practice each person or each interest group wishes to make an exception in the particular case in question and thus implores the government to rush any and all assistance, obviously augmenting governmental powers.

> Such persons will admit, as a general principle, that the public authority ought not to interfere in private concerns; but, by an exception to that rule, each of them craves its assistance in the particular concern on which he is engaged and seeks to draw upon the influence of the government for his own benefit, although he would restrict it on all other occasions. If a large number of men applies this particular exception to a great variety of different purposes, the sphere of the central power extends itself imperceptibly in all directions, although everyone wishes it to be circumscribed.
>
> Thus a democratic government increases its power simply by the fact of its permanence. Time is on its side; every incident befriends it; the passions of individuals unconsciously promote it; and it may be asserted that the older a democratic community is, the more centralized will its government become.[69]

For other reasons Tocqueville argued that centralization is indigenous to industrial society, or to be more precise, it *will* be indigenous as generations pass and industrial growth continues. The central gov-

68. Tocqueville, *Democracy*, 2: 311.
69. Ibid., pp. 310–12.

ernment will be summoned both to mediate disputes between owners and workers (although he never claimed government to be a neutral arbiter) and to alleviate the misery arising from the cycles of prosperity and poverty. The "one great cause" of governmental centralization in Europe will arise from industrialization. Industrialization has brought with it cycles involving "sudden alterations of plenty and want," and it has produced working conditions that frequently tend to "sacrifice the health and even the life" of members of the working class. As a result, Tocqueville suggested that industry would require governmental regulation, although one might wonder why local governments, instead of the national government, could not undertake this regulation. Nevertheless, the regulation of industry would be the greatest single cause of centralization. "Thus, the manufacturing classes require more regulation, superintendence, and restraint than the other classes of society, and it is natural that the powers of government should increase in the same proportion as those classes."[70]

Finally, not only will governments centralize for reasons unique to the new commercial society, they will also centralize for age-old reasons. For example, wars and crises always centralize; without the web of formal groups distinguishing aristocratic society, decentralization after a war or crisis is nearly impossible. War subverts the habits of participatory democracy, and these habits are the only protection for freedom that a democracy can substitute for aristocratic dispersal of groups.

> War does not always give over democratic communities to military government, but it must invariably and immeasurably increase the powers of civil government; it must almost compulsorily concentrate the direction of all men and the management of all things in the hands of the administration. If it does not lead to despotism by sudden violence, it prepares men for it more gently by their habits. All those who seek to destroy the liberties of a democratic nation ought to know that war is the surest and shortest means to accomplish it. This is the first axiom of the science.[71]

Other sorts of crises tend to centralize, especially the crisis that is the lifelong companion to an obsession for wealth: the perpetual fear of a drop in the standard of living. Eventually, argued Tocqueville, all democratic participation will be put aside, and government will be-

70. Ibid., p. 327.
71. For this quotation and the remaining paragraph in the text, see ibid., pp. 284, 318, 148–51.

come the watchman of the economy, the nation a machine for producing wealth.

Tocqueville of course feared the potential, arising from centralization, for plain old-fashioned tyranny. Since it is the "instinctive desire of every government to gather all the reins of power into its own hands," centralized government "fashions despotism and destroys citizenship."[72] But Tocqueville despised any centralization, even if benevolent *and* popularly elected; "to create a representation of the people in every centralized country is, therefore, to diminish the evil that extreme centralization may produce, but not to get rid of it."[73] Tocqueville feared oppression, but he feared a societal sedation even more. He always considered Russia as the most formidable enemy of liberty because its centralization both oppressed and anesthetized men and women. "Uniformity in liberty has always seemed boring to me, but what can be said of complete uniformity in servitude, of these [Russian] villages that are so perfectly alike, populated by people who are so perfectly similar, doing the same things, in the midst of the deepest slumber of intelligence? I confess to you in a whisper that I would prefer disordered barbarism."[74] Oppression is less dangerous than "the mania for regimentation" that squeezes all spirit from a people. "The modern bureaucrat," he said, must "efface" his personality. In the eighteenth century, "the craving to secure a place in the bureaucracy became a second nature with the Frenchman, and had much to do with the servile state to which people were reduced,"[75] and he worried that centralization would continue "till the very men who from time to time upset a throne and trample on a race of kings bend more and more obsequiously to the slightest dictate of a clerk."[76] This last passage, one of the most forceful in Tocqueville's writings, discloses his fear. By sapping popular energy, centralization might extinguish all capacity for action; Tocqueville's aristocratic ideal of heroism and grandeur kindled his contempt for the administration of things.

Centralized administration, Tocqueville felt, would help render a

72. Tocqueville, *The Old Regime*, p. 58; Yale Tocqueville Collection, C.V.b., Paquet No. 13, p. 1. The word Tocqueville actually used in this latter passage was not *citizenship* but *civisme* (in English, *civism*), a word, with wide circulation at the time of the French Revolution, that meant both good citizenship and having the proper disposition toward the French Revolution itself. It is a word that again reminds us how far removed we are from Tocqueville's vocabulary.

73. Tocqueville, *Democracy*, 2: 338.
74. Tocqueville, *Selected Letters*, p. 302.
75. Tocqueville, *The Old Regime*, pp. 63, 104.
76. Tocqueville, *Democracy*, 2: 332.

coup d'état more likely, but any significant political change less likely. A mere change of power became easy, because only one place must be vanquished. "Nothing is so favourable to revolution as centralization, because whoever can seize the central point is obeyed down to the extremities."[77] Like Weber, however, Tocqueville recognized that a functioning bureaucracy effectively resists all change by simply proceeding according to past rules, smothering both revolutionary change and innovative reform. Amidst the revolutions of 1830 and 1848, even when the head of the government bureaucracy had been severed, "its body survived intact and active."[78] Indeed, a bureaucratic machine "is hardly dependent on the worth of the men running it," and it will run even when "the central motor [is] shut off."[79]

CENTRALIZATION: THE INTERTWINING OF POLITICS AND ECONOMICS

Tocqueville's dislike for centralization led him to despise what he conceived to be socialism, a socialism distinguished by the regimentation suggested by Babeuf, Cabet, and Fourier—the kind of socialism that prompted the Saint-Simonians to declare "we call for order and proclaim the strongest and most unitary hierarchy for the future."[80] Professing a contempt for those "ultra-centralizers who wish to make the state the creditor of all its citizens," Tocqueville told Beaumont that such men form a "race which I detest even more, I believe, than the lackeys of the conservative party."[81] "To deliver to the government the direction of industry" seemed to Tocqueville the swiftest way to bring about centralization and all its pernicious effects.[82] Tocqueville, for example, fought Abbé Landmann's proposal to establish socialist communities in Algeria, because men, instead of working for themselves, would be merely "bees" toiling for the "hive."[83] In a speech delivered to the Constituent Assembly in September 1848, the period in Tocqueville's life when he was most hostile to working-class movements, he declared: "We come to the third and last trait [of socialists], the one which most clearly characterizes so-

77. Tocqueville, *Correspondence . . . Senior*, 2: 133.
78. Tocqueville, *The Old Regime*, p. 202.
79. Tocqueville, *The European Revolution and Correspondence with Gobineau*, p. 152.
80. Iggers, ed., *The Doctrine of Saint-Simon*, pp. 115–16.
81. Tocqueville, *Oeuvres* (M), vol. 8, pt. 1, *Correspondance . . . Beaumont*, p. 507.
82. Tocqueville, *Oeuvres* (M), vol. 11, *Correspondance . . . Royer-Collard . . . Ampère*, p. 60; *Oeuvres* (B), vol. 9, *Études économiques, politiques*, p. 78.
83. Tocqueville, *L'Algérie*, in *Oeuvres* (M), vol. 3, *Écrits et discours politiques*, p. 250.

cialists of every stripe, of every school. . . . It is the idea that the State must not only direct society, but must be, so to speak, the master of every man. . . . It is a new form of servitude."[84] It might be argued that Tocqueville ignored those thinkers who suggested that democratic, decentralized control of the economy was compatible with a form of socialism, but Tocqueville's message—that the national government must not direct economic affairs—is unmistakable.

But what kind of economy could Tocqueville envision as being consistent with his love of decentralization, since he argued that both capitalism and socialism tend toward centralization? His fear of socialism leading to extreme centralization led him to profess, with some wavering and with numerous qualifications, the views of the English political economists. In a passage in his notebooks, written just after he left England for Ireland in 1835, Tocqueville argued that freedom and trade promote each other. "Considering the world's history I can find some free peoples who have been neither manufacturers nor traders. But I can find no example of a manufacturing and, above all, a trading people who have not been free."[85] Although one can search in vain for any similar assertion once Tocqueville arrived back on the soil of his aristocratic ancestors (because he always seemed to see the world through the spectacles of the country he was visiting), this passage apparently substantiates the claim that Tocqueville believed a *laissez faire* economic policy promoted freedom. But, in fact, he equivocated about *laissez faire* principles.

Tocqueville's wavering manifested his conviction that political questions must not become subordinate to economic ones. "I believe, moreover, that there are political interests in favor of which it is wise to sacrifice, to a certain degree, industrial interests."[86] For example, Tocqueville affirmed the right of property and, in June of 1848, he worried that the insurgents would undermine "family, property, and civilization."[87] But he never suggested that the right of property was an unbreakable natural right. In fact, Tocqueville shared none of what he called the English Tory's "superstitious cult of the rights of property,"[88] because he believed that property was a right created by individuals acting politically, a right sustained only because, and as long as, it did indeed foster the general good. When, as in Ireland,

84. Drescher, ed., *Tocqueville and Beaumont on Social Reform*, p. 183.
85. Tocqueville, *Journeys to England and Ireland*, pp. 105–6.
86. Tocqueville, *Oeuvres* (B), vol. 7, *Nouvelle correspondance*, p. 202.
87. Alexis de Tocqueville, *Alexis de Tocqueville als Abgeordneter* (Hamburg, 1972), p. 129.
88. Tocqueville, *Journeys to England and Ireland*, p. 73.

most starved while others basked in superfluity, then the right of property must be modified. Thus, in the public interest, Tocqueville summoned the government (and somehow he did think this could be done without centralization) to disperse monopolies; to regulate industry when it threatened public interest; to oversee such public works as railroads, harbors, and canals; and to ensure a relatively equal industrial development in all French provinces.[89] In addition, government, and again wherever possible local government, must regulate wages if workers are being treated unfairly, relieve poverty, ensure legal aid and cheap insurance for the poor, extend education and hospitalization to all, and assist workers to form their own savings banks, credit unions, and mutual aid associations.[90]

To the extent that it fostered entrepreneurial characteristics— self-reliance, innovation, energy, and so forth—Tocqueville admired a *laissez faire* economy. Nonetheless, he despised the bourgeois economy for the poverty and degradation that he thought invariably traveled with it, a degradation always pretended to be an accident, but which, like an embarrassing little brother, was a blood relation.

> When one crosses the various countries of Europe, one is struck by a very extraordinary and apparently inexplicable sight. The countries appearing to be most impoverished are those which in reality account for the fewest indigents, and among the peoples most admired for their opulence, one part of the population is obliged to rely on the gifts of the other in order to live.[91]

Tocqueville continued by suggesting that the reader journey across England, marvel at the magnificent roads and the new houses, and imagine that one has arrived at the "Eden of modern civilization." But, if one looked closely enough, one would find that one-sixth of England's population was so poor as to require public charity.[92] The fact that modern industry seemed to bring poverty as well as wealth into the world was bad enough; even worse, the industry that created the cherished wealth of the middle classes degraded men and women, transformed them into brutes and savages, and reduced them to tools laboring fiercely to serve machines.

89. Tocqueville, *Oeuvres* (B), vol. 9, *Études économiques, politiques*, pp. 77, 573; *Democracy*, 2: 330; *Oeuvres* (M), vol. 8, pt. 2, *Correspondance . . . Beaumont*, p. 294.

90. Drescher, *Tocqueville and England*, ch. 7; Tocqueville, *Democracy*, 2: 200–201; for an excellent discussion of the relation between democracy and industrialization in Tocqueville's thought, see Seymour Drescher, *Dilemmas of Democracy* (Pittsburgh, 1968), ch. 3.

91. Drescher, ed., *Tocqueville and Beaumont on Social Reform*, pp. 1–2.

92. Ibid., p. 2.

A sort of black smoke covers the city. The sun seen through it is a disc without rays. Under this half daylight 300,000 human beings are ceaselessly at work . . . the crunching wheels of machinery, the shriek of steam from boilers, the regular beat of the looms, the heavy rumble of carts, those are the noises from which you can never escape in the sombre half-light of these streets. . . . From this filthy sewer pure gold flows. Here humanity attains its most complete development and its most brutish; here civilization works its miracles, and civilized man is turned back almost into a savage.[93]

The worker "loses the general faculty of applying his mind to the direction of the work," and after years of labor, "he no longer belongs to himself, but to the calling."[94] When Tocqueville had editorial control over the newspaper *Le Commerce,* he allowed Lamartine to express the same sort of anger Tocqueville expressed only in private notebooks. Society is tending, said Lamartine, "toward a passive role of *laissez faire* and *laissez passer,* the brutal axioms of the English system, and *laissez faire* and *laissez passer* invariably mean nothing less than *laissez souffrir* and *laissez mourir.*"[95] Finally, like his mentor Pascal and a successor such as Durkheim, Tocqueville objected—through *Le Commerce*—to what he considered the moral decay of a society consecrating itself to the impossible ideal of *laissez faire.* "By restricting man in the narrow and coarse sphere of material well-being, by exciting his needs and desires beyond all measure, one deprives work of its moral goal and its most satisfying reward. Nothing remains any longer but the love of gain."[96] Once more, Tocqueville's harshness toward the new bourgeois society places his political thought carefully alongside the concerns of his generation.

Because Tocqueville persistently postponed his often promised study of economics, he rarely quarreled with his English friends about economic issues, even though he had a strong distaste for the free-trade liberalism of people such as Cobden, Bright, and Senior. Without question, Tocqueville mistrusted large industry and the capitalist ethic, and although he always remained certain that these were morally and politically undesirable, he simultaneously suspected that they were economically unnecessary. When in Switzerland, for example, he eagerly embraced the Swiss model of successful, small industry—

93. Tocqueville, *Journeys to England and Ireland,* p. 96.
94. Tocqueville, *Democracy,* 2: 168–69.
95. *Le Commerce,* December 30, 1844; see also Roger Boesche, "Tocqueville and *Le Commerce*: A Newspaper Expressing His Unusual Liberalism," *Journal of the History of Ideas* 44 (April–June 1983): 277–92.
96. *Le Commerce,* January 7, 1845.

indeed the nearly cooperative industries within villages. "The political and moral advantages of this kind of manufacture seem evident; but the example of England seemed to prove that, with respect to economy (which is everything in commerce), this system was defective. Nonetheless we have just seen that the Swiss were competing against England and France, which have a centralization of commerce."[97] Since Tocqueville was horrified at the size of the French Ministry of the Interior, which employed only twelve hundred people, we can surmise his reaction to private industries employing tens of thousands.[98]

Tocqueville most feared a state cursed with the twin terrors of large aggregations of industrial power and a highly centralized government, two centralized powers that might alternate in teaching docility. "Manufactures govern us, [centralized governments] govern manufactures."[99] Indeed, "equality increasingly extends its dominion everywhere—except in industry, which is moving in a more aristocratic direction every day," and capital slowly becomes "concentrated in a few hands."[100] In his notes on Machiavelli's *History of Florence*, Tocqueville claimed that democracy cannot succeed in large manufacturing cities like Manchester or Liverpool. If a democratic nation empties its rural areas and undermines the importance of its small towns, democracy will fail. Industrial cities, Tocqueville suggested, must remain exceptions.[101]

Since Tocqueville consistently admired popular, participatory action—indeed he praised *les institutions communales* of American democracy[102]—he approved of private industry when it was characterized not by petty obligarchies but by individuals actively congregating in a cooperative endeavor. "Certain men happen to have a common interest in some concern; either a commercial undertaking is to be managed, or some speculation in manufactures to be tried; they meet, they combine, and thus, by degrees, they become familiar with the principle of association."[103] Tocqueville's affection was not for something abstract called "private enterprise," the right of corporate owners to act in their economic interests, but rather for the dispersal of power and the social energy that frequently surfaces in economic

97. Tocqueville, *Oeuvres* (M), vol. 5, pt. 2, *Voyages en Angleterre, Irlande, Suisse et Algérie,* p. 188.

98. Tocqueville, *Selected Letters,* p. 60.

99. Tocqueville, *Democracy,* 2: 331.

100. Drescher, ed., *Tocqueville and Beaumont on Social Reform,* p. 200.

101. Tocqueville, *Oeuvres* (B), vol. 8, *Mélanges, fragments,* p. 446.

102. Yale Tocqueville Collection, C.V.e., p. 9.

103. Tocqueville, *Democracy,* 2: 123, 330–31.

endeavors that successfully escape government control. He embraced any association, either for civic purposes or for industrial ones, in which people willingly and consciously associate themselves for some common goal. In his history of Cherbourg, he commended enthusiastically the ceaseless attempts of citizens to build a breakwater. "It had an audacious and grandiose character which struck contemporaries, and which merits the attention of posterity." Above all, their efforts brought them together, taught them cooperation, made them aware of their own powers and creativity. "All those who were present at this grand scene have retained the most lively memory of it, despite the years; they speak of it with as much warmth as if the thing had happened yesterday; there was in that, indeed, more than a ceremony: it was one of the most beautiful spectacles that man has ever been able to contemplate."[104] Such praise, even though the breakwater soon collapsed! He admired not the efficiency but the energy. If citizens of a parish, a county, or a community undertook an economic project in competition with private companies, Tocqueville approved.[105] Workers who united themselves in self-help associations or worker-controlled rather than state-controlled credit unions drew his praise.[106] All were economic enterprises that fostered decentralized, democratic mastery over one's world. In the end, of course, Tocqueville's economic thoughts were both inconsistent and confused, and he hardly offered a clear economic program for a modern industrial world. He was frustrated with the large enterprises of capitalism and was terrified of the claims of socialism.

Tocqueville's passion for decentralization had its roots in the French past, but it was nourished by his concern, shared by his generation, for the atomization of society and the resulting sensation of powerlessness. Decentralized political and economic participation push men and women from their private self-interested worlds into the public, teach them in a practical way how to master their surroundings, remind them of their interdependence and of the pleasures of cooperation, and militate against the docility and sterility encouraged by centralization. Cooperative, decentralized efforts— efforts that release the latent potentials for popular energy and that impel men and women to master their political world—are the first marks of a free nation.

104. Tocqueville, *Oeuvres* (B), vol. 9, *Études économiques, politiques*, pp. 153, 155.
105. Tocqueville, *Journey to America*, p. 288.
106. Tocqueville, *Democracy*, 2: 325; *The European Revolution and Correspondence with Gobineau*, p. 157; *Le Commerce*, December 30, 1844; Drescher, *Tocqueville and England*, ch. 7.

7 Freedom as Interdependence: The Paradox of Personal Independence

Revealing his debt to a long English tradition stretching back at least to Hobbes, Mill claimed that "the only freedom which deserves the name is that of pursuing our own good in our own way,"[1] a private and individualistic definition of freedom that has doggedly stalked us into our century. Tocqueville, borrowing from both the conservatives and the radical republicans in the French tradition, would have none of this definition, or, as will be clear later, would have only half of it. French conservatives such as Bossuet, de Maistre, or Bonald discovered in the unity of the closely knit societies of medieval times a critique of the self-interested individualism that they felt was implicit in both commercial societies and in definitions of freedom offered by modern liberalism. Out of political and military necessity, the far-reaching dispersal of the Middle Ages spawned a multitude of hierarchical but unified communities characterized by close ties among all citizens. Indeed, the group and the individual were nearly "inseparable," because "the solitary individual . . . could do but little."[2] In *L'Histoire des variations*, a book that Tocqueville greatly admired, Bossuet expressed his fear that the individualism inherent in Protestantism would generate a ceaseless questioning of all authority and a dangerous individual independence, eventually dissipating all cooperation, even in the most ordinary undertakings. "When each

1. John Stuart Mill, *On Liberty*, I.
2. Marc Bloch, *Feudal Society*, trans. L. A. Manyon, 2 vols. (Chicago, 1961), 1: 123–26.

does what he wants, and has for a rule only his own desires, all goes into confusion."[3] Montesquieu expressed an opinion later assumed by Rousseau, declaring that freedom could not equal personal independence. "We must continually present to our minds the difference between independence and liberty. . . . The independence of individuals is the end aimed at by the laws of Poland, thence results the oppression of the whole."[4] Rousseau's Emile similarly lamented that the people of Europe, "in their efforts after independence . . . become slaves."[5] Or as Rousseau said somewhat more dramatically in speaking of possible political regeneration in Poland:

> Liberty is a food that is good to taste but hard to digest: it sets well only on a good strong stomach. I laugh at those debased peoples that let themselves be stirred up by agitators and dare to speak of liberty without so much as having the idea of it; with their hearts still heavy with the vices of slaves, they imagine that they have only to be mutinous in order to be free. Proud, sacred liberty! If they but knew her, those wretched men; if they but understood the price at which she is won and held; if they but realized that her laws are stern as the tyrant's yoke is never hard, their sickly souls, the slaves of passions that would have to be hauled out by the roots, would fear liberty a hundred times as much as they fear servitude. They would flee her in terror as they would a burden about to crush them.[6]

THE DIFFERENCE BETWEEN FREEDOM AND INDEPENDENCE

In our century it is difficult to imagine the apparently modern Tocqueville motivated by Bossuet's Catholic distrust of Protestant individualism and influenced by Rousseau's nostalgic conviction that Roman republican freedom originated in personal discipline or even in individual self-sacrifice, but in fact he was. Using language that might please Bossuet, Montesquieu, or Rousseau, Tocqueville stated emphatically that freedom is more than the independence to do as one wishes. As he admired the American Revolution, he suggested that this revolution was not the result of a "vague or ill-defined craving for independence" but was rather the result of mature reflection and a reasoned "preference for freedom." Indeed, the American

---

3. Abbé Bossuet, *Extraits des oeuvres diverses* (Paris, 1899), p. 200. (From *Politique: tirée des propres paroles de l'Écriture Sainte.*) See also p. 325. (From *L'Histoire des variations des églises protestantes.*)

4. Montesquieu, *Spirit of the Laws*, XI, 3–5, 1: 150–51.

5. Rousseau, *Émile*, p. 436.

6. Rousseau, *The Government of Poland*, pp. 29–30.

Revolution distinguished itself by a "love of order" instead of forming an "alliance with the turbulent passions of anarchy." "It was never assumed in the United States that the citizen of a free country has a right to do whatever he pleases; on the contrary, more social obligations were imposed on him than anywhere else."[7] Tocqueville well knew that political communities could smother individual choice, and he is correctly remembered for his warnings against the tyranny of the majority. Nevertheless, Tocqueville thought that a free community can rightfully impose obligations and duties on its citizens, because it offers valuable resources to each individual, and, as thinkers as widely different as Socrates and Rousseau had suggested, such a community transforms the individual into something greater and better than he or she would have been outside this community. Thus, out of a sense of obligation and even a sense of self-interest, one should attend to the general good at least as much as to one's narrowly defined self-interest. Mere personal independence to chase one's desires cannot be the goal of a free society. "So wrong it is to confound independence with liberty. No one is less independent than a citizen of a free state."[8] In fact, Tocqueville expressly identified personal independence with selfishness and isolation, two conditions that are, as we shall see later, the companions of despotism.

In a quest for individual independence, thinkers begin to suggest that the essence of freedom lies in a private existence apart from one's fellow citizens and perhaps even society, a suggestion that only increases the tendency toward isolation and individual powerlessness that worried so many of Tocqueville's generation. On this issue Tocqueville thought that someone like Stendhal, pretending one could escape into freedom behind masks and prison walls, was offering remedies that would only aggravate the illness. Seizing an image whose forcefulness he never could fully imagine, Rousseau likened men who are alone to saplings in the middle of a highway.[9] Without the same image, Tocqueville had the same thought. "In the ages of equality all men are independent of each other, isolated, and weak."[10] He acknowledged that individuals in association with others can never do precisely everything they wish, but outside of associations individuals have no political freedom and find themselves powerless to accomplish anything. "If you are resolved not to submit to [association with others], you undoubtedly retain your individuality; but you

7. Tocqueville, *Democracy*, 1: 73.
8. Tocqueville, *The Old Regime*, p. 275.
9. Rousseau, *Émile*, p. 5.
10. Tocqueville, *Democracy*, 2: 17.

can do none of the good that you wish to others, and your object in fact becomes selfish."[11] Having recognized "their mutual dependence," individuals can cooperate to control decision making in their communities. "As soon as a man begins to treat of public affairs in public, he begins to perceive that he is not so independent as he had first imagined, and that in order to obtain their support he must often lend them his co-operation."[12] If each citizen runs off to the independence of Thoreau's woods, all soon become subjects. Only despotism "makes general indifference a sort of public virtue"; freedom "perpetually brings men together and forces them to help one another in spite of the propensities that sever them."[13] In an 1856 letter, Tocqueville expressed his hope that religion, by inculcating in each a public duty, could extract individuals from an obsession with private affairs and teach them public duties.

> I have often heard it said that my grandmother, who was a very saintly woman, after having recommended to her young son the exercise of all the duties of private life, did not fail to add: "And then, my child, never forget that a man above all owes himself to his homeland; . . . and that God demands of him that he always be ready to consecrate, if need be, his time, his fortune, and even his life to the service of the state and of the king.[14]

This is a paradox. No political thinker embraced individual independence more passionately than did Tocqueville. He lamented that "private independence" was becoming "more weak, more subordinate, and more precarious"; he detested Morelly's advocacy of the "total submerging of each citizen's personality in the group mind"; he deplored the collectivist attempts by Abbé Landmann to "direct the [Algerian] colonist as an infant"; he worried that individuals were being rendered a "mere bit of a social machine"; he attacked the socialists because "democracy extends the sphere of individual independence, socialism restricts it."[15]

Still one cannot dismiss Tocqueville's claim that "no one is less independent than a citizen of a free state," and the two apparently hostile positions must be reconciled. Tocqueville's adversary was not

11. Tocqueville, *Memoir*, 2: 80–81.
12. Tocqueville, *Democracy*, 2: 109–10.
13. Ibid., pp. 109, 111.
14. Tocqueville, *Selected Letters*, pp. 338–39.
15. Tocqueville, *Democracy*, 2: 321; *The Old Regime*, p. 164; *L'Algérie*, in *Oeuvres* (M), vol. 3, *Écrits et discours politiques*, p. 288; *Memoir*, 2: 380; Drescher, ed., *Tocqueville and Beaumont on Social Reform*, p. 187.

personal independence but a political ideology that, in its very attempts to secure individual independence, encouraged a self-interested and eventually selfish withdrawal from the public sphere. He opposed a cult of personal independence that, by urging such severance from the world, would penultimately establish the prerequisites for a new despotism and ultimately extinguish all personal independence. The paradox emerges. Tocqueville argued that those who equate freedom and personal independence might in fact beget the very collectivist despotism they fear, whereas those who advocate cooperative, democratic action among citizens will more likely bring to life what he called a "sturdy" or a "healthy" independence.[16] It's as if one were to say that the only way to get to Boston was by way of San Francisco.

> How bizarre! Whereas each private individual, exaggerating to himself his work and his independence, tended toward individualism, the public mind headed more and more, in a general and abstract way, toward a sort of political pantheism which, taking away from the individual even his own existence, threatened finally to merge him entirely into the common life of the body social.[17]

Tocqueville was disputing a political ideology that sought to justify, perhaps even to eulogize, the atomization of society that Tocqueville and his generation abhorred, an ideology that, however foreign to ancient democracies, entered the modern, Western world with the collapse of feudalism and with the emergence of what Tocqueville called the "bourgeois state."[18] By the time of our century, the popularized version of this ideology suggests that freedom is "doing your own thing" rather than learning from each other and immersing oneself in political struggles to influence the world.

THE DANGERS OF ISOLATION

As we saw in chapter 2, Tocqueville was greatly concerned with the increasing isolation of citizens from one another, and he warned that isolation and withdrawal were dangers to freedom, not avenues to freedom. Throughout his writings, he scattered images of the solitude that had descended upon the people of his century. He worried

16. Tocqueville, *The Old Regime*, pp. 108, xii.
17. Tocqueville, *Oeuvres* (B), vol. 9, *Études économiques, politiques*, pp. 15–16.
18. Tocqueville, *The European Revolution and Correspondence with Gobineau*, p. 152.

that people would become strangers to one another; he lamented his own "Benedictine" life; he declared that each person was enclosed in a "walled tomb" from which one listens but hears nothing; he feared the "silence" that was enfolding itself around each person in France; and he declared that "each is retired and as if buried in his private affairs."[19] In short, he offered a picture of solitude within society, loneliness even in a crowd. Each was as if locked in a house where "neither air nor light ever penetrate,"[20] and where, he feared, darkness would descend. All this was dangerous. Tocqueville shared none of his generation's Romantic fondness for the solitude of woods and mountains. Solitude, he said, was a "state against nature"; Kentucky landowners were "rendered half-savage by solitude"; and dispersal was a proper state for savages, not for free men and women who associate themselves in political communities.[21] Indeed, solitude gives birth to enervation, anxiety, inaction, and boredom; it softens the individual until he or she is ripe for submission.

This isolation contrasted glaringly with the close ties among individuals during the Middle Ages. After rustling through family papers dating back at least three centuries, Tocqueville wrote his nephew of "new proof of the sweet and paternal relations which, in those times, existed still between the upper and lower classes."[22] Only in the new world of commerce and industry, only in the new democracies, do people "acquire the habit of always considering themselves as standing alone." In the old aristocracies, one could not escape a web of ties to others. "Aristocratic institutions, moreover, have the effect of closely binding every man to several of his fellow citizens. . . . Aristocracy had made a chain of all the members of the community, from the peasant to the king; democracy breaks that chain and severs every link."[23]

The new word *individualism*, Tocqueville argued, by itself expressed the mistaken ideal—on the rise in the new bourgeois world—that people can be free by withdrawing from society. Indeed, the word did not exist until the old ties of aristocratic society had col-

---

19. Tocqueville, *The Old Regime*, p. xiii; *Oeuvres* (M), vol. 8, pt. 3, *Correspondance . . . Beaumont*, p. 336; *Oeuvres* (B), vol. 7, *Nouvelle correspondance*, pp. 298, 421; *Oeuvres* (M), vol. 8, pt. 2, *Correspondance . . . Beaumont*, p. 407; *Oeuvres* (B), vol. 7, *Nouvelle correspondance*, p. 288.

20. Tocqueville, *Memoir*, 2: 204.

21. Tocqueville, *Oeuvres* (B), vol. 9, *Études économiques, politiques*, p. 327; *Journey to America*, p. 285.

22. Tocqueville, *Oeuvres* (B), vol. 7, *Nouvelle correspondance*, p. 436.

23. Tocqueville, *Democracy*, 2: 105.

lapsed. "That word 'individualism,' which we have coined for our requirements, was unknown to our ancestors, for the good reason that in their days every individual necessarily belonged to a group and no one could regard himself as an isolated unit."[24] While subverting a sense of public duty individualism extolls private life, eventually threatening political freedom, because *"general apathy* which is the consequence of individualism" breeds a profound indifference toward the public realm.[25]

> *Individualism* is a novel expression, to which a novel idea has given birth. Our fathers were only acquainted with *égoïsme* (selfishness). Selfishness is a passionate and exaggerated love of self, which leads a man to connect everything with himself and to prefer himself to everything in the world. Individualism is a mature and calm feeling, which disposes each member of the community to sever himself from the mass of his fellows and to draw apart with his family and his friends, so that after he has thus formed a little circle of his own, he willingly leaves society at large to itself. . . .
>
> Selfishness blights the germ of all virtue; individualism, at first, only saps the virtues of public life; but in the long run it attacks and destroys all others and is at length absorbed in downright selfishness.[26]

Individualism was a new word appropriate to a new society witnessing centrifugal forces flinging individuals into private worlds and fastening them there.

Although Tocqueville often ascribed this tendency toward privatization to the collapse of the old aristocratic society and its ties, he recognized that the relish for wealth, an obsession he associated with the bourgeoisie, hastened the centrifugal forces that enticed each out of the public world. In a speech before the Chamber of Deputies in 1842 he lamented that no one seemed concerned with political decisions, that each seemed fascinated with his or her private interests, and that "more and more each seems to retire into himself and isolate himself."[27] In *Democracy in America* Tocqueville blamed the problem on the "perpetual striving" to keep or to increase one's private accumulation of wealth, a concern so absorbing that no one wished to be bothered with appeals for political ideals. "Do not talk to him of the interests and the rights of mankind; this small domestic concern ab-

24. Tocqueville, *The Old Regime*, p. 96.
25. Tocqueville, *Democracy*, 2: 388.
26. Ibid., p. 104.
27. Tocqueville, *Oeuvres* (B), vol. 9, *Études économiques, politiques*, pp. 375–76.

sorbs for the time all his thoughts and inclines him to defer political agitations to some other season."[28] The love of pleasures and wealth seduces people from the public sphere and sweetly settles them in private, attractive comfort, a process that, as we shall see later, opens the door to welcome the new despotism.

> There is, indeed, a most dangerous passage in the history of a democratic people. When the taste for physical gratifications among them has grown more rapidly than their education and their experience of free institutions, the time will come when men are carried away and lose all self-restraint at the sight of the new possessions they are about to obtain. . . . It is not necessary to do violence to such a people in order to strip them of the rights they enjoy; they themselves willingly loosen their hold. The discharge of political duties appears to them to be a troublesome impediment which diverts them from their occupations and business. If they are required to elect representatives, to support the government by personal service, to meet on public business, they think they have no time, they cannot waste their precious hours in useless engagements; such idle amusements are unsuited to serious men who are engaged with the more important interests of life. These people think they are following the principle of self-interest, but the idea they entertain of that principle is a very crude one; and the better to look after what they call their own business, they neglect their chief business, which is to remain their own masters.[29]

This sentiment blossomed, Tocqueville maintained, only with nineteenth-century dominance of the bourgeoisie. "Eighteenth-century man had little of that craving for material well-being which leads the way to servitude."[30]

The first danger to freedom from this self-imposed isolation is the evaporation of participatory politics. Because people consider themselves independent from one another, they have a strong but subtle disposition to perceive the whole as beyond their concern. Without the habit of association, people "fall back upon themselves" and withdraw. "Such men can never, without an effort, tear themselves from their private affairs to engage in public business."[31] In a letter to Royer-Collard, Tocqueville complained of egoism, "a sweet, peaceful, and tenacious love of one's private interests." Egoism is quite con-

28. Tocqueville, *Democracy*, 2: 268–69.

29. Ibid., p. 149.

30. Tocqueville, *The Old Regime*, p. 118; see also *The European Revolution and Correspondence with Gobineau*, p. 109.

31. Tocqueville, *Democracy*, 2: 310.

sistent with private virtues and private prosperity, but it seems to have led to "honest men and poor citizens."[32]

Equality, independence, and isolation contribute to the second danger to freedom. Once the political topography has become flattened, that is, once society has become transformed into an "unorganized aggregation of individuals" instead of a collection of well-established groups and classes, the government towers over these individuals, "isolates them and then influences each separately."[33] To Tocqueville, both the nature and the conception of society had changed dramatically in less than a century. No longer was society a vast conglomeration of groups united by common ties and a common ethic—that division of aristocratic society into guilds, trade corporations, parishes, provinces, families, classes, and so forth.[34] Instead society had been what Bossuet called "partialized" and was now seen as no more than a collection of individuals.[35] To use a crude simile, society once seemed to be a structure that resembled lumps of sugar, but now, with its bonds pulverized, it was more like thousands of scattered sugar grains. "Every individual," Tocqueville said, "stands defenseless and insulated in the face of this unscrupulous Executive with its thousands of armed hands and its thousands of watching eyes."[36] Once again individualism, isolation, and independence lead not to freedom but to powerlessness.

A Lesson from the Old Regime

Tocqueville seems to have written his *Old Regime* with the image of a vacuum in mind, because he argued that the French monarchy had maintained its power by isolating classes and groups from each other and by assuring monarchical domination of public concerns, or—to speak metaphorically—domination of public space. The monarchy divided classes and groups by playing upon natural jealousies and prejudices, thus leaving no unified power to oppose the central government. Only in the government office files did "the various classes of prerevolutionary France rub shoulders," because the nation was

---

32. Tocqueville, *Oeuvres* (M), vol. 11, *Correspondance . . . Royer-Collard . . . Ampère*, p. 64.

33. Tocqueville, *Correspondence . . Senior*, 2: 79; *Democracy*, 1: 90.

34. Tocqueville, *Democracy*, 2: 306; *The Old Regime*, p. 163.

35. Bossuet, *Extraits des oeuvres diverses*, p. 199; see Sewell, *Work and Revolution in France*, chs. 2 and 4.

36. Tocqueville, *Correspondence . . . Senior*, 2: 80; also *Journey to America*, p. 259.

"divided within itself into a great number of watertight compartments, small, self-contained units, each of which watched vigilantly over its own interests and took no part in the life of the community at large." The monarchy managed this forced privatization of society by suppressing general and then local democratic freedoms, consequently isolating citizens from one another and creating a vacuum into which its own functionaries could flow. "As our nation-wide freedoms succumbed, dragging down with them all local liberties, there was a tendency for the upper and middle classes to cooperate less and less in public affairs and thus to draw apart."[37]

Gradually the monarchy lost its effectiveness, and despite maintaining political power, it lost political authority. The nation, Tocqueville argued, awaited any group that could seize public attention, move into the public vacuum, and address public concerns. No organized groups or classes were involved in politics, and this left it to eighteenth-century writers who, although lacking in political experience and hence scattering misconceived ideas, eventually substituted these ideas about politics for practical political activity.

> Thus the philosopher's cloak provided safe cover for the passions of the day and the political ferment was canalized into literature, the result being that our writers now became the leaders of public opinion and played for a while the part which normally, in free countries, falls to the professional politician. And as things were, no one was in a position to dispute their right to leadership.[38]

Governments that construct their edifice of power on a foundation as capricious as animosity among groups and classes will perpetuate their power only as long as they maintain the division that assures their own occupation of the political space. The French monarchy had no allies for support, and when classes and groups finally emerged from isolation and joined together, the monarchy that had seemed so indestructible fell like a kite that suddenly lost the support of the wind.

> But once the bourgeois had been completely severed from the noble, and the peasant from both alike, and when a similar differentiation had taken place within each of these three classes, with the result that each was split up into a number of small groups almost completely shut off from each other, the inevitable consequence was that, though the nation came to seem a homogeneous whole, its parts no longer held together. Nothing had been left that could obstruct the central govern-

37. Tocqueville, *The Old Regime*, pp. 77, 86.
38. Ibid., p. 142.

ment, but, by the same token, nothing could shore it up. This is why the grandiose edifice built up by our kings was doomed to collapse like a card castle once disturbances arose within the social order on which it was based.[39]

Tocqueville offered a simple lesson. Because governments always attempt to depoliticize groups and individuals and, in doing so, attempt to occupy any resulting political vacuum, free nations must find ways to entice men and women from their private worlds so they might actively oppose these attempts. Freedom must "force each to leave his hole."[40] Again, however, Tocqueville left us with a political problem that is circular. Freedom alone, he said, is capable of combatting the threats to freedom. "For only freedom can deliver the members of a community from that isolation which is the lot of the individual left to his own devices and, compelling them to get in touch with each other, promotes an active sense of fellowship. . . . [Freedom] alone replaces at certain critical moments their natural love of material welfare by a loftier, more virile ideal; offers other objectives than that of getting rich."[41]

Tocqueville's example of democratic freedom was the United States, where citizens seized, and daily re-seized, public space. In fact, the United States was one of the few examples Tocqueville could offer in which citizens had the habit of public activity and had learned the enjoyments of public cooperation. "But if an American were condemned to confine his activity to his own affairs, he would be robbed of one half of his existence; he would feel an immense void in the life which he is accustomed to lead, and his wretchedness would be unbearable."[42] Although Tocqueville offered us few hints as to how to create these habits of public activity, he repeatedly suggested these habits were essential. For example, a twentieth-century reader who has become accustomed to the private automobile will read Tocqueville's claim about public transportation in the United States of 1831 with astonishment. "In all the journeys I have made in the United States I have never seen one single person in his own carriage or with his own horses. The wealthiest people travel in public conveyances without servants."[43] Although it is difficult to overcome the initial inertia brought about by the comforts of private life, once that is

39. Ibid., pp. 136–37.
40. Tocqueville, *Oeuvres* (M), vol. 8, pt. 3, *Correspondance . . . Beaumont*, p. 543.
41. Tocqueville, *The Old Regime*, p. xiv.
42. Tocqueville, *Democracy*, 1: 260.
43. Tocqueville, *Journey to America*, p. 226.

achieved, participation in public life becomes a pleasure. "Montesquieu somewhere alludes to the excessive despondency of certain
Roman citizens who, after the excitement of political life, were all at
once flung back into the stagnation of private life."[44]

Successful political movements and free communities must devise
centripetal forces to overcome the centrifugal ones that fling individuals into the comforts of private life. Montesquieu wrote that in
early Rome "men were always at work or in the public square, and
hardly ever remained at home." Tocqueville reported that in the
political excitement just before the French Revolution, "it seemed as
if everyone wished to escape whenever he could from his private
affairs."[45] Before the outbreak in June of 1848, the workers "no
longer lived in their houses, but in the public squares."[46] It is this kind
of public participation that individualism and isolation undermine.

THE THREAT TO FREEDOM OF THOUGHT, OR TYRANNY OF THE MAJORITY

While equating freedom with personal independence threatens
democratic freedom because it justifies a withdrawal from public participation, it also eventually subverts freedom of thought because,
paradoxically, it snuffs out a diversity of ideas. In France's aristocratic
past, according to Tocqueville in *Democracy*, a natural diversity of
ideas existed simply by virtue of the many diverse groups and classes.
"The Middle Ages were a period when everything was broken up,
when each people, each province, each city, and each family tended
strongly to maintain its distinct individuality." Such groups clung to
their individual view of the world, demanding of their members an
often unquestioning adherence to this view. The artisan, for example,
answered not to the standards of the marketplace but to the peculiar
standards of his guild. As these groups dissolved, however, individuals entered the economic marketplace to sell skills and select
ideas. Stripped of the support and protection of the traditional
group, alone in this competitive marketplace, the individual overwhelmingly felt insignificant. "The same equality that renders him
independent of each of his fellow citizens taken severally exposes him

44. Tocqueville, *Democracy*, 1: 260.
45. Montesquieu, *Considerations on the Causes of the Greatness of the Romans and Their
Decline*, trans. David Lowenthal (Ithaca, 1965), p. 24; Tocqueville, *The European Revolution and Correspondence with Gobineau*, p. 36.
46. Tocqueville, *Recollections*, p. 163.

alone and unprotected to the influence of the greater number. . . . A sort of enormous pressure of the mind of all upon the individual intelligence."[47] Again the paradox. In an age when people declared themselves autonomous, when they prided themselves on their individuality, heteronomy flourished and they conformed to the common language even in the very speech that proclaimed their autonomy.

> After the old social hierarchy had been destroyed, each Frenchman was more enlightened, more independent, more difficult to govern by compulsion; but, on the other hand, natural and necessary ties no longer existed among them. Each conceived a more vivid and more proud sentiment of his liberty: but it was more difficult for him to unite himself with others to defend it; he was dependent on no one, but he could count on no one. The same social movement which had broken his shackles had isolated his interests, and he could be taken aside to be constrained and corrupted separately.[48]

Only with this in mind can one understand adequately Tocqueville's idea of the tyranny of the majority and his famous statements that "freedom of opinion does not exist in America" and "I know of no country in which there is so little independence of mind and real freedom of discussion as in America."[49] It was not simply that Americans were more "conformist" than other peoples. He argued that, while artisans used to conform to the standards of their guild and aristocrats to the manners of their class, Americans conformed to a uniform pattern of ideas and sentiments that embraced the entire society.

> In aristocracies men often have much greatness and strength of their own; when they find themselves at variance with the greater number of their fellow countrymen, they withdraw to their own circle, where they support and console themselves. Such is not the case in a democratic country; there public favor seems as necessary as the air we breathe, and to live at variance with the multitude is, as it were, not to live. The multitude require no laws to coerce those who do not think like themselves: public disapprobation is enough; a sense of their loneliness and impotence overtakes them and drives them to despair.[50]

If this analysis is correct, then to encourage withdrawal from public participation merely isolates individuals, magnifies the sensation of

47. Tocqueville, *Democracy*, 1: 451; 2: 50, 11.
48. Tocqueville, *Oeuvres* (B), vol. 9, *Études économiques, politiques*, p. 13.
49. Tocqueville, *Democracy*, 1: 275, 273.
50. Ibid., 2: 275–76.

powerlessness, and ultimately hastens conformity and manipulation. To borrow from Laski, one will establish individualism but not individuality.[51] Left alone, lacking the cultural tools needed to make a free choice, overwhelmed by the pressures of society, and seduced by the comforts of private life, individuals will snatch the ideas offered to them by society, especially when these ideas are wrapped with a promise of freedom and independence.[52] But how to sustain diversity in democratic society? In part, by equipping citizens to make intelligent choices (the topic of the following two chapters), and by bringing individuals together. The paradox begins to be resolved; authentic personal independence—which Tocqueville always wanted—emerges in cooperative, democratic interaction.

FREEDOM: FRIENDS ACTING TOGETHER

For Tocqueville, the idea of friends acting in common, rather than that of individuals constitutionally secured against interference in their private affairs, lies at the heart of a free society. Once again, he drew upon the French tradition. Bodin declared friendship to be the "foundation" of society, the binding force that ties people together; Montaigne wrote, "Aristotle says that good lawgivers have paid more attention to friendship than to justice. Of a perfect society friendship is the peak."[53] Rousseau, whose fictional characters invariably transformed themselves from lovers into friends, argued that love is a private virtue not suited to freedom, whereas friendship was a noble, political virtue. Geneva, said Rousseau, made "friends, citizens, and soldiers out of the same men."[54] All these thinkers borrowed from a tradition of thought extending back to Aristotle and Tacitus, who

51. Laski, "Alexis de Tocqueville and Democracy."

52. Consider Graña: "For de Tocqueville, this was the consequence of the political and economic dissolution of the old class differences. He had very little of the eighteenth-century confidence in the individual to summon a meaningful universe by the power of a single-handed rationality. He thought that, deprived of a model of public behavior and a 'self-image' issuing from a traditional group style of existence, the individual would be forced to 'make himself,' which meant in effect that he would enter the race for acquisition as the only instrument of self-expression. What de Tocqueville was saying and what the anti-market literary view maintained was that a socially rising but cultureless person had no choice but to be economically aggressive." (*Bohemian versus Bourgeois*, pp. 106–7.) See also Williams, *Culture and Society*, passim.

53. Bodin, *Six Books of the Commonwealth*, VI, 4; III, 7; IV, 7; pp. 191, 98, 141; Michel de Montaigne, *Essays*, trans. and selected by J. M. Cohen (Baltimore, 1958), I, 28.

54. Rousseau, *Politics and the Arts*, p. 105.

both contended that love was a private virtue welcomed by despots. Friendship binds people together in forceful cooperation, whereas love consoles people in their powerlessness; friendship gives birth to energy and action, whereas love comforts people with a pleasant passivity. Fénelon represented this view in calling love a "tyranny" and an "incurable disease," fastening people to the "sordid pleasures of sensuality" and denying them the "sublime enjoyments of wisdom, virtue, and honour."[55]

Ampère told us what we suspected, that his friend Tocqueville "was never of the family of René," that is, that Tocqueville never shared the conviction of his generation that romantic love cured despair and loneliness, constituted a pleasurable and self-sufficient world, and offered a panacea for the world's troubles.[56] As we saw in chapter 5, Tocqueville disliked this escape to the private. Friendship, he suggested, is a political virtue that promotes freedom and is, concomitantly, "the greatest and most manly enjoyment that I know." One month before his death, Tocqueville wrote to a friend, "I would give all the beauties of nature in exchange for the conversation of my friends."[57] In addition to enjoyment, friendship gives strength and confidence for entering the political arena—an idea Tocqueville expressed to one of his oldest friends, Kergorlay. "I have never felt more deeply than while reading [your letter], the value of the friendship that unites us. Let us hold on to that feeling with all our might, my dear Louis: it alone in this world is firm and stable. As long as we can support ourselves on each other with confidence this way, we will never be weak; and if one of us falls, he will at least soon be lifted up again."[58] Friends who unite themselves also overcome powerlessness and isolation. To his closest friend, Beaumont, Tocqueville wrote that in an era of "dispersal, jealousies, and resentment," friendship was an "enormous force" that could accomplish a great deal.[59]

No political thinker would deny that friends both enlighten and bestow confidence. But friendship offered Tocqueville a model for free, political action in cooperation with others. He extended this model to argue that *only* in interaction with others, especially but not exclusively in political interaction, can we recognize our own poten-

55. Fénelon, Meffire François de Salignac de La Mothe, *The Adventures of Telemachus*, no trans. given, 3d ed. (Dublin, 1777), pp. 108, 110.
56. Tocqueville, *Oeuvres* (M), vol. 11, *Correspondance . . . Royer-Collard . . . Ampère*, p. 446.
57. Tocqueville, *Memoir*, 1: 327, 2: 441.
58. Tocqueville, *Selected Letters*, p. 35.
59. Tocqueville, *Oeuvres* (M), vol. 8, pt. 1, *Correspondance . . . Beaumont*, p. 538.

tial, augment and diversify our personal talents, and discover new ideas. People develop by communicating. As Rousseau asked, "How far could men improve or mutually enlighten one another when, having no fixed habitation, and no need of one another's assistance, the same persons hardly met twice in their lives?"[60] Michelet echoed this sentiment: "Life is kindled and magnetized by life, extinguished by isolation. The more it is mixed with lives different from itself, the more it becomes interdependent with other existences, the more it exists with force, happiness, fecundity."[61] Left to himself, Baudelaire argued, an artist seeking success will feel secure only in imitating the common standard of work. In schools, that is, in groups that extend to the individual the support of a distinct perspective, originality blossoms. "The present state of painting is the result of an anarchic liberty that glorifies the individual, however weak, to the detriment of groups, in other words schools." As a result, "individuality—this right of small property—has eaten up collective originality."[62] Or, as Laski paraphrased Bonald: "The only man who has an opportunity to develop his powers is a member of a group."[63]

This position perhaps sprang from Aristotle who argued that the many, from sharing ideas and experiences, are generally more rational than the individual. "And as a feast to which all the guests contribute is better than a banquet furnished by a single man, so a multitude is a better judge of many things than any individual."[64] Hobbes, however, brought a reversal of immeasurable importance, because he and the entire liberal tradition subsequent to him depicted the independent individual as rational and the group as irrational and threatening. For Aristotle, it was the individual tyrant that most threatens political freedom; for Hobbes, it was the crowd. Although Tocqueville confessed his instinctive distaste for the crowd or "mob,"[65] he agreed with Aristotle that isolated individuals are irrational, unsure finally of even their common sense, and in the end dominated by their passions and vulnerable to opinions pressed upon them by society. Individuals in groups can sometimes, but certainly not always, rationally sustain an independent view of the world. For example, people will vote sensibly, Tocqueville argued, if given the right information and an "oppor-

60. Rousseau, *The Social Contract* and *Discourses*, from *A Discourse on the Origin of Inequality*, p. 213.

61. Michelet, *Le Peuple*, pp. 116–18.

62. Baudelaire, *Selected Writings on Art and Artists*, pp. 290, 103–4.

63. Laski, *Authority in the Modern State*, p. 137.

64. Aristotle, *Politics*, III, 15 (trans. Benjamin Jowett). From *The Basic Works of Aristotle*, ed. Richard McKeon (New York, 1941).

65. Tocqueville, *Democracy*, 1: 271.

tunity of getting together and deciding on one policy rather than another."[66] Isolated in tiny villages, peasants are easily manipulated by the local authorities; but when assembled in larger districts, they actively and consciously maintain an independent point of view.[67] Thus, Tocqueville regarded the township as the "natural" organization of human beings, "the ultimate *individual* in the American system."[68] Only through interaction and participation in the public sphere can men and women of modern societies successfully replace the diversity so easily sustained in aristocratic society. In groups one finds genuine personal independence and a healthy individualism.

> Feeling and opinions are recruited, the heart is enlarged, and the human mind is developed only by the reciprocal influence of men upon one another. I have shown that these influences are almost null in democratic countries; they must therefore be artificially created, and this can only be accomplished by associations. . . . As soon as several of the inhabitants of the United States have taken up an opinion, they look for mutual assistance; and as soon as they have found one another out, they combine. From that moment they are no longer isolated men, but a power seen from afar, whose actions serve for an example and whose language is listened to.[69]

The only alternative to creating an opinion about the world cooperatively and actively is accepting passively the opinions forced through the window of one's isolated sphere.

After learning from others in public cooperative activities, and after borrowing from the resources offered by a rich cultural heritage, individuals can choose freely among the wealth of diversity in the world. "In free and enlightened democratic times there is nothing to separate men from one another or to retain them in their place. . . . They communicate and intermingle every day; they imitate and emulate one another. This suggests to the people many ideas, notions, and desires that they would never have entertained if the distinctions of rank had been fixed and society at rest."[70] In political and public interaction with others, rather than a self-interested withdrawal from society, men and women find independence, individualism, intelligence, and self-confidence. "One of the happiest consequences of the absence of government . . . is the *ripening of indi-*

66. Tocqueville, *The Old Regime,* p. xi.
67. Tocqueville, *Memoir,* 2: 222–23.
68. Tocqueville, *Democracy,* 1: 62; *Journey to America,* p. 152.
69. Tocqueville, *Democracy,* 2: 117–18.
70. Ibid., p. 40.

vidual strength which never fails to follow from it. Each man learns to think and act for himself without counting on the support of any outside power which, however watchful it be, can never answer all the needs of man in society."[71] The paradox is resolved. However circuitous a journey, Tocqueville's quest for authentic independence ends successfully.

71. Tocqueville, *Journey to America*, pp. 38–39. (My emphasis.)

8 Freedom as Self-Mastery: The Necessity of Culture

"**D**o what thou wilt,**"** that famous dictum by Rabelais, formed a first link in a minor chain of French thought that perceived human beings as bundles of desires to be satisfied. Holbach characterized people as being led by desires. Condillac, who in one passage equated pleasures with needs, exemplified a sensualist philosophy that borrowed from Locke to attack the rationalism of Plato and Descartes, while suggesting to a nascent commercial society that individuals both become knowledgeable and enjoy life by means of their senses.[1] In the nineteenth century, this view culminated in France with Fourier and the Saint-Simonians. Fourier argued that individuals were deprived because "their passions are unfilled, their senses are not appeased," and, as Manuel pointed out, Fourier's notion of freedom included a sort of "permanent orgasm" in which the individual willingly yielded "blindly to his passions."[2] Since God or Nature made human beings desiring animals, Fourier and the Saint-Simonians both argued, the repression of desires brings sickness, and their release brings health. Once people express passions that are natural and not socially distorted, a social harmony will spring forth, a harmony in which freedom does in fact issue from "do what thou wilt."

1. Paul Henry Thiry, Baron d'Holbach, *The System of Nature, or Laws of the Moral and Physical World,* trans. H. D. Robinson (Boston, 1889), p. 41; E. B. de Condillac, *Treatise on the Sensations,* trans. Geraldine Carr (Los Angeles, 1930), p. 238.
2. Manuel, *The Prophets of Paris,* pp. 217, 228; Fourier, *Design for Utopia,* p. 48.

PERSONAL FREEDOM AS THE CONTROL OF DESIRES

This notion of freedom and this conception of human beings as mere bundles of desires waiting to be satisfied conflicted sharply with that part of the French tradition that influenced Tocqueville. "Of course, there is hardly any place for virtue," argued Bodin, "in a city where each man indulges his own habits and desires so eagerly."[3] Fénelon added that a king who can chase his inclinations with impunity is a "slave to his own passions."[4] Arguing that only a savage is led predominantly by desires, Rousseau contended that a free man must master himself and his desires. "For the mere impulse of appetite is slavery, while obedience to a law which we prescribe to ourselves is liberty."[5] Tocqueville's analysis was almost precisely Rousseau's, for he argued that desires rule savages and slaves, whereas free individuals willfully and rationally master these passions. For example, Tocqueville regarded the American slave as ruled entirely from without. "His mind remained utterly undeveloped. His life has been passive, thoughtless, and unthinking." When freed, the slave became the "prey" of his own desires.[6]

> If he becomes free, independence is often felt by him to be a heavier burden than slavery; for, having learned in the course of his life to submit to everything except reason, he is too unacquainted with her dictates to obey them. A thousand new desires beset him, and he has not the knowledge and energy necessary to resist them: these are masters which it is necessary to contend with, and he has learned only to submit and obey. In short, he is sunk to such a depth of wretchedness that while servitude brutalizes, liberty destroys him.[7]

If cooperative, democratic mastery of the political world constitutes the first prerequisite for political freedom, mastery of one's passions must be the second; as a result, Tocqueville's distaste for a conception of human beings that portrays them as mere consumers of pleasures is ubiquitous. He admired the old French aristocracy for its immunity to the "intoxication of unreflecting passions," he despised the Islamic religion for what he regarded as its approval of coarse and sensual pleasures, and he struggled against socialism because he perceived it as an "energetic and continuous appeal to man's material

3. Bodin, *Method for the Easy Comprehension of History*, p. 276.
4. Fénelon, *The Adventures of Telemachus*, p. 84.
5. Rousseau, *The Social Contract*, I, 8.
6. Tocqueville, *On the Penitentiary System*, p. 161.
7. Tocqueville, *Democracy*, 1: 345.

passions," indeed an attempt at "rehabilitating the flesh."[8] Never, he lamented, had a "more gross and more vulgar sensualism" reigned than in the popular literature of his day, and he referred to Balzac's work as "literary pork."[9]

Although Tocqueville was no ascetic who condemned the pleasures of this world—indeed he pointedly said that people must gratify both body and soul, since the angel unfortunately can never predominate over the animal[10]—he clearly regarded the chase for pleasure as something inferior. One could expect as much, for those who most influenced him agreed strongly. Beaumont said there was no one whom Tocqueville "studied with more perseverance and more interest than Pascal. The two minds were made for one another."[11] Pascal declared desire to be the foundation of all evil, urged religion to cure "pride and lust," fostered a struggle against both self-interest and the "lust of the eyes," and condemned the Jesuits for "the scandalous and unmeasured license which they are introducing into public manners."[12] Fénelon maintained that great nations with an abundance of gold, jewelry, and fine delicacies must be unhappy, because the citizens must have become enslaved in their everlasting desires. "These superfluities . . . effeminate, intoxicate, and torment those who possess them. . . . [Their torment is the] unavoidable consequence of the innumerable artificial wants, to which they are enslaved, and upon which they make all their happiness depend."[13] Similarly, Montesquieu admired the Stoics because they embraced the source of "true greatness—the contempt of pleasure and pain."[14] Rousseau depicted virtue as a "state of warfare" in which one must "vanquish" desires by "resisting them."[15] Rousseau's character Emile pleaded, "make me free by guarding me against the passions which do me violence; do not let me become their slave; compel me to become my own master and to obey, not my senses, but my reason." Rousseau reported that "many men were mad enough to purchase a

8. Tocqueville, *Democracy*, 1: 245; *Memoir*, 1: 325; Drescher, ed., *Tocqueville and Beaumont on Social Reform*, p. 182.

9. Tocqueville, *Oeuvres* (M), vol. 8, pt. 3, *Correspondance . . . Beaumont*, p. 545; *Oeuvres* (M), vol. 15, pt. 1, *Correspondance . . . Corcelle*, p. 185.

10. Tocqueville, *Memoir*, 1: 304.

11. Ibid., p. 49 (from Beaumont's *Memoir*).

12. Blaise Pascal, *Pensées*, Brunschvicg ed., trans. W. F. Trotter, (New York, 1958), (Br) 430; Mesnard, *Pascal: His Life and Works*, pp. 98, 26; Blaise Pascal, *The Provincial Letters*, in *The Pensées* and *The Provincial Letters*, trans. Thomas M'Crie (New York, 1941), p. 475.

13. Fénelon, *The Adventures of Telemachus*, p. 140.

14. Montesquieu, *The Spirit of the Laws*, XXIV, 10, 2: 33.

15. Rousseau, *Eloisa*, 4: 154, 145.

night with Cleopatra at the price of their life, and this is not incredible in the madness of passion."[16]

This disdain for mere pleasure was, for Tocqueville, the cornerstone of an aristocratic ideal that suggested great individuals exhibit a contempt for mere life while striving for the good life that comes from mastering oneself, an ideal admirably expressed by Montaigne. "Have you been able to reflect on your life and control it? Then you have performed the greatest work of all. . . . Our duty is to compose our character."[17] Tocqueville repeatedly embraced this aristocratic ideal. Aristocracies, he said, displayed a "haughty contempt of little pleasures," even while indulging in them, whereas democracies seem to glorify petty pleasures and material comforts and "are extremely eager in the pursuit of actual and physical gratification."[18] Tocqueville argued that for a man to "think and act for himself," he must knowledgeably determine what is good, cultivate his own confidence and talents, and ensure that "his passions do not prevent him from carrying it out."[19] In a more religious passage, his debt to Pascal is apparent. "Don't you see the incomparable beauty of that rare, open struggle of the spirit against the ruling flesh?"[20]

In part, these thinkers claimed that happiness would never emerge in attempts to satisfy desires. Montesquieu said, "It is with lust as with avarice, whose thirst increases by the acquisition of treasure." Rousseau wondered, "what is the fate of those sons of sensuality, who indiscreetly multiply their torment by their pleasures?" suggesting that "the passions are sisters and . . . one alone suffices for arousing a thousand."[21] Happiness must lie not in augmenting our means of satisfaction, for this is invariably tracing a circle without end, but in lowering or suppressing our appetites. "The art of satisfying our desires," said one of Rousseau's characters, "lies not in indulging, but in suppressing them."[22]

Tocqueville unquestionably shared this view. In modern democracies, he suggested, individuals never procure the comforts of the world "without exertion, and they never indulge in them without apprehension. They are therefore always straining to pursue or re-

16. Rousseau, *Émile*, pp. 290, 289.
17. Montaigne, *Essays*, III, 13.
18. Tocqueville, *Democracy*, 2: 45–46.
19. Tocqueville, *Journey to America*, p. 39.
20. Tocqueville, *The European Revolution and Correspondence with Gobineau*, p. 207.
21. Montesquieu, *The Spirit of the Laws*, XVI, 6, 1: 254; Rousseau, *Eloisa*, 2: 259; Rousseau, *Politics and the Arts*, p. 21.
22. Rousseau, *Eloisa*, 3: 229.

tain gratifications so delightful, so imperfect, so fugitive." Unfortunately, "every passion gathers strength in proportion as it is cultivated, and is increased by all the efforts made to satiate it," like a blackmailer who returns again and again, promising each successive time is the last. "Fortune awaits [Americans] everywhere, but not happiness." Citizens of the United States, especially in the North, are taught both "to place wealth above all pleasures of the intellect or the heart," and that happiness is a private phenomenon, that "individual selfishness is the source of general happiness."[23] Because happiness, Tocqueville argued, cannot come from wealth or pleasure, or from self-interest, Americans have misplaced their efforts and set in motion an endless series of anxieties and dissatisfactions.

> In America I saw the freest and most enlightened men placed in the happiest circumstances that the world affords; it seemed to me as if a cloud habitually hung upon their brow, and I thought them serious and almost sad, even in their pleasures. . . .
>
> At first sight there is something surprising in this strange unrest of so many men, restless in the midst of abundance. The spectacle itself, however, is as old as the world; the novelty is to see a whole people furnish an exemplification of it.
>
> Their taste for physical gratifications must be regarded as the original source of that secret disquietude which the actions of Americans betray and of that inconstancy of which they daily afford fresh examples. He who has set his heart exclusively upon the pursuit of worldly welfare is always in a hurry, for he has but a limited time at his disposal to reach, to grasp, and to enjoy it.[24]

What limited happiness life can offer, Tocqueville suggested, arises only from restricting one's desires. "It is only by resisting a thousand petty selfish passions of the hour that the general and unquenchable passion for happiness can be satisfied."[25] Happiness also requires, beyond mere self-interest, a touch of virtue and the fulfillment of one's duty, as he wrote in a letter to Kergorlay. "I am feeling more and more what you tell me about the pleasures of the conscience. . . . There is only one great goal in this world, one which merits the efforts of man: that is the good of humanity."[26]

23. For the preceding quotations see Tocqueville, *Democracy*, 2: 137, 164; 1: 305, 411.
24. Ibid., 2: 144–45.
25. Ibid., p. 159.
26. Tocqueville, *Oeuvres* (M), vol. 13, pt. 1, *Correspondance . . . Kergorlay*, p. 345.

THE RELATION BETWEEN POLITICAL FREEDOM AND PERSONAL MASTERY OF DESIRES

Notwithstanding its value to personal happiness and personal freedom, the mastery of one's desires was cherished by French thinkers because it was indispensable to broader political freedom. Tacitus, who influenced French thought significantly, assumed that a free republic required a demanding morality and that slavery sprang from "craving for luxury and idleness and loathing discipline and toil."[27] While Montesquieu suggested that "incontinency may be considered as the last of miseries" for a popular state and a "certain forerunner" of despotism, Rousseau argued that states that mistake freedom for "unbridled license to which it is diametrically opposed" eventually "hand themselves over to seducers, who only make their chains heavier than before."[28]

Until the last two centuries, as Bloom points out,[29] political thinkers generally assumed that republics necessitated censorship—protection against any subversion of private morality—to maintain freedom, that only despotisms allowed people relentlessly to chase their desires. Consider Montesquieu's description of a free republic:

> We must not imagine that criminal actions only are destructive of virtue; it is destroyed also by omissions, by neglects, by a certain coolness in the love of our country, by bad examples, and by the seeds of corruption: whatever does not openly violate but elude the laws, does not subvert but weaken them, ought to fall under the inquiry and correction of the censors.[30]

Only censorship could sustain the strict morality fundamental to republics. The concept of a "victimless crime," the invention of a society consecrated to a self-interested consumption of pleasure and wealth, would never have been tolerated, since these thinkers considered every action, even the most private, to have a public effect. Each action invariably provided an example that either strengthened or weakened public morality. Again, as Montesquieu said, "there are bad examples which are worse than crimes, and more states have perished by the violation of their moral customs than by the violation of their

27. Tacitus, *The Complete Works*, ed. Moses Hadas, trans. Alfred John Church and William Jackson Brodribb (New York, 1942), p. 14. (*Annals*, I, 16.)
28. Montesquieu, *The Spirit of the Laws*, VII, 8, 1: 101; Rousseau, *The Social Contract* and *Discourses*, p. 178. (From *A Discourse on the Origin of Inequality*.)
29. Allan Bloom in his Introduction to Rousseau, *Politics and the Arts*.
30. Montesquieu, *The Spirit of the Laws*, V, 19, 1: 69.

laws."[31] Rousseau admired Plutarch's description of Cato, the harsh censor and protector of public morality. "For the Romans thought that no marriage, or rearing of children, nay, no feast or drinking-bout, ought to be permitted according to every one's appetite or fancy. . . ."[32] This discussion explains Tocqueville's persistent questioning, in Ireland, in England, and in the United States, of the state of morality, and it explains his claim that "no free communities ever existed without morals."[33] In one passage Tocqueville approved censorship in the interest of morality, and in another he stated that the "degree of a nation's prosperity" depends on its "morality."[34] Religion, for Tocqueville, supplanted Cato's code of honor; "liberty cannot be established without morality, nor morality without faith."[35]

Political freedom requires mastery of one's passions, because, without such mastery, desires and passions will fling individuals apart and undermine the cooperation needed to control one's world. After quoting his friend Lieber's description of how men and women in the United States gather at a moment's notice to attend to the public interest, Tocqueville asked, "To what do you attribute the incredible control which people get here over their passions?"[36] Tocqueville simply *assumed* that controlling one's world and controlling oneself went hand in hand. "In reading the historians of aristocratic ages, and especially those of antiquity, it would seem that, to be master of his lot and to govern his fellow creatures, man requires only to be master of himself. In perusing the historical volumes which our age has produced, it would seem that man is utterly powerless over himself and over all around him."[37] Dominated by desires, guided by obsessions with accumulating wealth, and haunted by unknown fears, individuals in democratic times find themselves to be slaves to their appetites, incapable of freely and rationally shaping their lives.

If satisfying desires becomes one's exclusive preoccupation, then one becomes vulnerable to any power that offers these satisfactions, like an addict doing the bidding of his supplier. For this reason,

31. Montesquieu, *Considerations on the Causes of the Greatness of the Romans and Their Decline*, p. 86.

32. Plutarch, *Lives of the Noble Romans*, selected and ed. Edmund Fuller, trans. John Dryden and Arthur Hugh Clough (New York, 1969), p. 132. (From "Marcus Cato.")

33. Tocqueville, *Journeys to England and Ireland*, pp. 123, 36–37; *Journey to America*, p. 43; *Democracy*, 2: 209.

34. Tocqueville, *Journeys to England and Ireland*, p. 49; *Oeuvres* (M), vol. 3, *Écrits et discours politiques*, p. 119. (From *Abolition de l'esclavage*.)

35. Tocqueville, *Democracy*, 1: 12.

36. Tocqueville, *Journey to America*, p. 43.

37. Tocqueville, *Democracy*, 2: 93.

despotism has always been associated with the license to do as one pleases, as long as these private actions did not threaten governmental power. Whereas Montesquieu declared "the Greeks abandoned themselves to senseless delight and believed themselves to be free in reality because the Romans declared them so," Rousseau claimed that Europeans were "fashioned for license, that is to say for servitude."[38] Like Rousseau, Tocqueville characterized his time as one of "license and servility" and worried that an "undisciplined and depraved democracy" would lead to a "yoke heavier than any that has galled mankind since the fall of the Roman Empire."[39] Tocqueville argued that people who are slaves to their desires will barter their political freedom for a momentary satisfaction. For example, he scoffed at a ruler in India who, after consigning his government to the English, "jumped for joy," exclaiming "I can have new dancers!"[40]

In addition, frivolity destroys political energy. A life consecrated to satisfying desires, or what Montesquieu called "continual pursuit of amusement," renders people petty, dissipates all public energy because of countless private pleasures, and strips a nation of bold action and grand purpose. For these thinkers, a free nation was a serious nation, hardly aware of our modern preoccupation with "having fun." As Montesquieu said, "man is like a spring that works better the more it is compressed."[41] In a remarkable passage that prefigured Freud, Montesquieu argued that the repression of private pleasure channels our energy into public activity.

> The less we are able to satisfy our private passions, the more we abandon ourselves to those of a general nature. How comes it that monks are so fond of their order? It is owing to the very cause that renders the order insupportable. Their rule debars them from all those things by which the ordinary passions are fed; there remains therefore only this passion for the very rule that torments them.[42]

Similarly, Tocqueville scorned his brother for craving to be "distracted from morning to night"; he declared that Danton's passion for a young girl caused his demise; and he ridiculed any people that had

38. Montesquieu, *Considerations on the Causes of the Greatness of the Romans and Their Decline*, p. 60; Jean-Jacques Rousseau, *Collection complète des oeuvres de J. J. Rousseau*, vol. 1, *Considérations sur le gouvernement de Pologne* (Geneva, 1782), p. 436.

39. Tocqueville, *Oeuvres* (M), vol. 11, *Correspondance . . . Royer-Collard . . . Ampère*, p. 11; *Memoir*, 1: 377.

40. Tocqueville, *Oeuvres* (M), vol. 3, *Écrits et discours politiques*, p. 519. (From *L'Inde*.)

41. Quoted in Loy, *Montesquieu*, p. 27.

42. Montesquieu, *The Spirit of the Laws*, V, 2–3, 1:40–41.

become indifferent to political goals by substituting for them mere "delights" and "frivolity."[43] Although he did fear that nations might become degraded and debauched, he feared even more that they might be enervated by such frivolity until finally all effective political action would be impossible. Like Montesquieu, Tocqueville contended that amusements extinguish the source of political action. In *Democracy* he wrote that people "gratify a number of petty desires without indulging in any great irregularities of passion, thus they are more apt to become enervated than debauched. . . . By these means a kind of virtuous materialism may ultimately be established in the world, which would not corrupt, but enervate, the soul and *noiselessly unbend its springs of action.*" In passages directed against Rousseau's claims that free people gather joyfully for dancing and play, Tocqueville asserted that "all free nations are serious because their minds are habitually absorbed by the contemplation of some dangerous or difficult purpose." Indeed, Tocqueville doubted that one could discover democracies "in which citizens met in the public places with garlands or roses and spent almost all their time in dancing and theatrical amusements."[44]

CULTURE AS A PREREQUISITE FOR FREEDOM

If individuals left to themselves merely pursue, and become tormented by, their desires, how can these desires be mastered? Only from without—by means of a culture that offers the tools embodied in traditions, customs, and laws, all of which enable individuals to master themselves and then their communities. It is a classically conservative argument, and Burke put it most ably in declaring that individuals have a right to be restrained.

> Men are qualified for civil liberty in exact proportion to their own disposition to put moral chains upon their own appetites . . . It is ordained in the eternal constitution of things, that men of intemperate minds cannot be free. Their passions forge their fetters. . . .
>
> The inclinations of men should frequently be thwarted, their will controlled, and their passions brought into subjection. This can only be

---

43. Tocqueville, *Oeuvres* (M), vol. 8, pt. 3, *Correspondance . . . Beaumont*, p. 495; *Correspondence . . . Senior*, 2: 57; *The European Revolution and Correspondence with Gobineau*, p. 127.

44. Tocqueville, *Democracy*, 2: 141, 233. (My emphasis.) Contrast with Rousseau, *Politics and the Arts*, pp. 125–27.

done by a *power out of themselves*. . . . In this sense the restraints of men, as well as their liberties, are to be reckoned among their rights.[45]

Similarly, Montesquieu argued that freedom does not consist in doing what pleases but rather doing what one ought to do—something taught to an individual by a culture or society.[46]

In French conservative thought, Bossuet argued that although nature ensures that individuals of potential courage and intellect are born in every age, only a healthy culture or a national "spirit" can actualize this potential.[47] Distinguishing between *natif,* the condition of people at birth or in a state of nature, and *naturel,* the state of perfection natural or proper to a person and toward which one ought to tend, Bonald asserted that "it is only in society that man can realize the full development of his physical and mental being; society is the natural state of man, it is his true nature."[48] Thus, like Aristotle, Bonald defined the natural state not as a beginning but as an end, that is, an essence toward which human beings tend and ought to tend, a potential that commands its own actualization. "The natural state or *la nature* is, on the contrary, a state of development, of accomplishment, of perfection: it is the end toward which his being tends naturally; . . . it is the state of civilization as opposed to barbarism."[49]

In this case, conservative thought overlaps with the thought of one of its enemies: Rousseau. Rousseau vacillated dexterously when he considered the value of human customs and culture, arguing first that customs distort and mutilate a naturally good human being, crushing what is kind and creative into something selfish and insipid. "God makes all things good; man meddles with them and they become evil. . . . [Man] destroys and defaces all things . . . he will have nothing as nature made it, not even man himself who must learn his paces like a saddle horse, and be shaped to his master's taste like the trees in his garden."[50] Second, after realizing that it is too late to reenter a natural state, Rousseau maintained that only a better society, better customs, a better culture could extract individuals from disaster. Born into the world to be mere human beings, completed by culture to be

45. Robert B. Dishman, ed., *Burke and Paine on Revolution and The Rights of Man* (New York, 1971), p. 138. The first passage is from a *Letter to a Member of the National Assembly* (1791), and the second is from *Reflections on the Revolution in France.*

46. Montesquieu, *The Spirit of the Laws,* XI, 3, 1: 150.

47. Bossuet, *Extraits des oeuvres diverses,* p. 148. (From *Discours sur l'histoire universelle.*)

48. Quoted in Moulinié, *De Bonald,* p. 148.

49. Quoted in ibid., pp. 147–48.

50. Rousseau, *Émile,* p. 5.

intelligent men and women, people approach a perfection only in a healthy culture. "We are born, so to speak, twice over; born into existence, and born into life; born a human being, and born a man."[51] Only in a culture, Rousseau argued, do people exchange natural liberty for civic liberty, rule by desire for rule by reason.

> The passage from the state of nature to the civil state produces a very remarkable change in man, by substituting justice for instinct in his conduct, and giving his actions the morality they had formerly lacked. Then only, when the voice of duty takes the place of physical impulses and the right of appetite, does man, who so far had considered only himself, find that he is forced to act on different principles, and to consult his reason before listening to his inclinations. Although, in this state, he deprives himself of some advantages which he got from nature, he gains in return others so great, his faculties are so stimulated and developed, his ideas so extended, his feelings so ennobled, and his whole soul uplifted, that, did not the abuses of this new condition often degrade him below that which he left, he would be bound to bless continually the happy moment which took him from it for ever, and, instead of a stupid and unimaginative animal, made him an intelligent being and a man.[52]

Tocqueville agreed both with the conservative French tradition and with Rousseau. Individuals are completed by culture, and freedom entails the external influence of this culture. In one passage he expressly approved of a definition of freedom offered by John Winthrop. Winthrop again made a distinction between natural liberty, which is shared by both man and beasts and involves nothing more than the ability to do as one wants whether that action is good or evil, and civil liberty, "a liberty to that only which is good, just, and honest."[53] Customs and cultures must restrain the license inherent in natural liberty and impart the controls needed for civic liberty. Certainly, as in India, a culture can stifle and stupefy individuals, and to this extent Tocqueville shared Rousseau's conviction that custom can tyrannize. But for good or ill, Tocqueville argued, a civilization completes people, fashions them into something more than they were at birth. Many liberal thinkers worried about society intruding upon individual independence, even manipulating individuals. Tocqueville recognized, however, that societies always intrude upon individuals and that no society can ever avoid manipulating people. The question

51. Ibid., p. 172.
52. Rousseau, *The Social Contract*, I, 8.
53. Tocqueville, *Democracy*, 1: 44.

becomes not whether there is manipulation, but what kind of manipulation and whether it is good or bad.

> The individual takes the trouble to be born; for the rest, society takes him in its arms like a nurse; it watches over his education; it opens before him the roads to fortune; it sustains him in his march. . . . What I have said is sufficient to let you know that in my opinion one cannot say absolutely that man becomes better in becoming civilized, but rather that man in becoming civilized gains all at once both virtues and vices that he did not previously have; he becomes another person, that is the clearest I can make it.[54]

Turning people loose does not constitute freedom. Slaves gain freedom not at the moment of independence but after they have been given the cultural tools to master rationally their desires and to shoulder the "arduous and manly habits of liberty." "It is France's duty and honor to civilize, enlighten, and moralize as well as to enfranchise," for France "labors to create civilized societies, not hordes of savages."[55]

If all cultures manipulate to some extent, and if some cultures smother everything that is good in human beings while other cultures offer the precise tools needed for freedom and morality, then clearly we must wonder what kind of culture Tocqueville admired.

TOCQUEVILLE'S ARISTOCRATIC HERITAGE

Without question, Tocqueville looked to French aristocratic culture to foster a higher sort of personal freedom, often important to political freedom, and to unfold human intellectual and creative potential, while curbing desires for wealth and pleasure. Many of the eighteenth-century philosophes, assuming without hesitation that Paris was the cultural capital of the world, betrayed a secret, and sometimes not so secret, conviction that genius germinated and flourished only in a fertile cultural soil, which was, of course, Paris. Every age has statesmen and heroes, Voltaire boasted, but "the thinking man, and what is still rarer, the man of taste," emerged only in four ages in the history of the world, with the Age of Louis XIV most nearly approaching perfection.[56] D'Alembert openly argued that genius

---

54. Quoted in Edward T. Gargan, *Alexis de Tocqueville: The Critical Years, 1848–1851* (Washington, D.C., 1955), pp. 6–7. (From an unpublished letter to Stoffels.)

55. Drescher, ed., *Tocqueville and Beaumont on Social Reform*, pp. 117, 134, 117.

56. Jean François Marie Arouet de Voltaire, *The Age of Louis XIV*, trans. Martyn P. Pollack (London, 1961), pp. 1–2.

blossomed only in a healthy culture. Nature, he said, was always the same, scattering geniuses in more or less equal numbers across time. But great individuals, left to themselves and scattered apart, obtained from their societies "no cultivation of their abilities." We improve ourselves by reading and "from association with others. . . . It is like the air one breathes without thinking about it, to which one owes life."[57] Great individuals who are without the benefits of society resemble seeds planted in poor soil.

Tocqueville, who was an aristocrat himself and who was born into a family whose aristocratic roots extended past the fifteenth century, grew up admiring French aristocratic culture. Although some, in seeking to paint Tocqueville as just another liberal, deemphasize his aristocratic nature, it must be confronted. Imagine this man who occasionally called himself a democrat, but who once, while wanting to leave a gathering, felt compelled to remain because he could find no doorman to open the door for him![58] However his political sentiments evolved, Tocqueville clung to the tastes and manners of an aristocrat. "I have an intellectual taste for democratic institutions, but I am an aristocrat by instinct, which means that I scorn and fear the crowd."[59] In another passage, he confessed that he was comfortable only in the company of aristocrats. Even though he disagreed with them, he knew how to act and what to say, while even members of the bourgeoisie who shared his ideas always left him ill at ease.[60] Similarly, he avowed a certain disdain for "mediocre" people, not a characteristic unique to French aristocrats to be sure, but in Tocqueville it emerged with an aristocratic flavor.

> Whenever there is nothing in a man's thoughts or feelings that strikes me, I, so to speak, do not see him. I have always supposed that mediocrities as well as men of parts had a nose, mouth and eyes, but I have never been able to fix in my memory the forms that those features take in each particular case. . . . It is not that I despise them, but I have so little truck for them, feeling that they are like so many cliches.[61]

Although he stressed that the "loss" of aristocratic manners should not be accorded "too much importance," his admiration for these

57. Jean Le Rond d'Alembert, *Preliminary Discourse to the Encyclopedia of Diderot*, trans. Richard N. Schwab and Walter E. Rex (New York, 1963), p. 61.

58. Tocqueville, *Oeuvres* (M), vol. 8, pt. 1, *Correspondance . . . Beaumont*, p. 101.

59. Quoted in Gargan, *Alexis de Tocqueville*, pp. 40–41. (From an unpublished fragment.)

60. Tocqueville, *Recollections*, p. 269.

61. Ibid., p. 104.

manners surfaced conspicuously. "Those manners threw a pleasing illusory charm over human nature; and though the picture was often a false one, it could not be viewed without a noble satisfaction."[62] Tocqueville confided to a friend that "the loss of our aristocracy is a misfortune from which we have not even begun to recover," because the Legitimists, heirs to the aristocratic heritage, lack the former "cultivation" and "intelligence."[63]

As we saw in chapter 4, Tocqueville persistently criticized bourgeois society for its vulgarity and lack of culture; its twin dangers were "tyranny" and "imbecility."[64] The bourgeoisie offered, in part, a consumer culture, hardly one that sought to restrain individual desires and channel them into intellectual activity. Several times Tocqueville lamented that he lived in a nation that no longer read books. "We have ceased to be what we were in a remarkable degree during two centuries—a literary nation. . . . The influential classes are no longer those who read."[65] Similarly, "the charming art of conversation" was a lost art, while the serious intellectual salons had closed forever.[66] He gave as an example the way in which eighteenth-century Parisian society received Hume. Hume was awkward, he spoke bad French, he had none of the polish now required in conversation. In the nineteenth century he would pass for an "intelligent bore." And yet if the form was lacking, the substance remained, and the eighteenth century accepted Hume for the extraordinary intellect he was. "Hume was, for years, the lion of all the salons of Paris. The fashionable beauties quarrelled for the fat philosopher." To Tocqueville, this an-

---

62. Tocqueville, *Democracy*, 2: 228–31.

63. Tocqueville, *Correspondence . . . Senior*, 2: 83.

64. Tocqueville, *Memoir*, 1: 315.

65. Ibid., p. 351; *The European Revolution and Correspondence with Gobineau*, p. 293; *Oeuvres* (B), vol. 7, *Nouvelle correspondance*, p. 349.

66. Tocqueville, *Memoir*, 2: 372. To Ampère, Tocqueville wrote: "You saw that M. Molé passed away. His death is going to close one of the last salons where one could converse. Certainly, neither his son-in-law nor his daughter will be able to continue. With him we had the aristocracy that loved ideas and letters; with them, we will have the aristocracy that loves fancy attire, beautiful uniforms, great names, titles, and pious books, all of which is mixed and kneaded together. A bad mixture which I will hardly approach." [*Oeuvres* (M), vol. 11, *Correspondance . . . Royer-Collard . . . Ampère*, pp. 304–5; see also *Oeuvres* (M), vol. 15, pt. 2, *Correspondance . . . Corcelle*, p. 157, for similar comments, upon the death of Molé, about the loss of that "ancient French taste for pleasures of the mind."] It is worth recalling that Tocqueville himself, to some extent, had been launched upon the Parisian intellectual world by his much older cousin Chateaubriand, when, after the first part of *Democracy in America* had been published, Tocqueville was invited to Madame Récamier's salon in 1835 to hear Chateaubriand, "le grand homme," read his *Mémoires*. [See *Oeuvres* (M), vol. 8, pt. 1, *Correspondance . . . Beaumont*, pp. 151–53; also Jardin, *Alexis de Tocqueville*, p. 218.]

ecdote epitomized the change between centuries; boredom had become the companion of commercial progress. "If the brilliant talkers and writers of that time were to return to life, I do not believe that gas, or steam, or chloroform, or the electric telegraph, would so much astonish them as the dullness of modern society, and the mediocrity of modern books."[67]

In a famous passage comparing democracy and aristocracy, Tocqueville lamented the loss of culture and grandeur in democracy:

> Do you wish to give a certain elevation to the human mind and teach it to regard the things of this world with generous feelings, to inspire men with a scorn of mere temporal advantages, to form and nourish strong convictions and keep alive the spirit of honorable devotedness? Is it your object to refine the habits, embellish the manners, and cultivate the arts, to promote the love of poetry, beauty, and glory? Would you constitute a people fitted to act powerfully upon all other nations, and prepared for those high enterprises which, whatever be their results, will leave a name forever famous in history? If you believe such to be the principal object of society, avoid the government of the democracy, for it would not lead you with certainty to the goal.
>
> But if you hold it expedient to divert the moral and intellectual activity of man to the production of comfort and the promotion of general well-being; if a clear understanding be more profitable to man than genius; if your object is not to stimulate the virtues of heroism, but the habits of peace; if you had rather witness vices than crimes, and are content to meet with fewer noble deeds, provided offenses be diminished in the same proportion; if, instead of living in the midst of a brilliant society, you are contented to have prosperity around you; if, in short, you are of the opinion that the principal object of a government is not to confer the greatest possible power and glory upon the body of the nation, but to ensure the greatest enjoyment and to avoid the most misery to each of the individuals who compose it—if such be your desire, then equalize the conditions of men and establish democratic institutions.[68]

Although he respected democracy, Tocqueville might well have said with Stendhal's Lucien Leuwen, "I need the pleasures of a time-honoured civilization."[69]

According to one author, Tocqueville was suggesting that "the quality of being a man was uniquely an aristocratic possession,"[70] and while the claim is too strong, it has a kernel of truth. Tocqueville did

67. Tocqueville, *Correspondence . . . Senior*, 2: 85.
68. Tocqueville, *Democracy*, 1: 262.
69. Stendhal, *Lucien Leuwen*, 1: 71.
70. Edward T. Gargan, *De Tocqueville* (New York, 1965), p. 72.

think that a healthy aristocratic culture imparted some sort of cultivation or education that restrained passions and enabled an individual to become what he or she ought to become. As he said in one passage, "a certain influence of traditions, in a word the aristocratic element, was very necessary in a free government."[71] Like Aristotle, Tocqueville assumed that freedom of thought required leisure, a leisure clearly unavailable to those who labored from dawn to dusk for sustenance. In an 1842 letter, Tocqueville referred to an acquaintance as a decent man, but added, because "he is obliged to work for his bread, he is forced to fill rather an inferior position."[72] In *Democracy*, Tocqueville argued that only with freedom from the necessity to labor can individuals develop intellectual capacities. "Whatever may be the facilities of acquiring information, whatever may be the profusion of easy methods and cheap science, the human mind can never be instructed and developed without devoting considerable time to these objects."[73] But this capacity of leisure, and hence the opportunity for cultivating one's intelligence, have always hitherto been the property of an aristocracy, hardly available in ages of even remote equality.

CAN DEMOCRACY ACCOMMODATE THE BEST OF ARISTOCRATIC CULTURE?

Tocqueville's dream, which he himself almost always regarded as a pleasant fantasy, was to unite democratic freedom and aristocratic culture, as if he were frustrated by the knowledge that not everyone in the world could be a French gentleman. Although in the first part of *Democracy* (1835) he argued that equality gave birth to a decline in art and literature, in the second part (1840) he ventured to dispute those who perceived a decline in art and literature as the "natural and inevitable result of equality." Instead, he attributed the poor quality of literature in the United States to "their strictly Puritanical origin, their exclusively commercial habits." Once again, not democratic equality per se, but the bourgeois preoccupation with accumulating wealth most threatened works of the mind; in some other democracy, one not so restricted by the commercial characteristics of the nineteenth century, intellectual accomplishments could penetrate all classes.

71. Tocqueville, *Oeuvres* (B), vol. 8, *Mélanges, fragments*, p. 488.
72. Tocqueville, *Memoir*, 1: 335.
73. Tocqueville, *Democracy*, 1: 207.

Not only will the number of those who can take an interest in the productions of the mind be greater, but the taste for intellectual enjoyment will descend step by step even to those who in aristocratic societies seem to have neither time nor ability to indulge in them. When hereditary wealth, the privilege of rank, and the prerogatives of birth have ceased to be and when every man derives his strength from himself alone, it becomes evident that the chief cause of disparity between the fortunes of men is the mind. Whatever tends to invigorate, to extend, or to adorn the mind rises instantly to a high value. . . .

The number of those who cultivate science, letters, and the arts, becomes immense. . . . What is done is often imperfect, but the attempts are innumerable; and although the results of individual efforts are commonly very small, the total amount is always very large.[74]

In reading this passage, one cannot help but conclude that Tocqueville was engaging in some wishful thinking, because his own analysis seems to lead to the conclusion that great intellectual work will be rare in the kind of democracies he describes. He generally maintained that intellectual achievement confined itself to historical epochs that had three specific conditions, only one of which modern democracies could provide.

First, only periods of enormous political action, even if that action was confined to a minority of the population, have been able to generate extraordinary cultural achievements, and this is the one prerequisite for intellectual endeavor of which modern democracy can boast. Tocqueville scoffed at those who believed that a people denied any access to political activity could withdraw to produce great intellectual achievements.

It would seem that civilized people, when restrained from political action, should turn with that much more interest to the literary pleasures. Yet nothing of the sort happens. . . . Those who believe that by making people withdraw from greater objects they will devote more energy to those activities that are still allowed to them, treat the human mind along false and mechanical laws. In a steam engine or a hydraulic machine, smaller wheels will turn smoother and quicker as power to them is diverted from the larger wheels. But such mechanical rules do not apply to the human spirit. Almost all of the great works of the human mind were produced during centuries of liberty.[75]

Once people lose interest in "public affairs," the taste for literature diminishes.[76] Tocqueville maintained that the greatest periods of ar-

74. Ibid., 2: 36, 38, 40–41, for the preceding quotations.
75. Tocqueville, *The European Revolution and Correspondence with Gobineau*, p. 168.
76. Tocqueville, *Correspondence . . . Senior*, 2: 157.

tistic achievement have been those historical eras distinguished by political dissension and even turmoil—such as Athens in the fifth and fourth centuries B.C., Rome in the first century B.C., Renaissance Italy, and of course eighteenth-century France. In discussing Renaissance Florence, Tocqueville noted that the "arts, sciences, and letters reached a surprising degree of perfection" only in those times of political turmoil, political passion, and even revolution. "To such an extent is liberty a powerful agent, even when one knows only incompletely how to use it! Since Florence has become peaceful and servile, its powers, its riches, its scope and its enlightenment have, on the contrary, not ceased to diminish."[77]

The second prerequisite for intellectual achievement is leisure, at least for some. But the leisure of both the Athenian upper class and also the old French aristocracy was purchased by the labor of slaves, servants, peasants, and/or women. Yet Tocqueville himself argued that modern democracies were gradually presenting a spectacle unique in the history of the world: societies without a leisure class, or, to be more precise, without a class somehow detached from the process of production. In the United States, a startled Tocqueville announced, everyone worked. "Among a democratic people, where there is no hereditary wealth, every man works to earn a living. . . ."[78] Even those with great wealth, he argued, continue working because of their restlessness even amidst abundance, the obsession with acquiring more and more. Thus Tocqueville's own analysis seems to suggest that modern democracies cannot establish the leisure imperative to great intellectual endeavors. The wealthiest of individuals, with rare exceptions, will remain in the endless cycle of production and consumption.

The third requirement for intellectual achievement is a national ethos that suggests individuals have a higher goal in life than mere enjoyment of comfort and pleasure. All great cultures have been devoted to some ideal of human perfection—or at least perfection for some. By nature, human beings distinguish themselves from animals, not by an ability to enjoy but by a capacity to improve. "If men were ever to content themselves with material objects, it is probable that they would lose by degrees the art of producing them; and they would enjoy them in the end, like the brutes, without discernment and without improvement." In suggesting that there is a goal "towards which the human race ought ever to be tending," and in suggesting that the educator must awaken the "sleeping powers" in the child, Tocqueville

77. Tocqueville, *Oeuvres* (B), vol. 8, *Mélanges, fragments*, p. 443.
78. Tocqueville, *Democracy*, 2: 161; see Aron, *Main Currents in Sociological Thought*, 1: 286–87.

demonstrated that he thought with the category of perfectibility in mind.[79] Indeed, he considered it foolish to "impose limits on human perfectibility."[80]

Even though Tocqueville claimed that American democracy had nearly boundless faith in human perfectibility, he again suggested that, as commerce increased, all democracies would replace this faith with a concern for industrial productivity. Industrialization and urbanization were transforming the peasants of France, who had once owned land and maintained a confident independence, into industrial workers, a metamorphosis that Tocqueville apparently felt was much like the butterfly becoming the caterpillar. "What can be expected of a man who has spent twenty years of his life in making heads for pins? . . . he no longer belongs to himself, but to the calling he has chosen." In an ardent quest for productivity and profit, the potentials of individuals to become creative masters of their world vanish, and the "mighty human intelligence which has so often stirred the world" concentrates on efficient motion to produce things. Rural American democracy fostered free, self-confident, and self-reliant individuals not trapped by the division of labor. An individual American often built his own home, plowed his own field, made his own clothes and tools, and even engaged in a variety of occupations ranging from lawyer to physician. "This is prejudicial to the excellence of the work," remarked Tocqueville, "but it powerfully contributes to awaken the intelligence of the workman."[81] Once more, however, Tocqueville's own picture of the future offers us an urban world in which these pioneer virtues will have no place.

This third prerequisite for great intellectual achievement seems to be missing in modern democracies, if we accept Tocqueville's analysis in lieu of his wishes. The demands of the economy, and the perception that the purpose of human beings is to consume goods and pleasures while a man "does what he wilt," all combine to bring a world that produces things, not great individuals. "It would seem as if the rulers of our time sought only to use men in order to make things great; I wish that they would try a little more to make great men," and indeed, "the great object in our time is to raise the faculties of men, not to complete their prostration."[82] For a while, the requirement of production might establish a commercial culture that does restrain the chase for pleasure, by demanding postponement of gratification.

79. Tocqueville, *Democracy*, 2: 157, 153; 1: 27.
80. Drescher, ed., *Tocqueville and Beaumont on Social Reform*, p. 8.
81. For the preceding quotations see Tocqueville, *Democracy*, 2: 168–69, 1: 442–43.
82. Ibid., 2: 347, 93.

In the long run, however, the consumer society will win, because, Tocqueville felt, bourgeois society can conceive of human beings only as consumers of satisfactions.

Once more, Tocqueville's hostility to the bourgeoisie rises to the surface, and he seems to suggest that one could not recapture the best of an aristocratic and intellectual culture in modern democracies. Nevertheless, Tocqueville noted a second kind of culture—a popular culture embodied in a nation's mores—that, if it could not produce intellectual greatness, might teach people to control their desires in order to establish democratic and political freedom.

9 Freedom Preserved by Mores, Not Laws

Our previous chapter left us with a question. Although Tocqueville dreamed of reconciling democratic freedom with aristocratic culture, he understood that this was impossible. Although he wished it to be otherwise, Tocqueville admitted that the unfolding of intellectual powers through art, ideas, and literature will elude most citizens. What kind of culture, then, will furnish these citizens with the democratic habits, confidence, practical knowledge, popular initiative and creativity, and ability to cooperate that are necessary for controlling one's personal passions and for exerting control over one's world? In passing from natural independence to civil freedom, from an unhindered chase after one's desires to a mastery of these desires, individuals must rely on customs and traditions that, if they are good, promote individual potential and democratic freedom. Most people are fashioned for freedom by mores.

CONSTITUTIONAL GUARANTEES OF FREEDOM: NECESSARY BUT NOT SUFFICIENT

Despite some equivocation, Tocqueville did seek to establish liberalism's cherished legal safeguards for individual freedom, and here he supported freedom of speech and press, freedom to associate, trial by jury, right to private property, and so forth. While recognizing that legal protection for these freedoms is necessary, Tocqueville strongly asserted that such protection is not sufficient, that without the habits of freedom inculcated by customs and mores, constitutional guarantees will not prove durable. For the moment, let us briefly summarize Tocqueville's support for legal safeguards of individual rights.

Although Tocqueville approved of legal protection for a free press, he did so with some hesitation—wishing, as he put it in *Democracy*, to find "an intermediate and yet tenable position between the complete independence and the entire servitude of opinion." Yet as long as a society ensured a wide diversity of publications, as long as it inhibited a handful of sources from dominating public opinion, Tocqueville found no danger, and many advantages, in complete freedom of the press. "The more I considered the independence of the press in its principal consequences, the more I am convinced that in the modern world it is the chief and, so to speak, the constitutive element of liberty. A nation that is determined to remain free is therefore right in demanding, at any price, the exercise of this independence." One qualification is crucial. Once "centralization" of information is entrenched, once the nation relies on two or three sources for information or a city relies on one major newspaper, then freedom of opinion has become illusory, because opinions are not popularly made but hierarchically "formed." Genuine freedom of the press is directly proportional to the number and variety of news sources, for centralized sources tend to give everyone the same opinion. "Nothing but a newspaper can drop the same thought into a thousand minds at the same moment."[1] Centralization of government invariably brings centralization of news sources; the former restricts freedom while the latter gives the illusion of freedom.

For three broadly different reasons, Tocqueville did approve restrictions of the press. First, restriction was sometimes reasonable in public emergencies—for example, wars. During the tumultuous, but not violent, days of August 1848, he approved a measure to censor some publications, although he fumed righteously when these restrictions descended upon journals he considered harmless.[2] He explained why he introduced legislation to suspend the clubs of Paris and restrict the press: "For my part, I believe that it was wise and necessary to make great concessions to the fears and legitimate resentments of the nation, and that, after such a violent revolution, the only way to save freedom was to restrict it."[3]

1. For the preceding quotations see Tocqueville, *Democracy*, 1: 188, 200, 192–94; 2: 119.
2. Tocqueville, *Oeuvres* (M), vol. 8, pt. 2, *Correspondance . . . Beaumont*, p. 39.
3. Tocqueville, *Recollections*, p. 272.

Second, Tocqueville, like Mill,[4] approved restrictions of the press for countries lacking political maturity; thus, for example, Algeria should not be allowed a free press, because such institutions are "not necessary to the small infancy of societies."[5] Twice he suggested that a "temporary dictatorship under firm and enlightened guidance" might help Ireland, and he cautiously preferred despotism to what he described as the misery and crime of South America.[6] Legal protection of a free press, for Tocqueville, was not an absolute good that should be applied in all times and places.

Third, Tocqueville apparently also approved censorship for purposes of public morality. After stumbling upon a controversy over restrictions on the theater in London, he wrote of those advocating the restrictions, "from the point of view of public morality I believe they were right."[7] In another instance, he found the tyranny of the majority "unquestionably good," to the extent that it proscribed anyone from publishing "licentious books."[8] The evidence is inconclusive on this point, but Tocqueville regarded morality as so important to a republic that one can easily imagine him—or Jefferson for that matter—denying the right to publish "licentious books," although Tocqueville well knew that this would leave him with the problem of who would decide what is "licentious."

When we turn to his discussion of freedom of association, we again find that Tocqueville wavered about whether this freedom should be unlimited. Even after depicting all the advantages of associations—protecting individuals from centralization, maintaining diversity of opinion, encouraging participation, and so forth—Tocqueville still announced that "I doubt whether, in any country or in any age, it is wise to set no limits to freedom of association." But he added immediately that whoever argued for restrictions on associations and contended that such restrictions would generate prosperity and tranquillity must realize "at what price these blessings are purchased." Indeed, "I can understand that it may be advisable to cut off a man's arm in order to save his life, but it would be ridiculous to assert that he will be as dexterous as he was before he lost it."[9]

4. John Stuart Mill, *On Liberty*, I; *Considerations on Representative Government*, II.
5. Tocqueville, *Oeuvres* (M), vol. 3, *Écrits et discours politiques*, pp. 275–77. (From *L'Algérie*.)
6. Tocqueville, *Journeys to England and Ireland*, pp. 149, 143; *Democracy*, 1: 240.
7. Tocqueville, *Journeys to England and Ireland*, p. 49.
8. Tocqueville, *Democracy*, 1: 275.
9. Ibid., 2: 128.

Tocqueville incessantly and steadfastly maintained that modern societies must assure rights to trial by jury, free legal counsel, bail, protection from arbitrary arrest, secret voting, freedom of assembling to worship "without . . . the authorization of the superintendent of police," an open trial, and private property (England most outraged him when seizing property in India).[10] He never advocated the right of women to vote but urged that France march slowly and deliberately toward full male suffrage. In judicial matters, Tocqueville adhered aggressively to Montesquieu's maxim that "the trouble, expense, delays" of a judiciary process actually foster liberty, because with each delay, with every subsequent appeal, another source of reason and justice can review and pronounce upon the case.[11] The English system of law, although slow, costly, and complicated, at least assured the "guarantees of the individual against the state."[12] Similarly, a judiciary independent of political power and pressure helps ensure individual liberties, and, if coupled with an independent judicial review, can guard against any possible "tyranny of political assemblies."[13]

Tocqueville also incorporated Montesquieu's dictum, borrowed from Polybius and bequeathed to Madison, that "power should be a check to power," that the various institutions and branches of government should all be counterpoised to one another in the interest of checking abuses.[14] "*Even in America,*" Tocqueville wrote, people recognized that a "completely democratic government is so dangerous" that they institutionalized precautions in order to delay, to review, and to eliminate all irrationalities, passions, and mistakes: for example, "the establishment of two chambers, the governor's veto, and above all the establishment of the judges. . . ." Unless a people elects representatives possessing an independence of judgment, that is, if a people seeks to meddle directly with national politics, it will "fall back into the chaos of the republics of antiquity."[15] The indirect elections

10. Ibid., 1: 294–95; Drescher, ed., *Tocqueville and Beaumont on Social Reform*, p. 55; *On the Penitentiary System*, p. 184; *Oeuvres* (M), vol. 6, pt. 1, *Correspondance anglaise*, pp. 127, 132; *Journeys to England and Ireland*, p. 234; *Oeuvres* (B), vol. 9, *Études économiques, politiques*, pp. 417–18; *Oeuvres* (M), vol. 3, *Écrits et discours politiques*, p. 278 (from *L'Algérie*); *Oeuvres* (M), vol. 6, pt. 1, *Correspondance anglaise*, pp. 254, 264; Drescher, *Tocqueville and England*, ch. 7.

11. Montesquieu, *The Spirit of the Laws*, VI, 2, 1: 74.

12. Tocqueville, *The Old Regime*, p. 286.

13. Tocqueville, *Journeys to England and Ireland*, p. 83; *Journey to America*, p. 303; *Democracy*, 1: 102–9, 2: 326, 1: 107.

14. Montesquieu, *The Spirit of the Laws*, XI, 4, 6, 1: 150, 160.

15. Tocqueville, *Journey to America*, pp. 148, 175.

of Senators should be the model for all national elections or else modern republics "run the risk of perishing miserably among the shoals of democracy."[16]

THE IMPORTANCE OF MORES

Constitutional or legal protections of individual rights and liberties are indispensable to freedom in the modern world, but, as we noted previously, Tocqueville did not consider them sufficient. Tocqueville concerned himself less with branches of government than with the roots of a political culture. Because freedom in a modern democracy entails participation in public affairs, participation must become a habit, something one does as if it were part of the natural course of things. "The habit of dealing with all matters by discussion, and deciding them all, even the smallest, by means of majorities, that is the hardest habit of all to acquire. But it is only that habit which shapes governments that are truly free. . . ." But if freedom is a habit, it is just as much a prism through which one sees the world—a set of unquestioned assumptions involving self-confidence, a sense that the political world will yield to democratic efforts to influence it, a sense of responsibility, self-reliance, and so forth.

> We Europeans think we can make republics by organizing a great political assembly. But on the contrary, of all forms of government a republic is the one that grows most from roots in the whole of society. Consider this country. The republic is everywhere, in the streets as much as in Congress. If there is something blocking the public way, the neighbors on the spot form a body to discuss it; they appoint a commission and put the trouble to rights by their collective effort sensibly directed. . . . The people have something of the republic in the marrow of their bones. . . .[17]

Free societies offer both this habit of participation and this prism of personal assumptions expressed not in classrooms but by means of customs or mores (which Tocqueville expressly equated[18]) that surround one from birth and are taken for granted as much as the air we breathe.

16. Tocqueville, *Democracy*, 1: 212.
17. Tocqueville, *Journey to America*, pp. 45, 42–43 (here Tocqueville was quoting his friend Francis Lieber).
18. Tocqueville, *Democracy*, 1: 310.

As a consequence, Tocqueville belittled those "excessive admirers of the division of powers,"[19] because he contended that societies preserve freedom not by balancing power but by dispersing it, not by legal safeguards of personal rights but by mores that assure a ubiquitous personal ethic that leads individuals automatically to respect these rights. In New England townships, "democracy has gradually penetrated into their customs, their opinions, and their forms of social intercourse; it is to be found in all the details of daily life as well as in the laws."[20] By contrast, Tocqueville was exasperated with France. "What greater impotence than that of institutions, when ideas and mores do not nourish them!"[21]

When reading Hobbes, one everywhere discovers geometrical images and analogies until it eventually seems possible to draw Hobbes's state—to draw lines of information and influence, to graph the movements of individuals, to sketch the institutional forces that pull and balance, to add circles in which private individuals wish to be left alone. Improving the body politic—or should we say the machine politic—becomes a question of mechanics: a lever added here, a force increased there, and dysfunctions vanish. Although he recognized the necessity of checks and balances, Tocqueville had absorbed the French sociological tradition of Bodin, Montaigne, and, to an extent, Montesquieu. With this tradition, he accepted all the time-honored metaphors that convey an organic conception of society. Tocqueville's prevailing political image involved not mechanics but health; one does not construct societies but rather one lets them grow, and with growth occasionally comes disease. Just as health invigorates all parts of the body, disease enervates. "I consider my country as a sick man whom we cannot, it is true, hope to cure at once, but whose malady one may greatly alleviate. . . ."[22] Restoration, however, necessitates more than new laws, for it requires a regeneration of the life-enhancing mores of a nation. The significance of this distinction cannot be overstressed. To judge whether a country is free, Locke or Madison might investigate its laws, its institutions, and whether the constitution legally assures private rights. Tocqueville, however, examined a more nebulous thing called "character" or "spirit" or "mores": not efficient

19. Tocqueville, *Oeuvres* (M), vol. 11, *Correspondance . . . Royer-Collard . . . Ampère*, p. 101.

20. Tocqueville, *Democracy*, 1: 333.

21. Tocqueville, *Oeuvres* (M), vol. 8, pt. 3, *Correspondance . . . Beaumont*, p. 543.

22. Tocqueville, *Correspondence . . . Senior*, 1: 90. Tocqueville elsewhere likened himself to a doctor attempting a dangerous cure on a very sick patient. (Yale Tocqueville Collection, C.V.j., Paquet No. 2, Cahier No. 2, p. 18.)

motion but health; not line but color; not quantifiable statistics but unquantifiable quality or character. How else can one understand his claim of prerevolutionary France that "liberty disappeared from institutions, and maintained itself more than ever in the manners . . ."?[23] Could Locke or Madison even conceptually grasp this proposition?

Tocqueville suggested that constitutional liberties are most important because they often shakily prop up a faltering political order until a new generation can establish freedom on a stronger foundation, like old boards that support the ceiling of a mine until more durable timbers can be found. "The great utility of popular institutions is to sustain liberty during those intervals wherein the human mind is otherwise occupied—to give it a kind of vegetative life, which may keep it in existence during those periods of inattention. The forms of a free government allow men to become temporarily weary of their liberty without losing it."[24] Tocqueville persistently clung to his conviction that "laws are always unsteady so long as they are not based for support on morals. Mores are the only tough and durable power among a people."[25] Although good laws tend to accompany a free society, they cannot create such a society. "I am quite convinced that political societies are not what their laws make them, but what sentiments, beliefs, ideas, habits of the heart, and the spirit of men who form them, prepare them in advance to be. . . ."[26] Indeed, healthy manners and customs can sometimes best defend individual rights; under the ancient French monarchy, citizens were "better defended by the state of usages and manners than the citizens of free countries are often protected by their laws."[27]

Having grown despite the storms of history, having been modified by the demands of the past, mores are necessarily tenacious, like a large oak that one can uproot only with long effort and without ever finding the tips of its deepest roots. This tenacity can enhance freedom, as in the United States, or enervate it, as in Germany. "Private life in Germany evidently has very engaging aspects. But what poor citizens! When I see the long use they have made of absolute power, the gentleness of that power, the tradition of liberty so effaced in the mores, the centralization, the universal passion for places and the

23. Tocqueville, *Memoir*, 1: 243. (From "France before the Revolution.")
24. Ibid., p. 250. (From "France before the Revolution.")
25. Tocqueville, *Journey to America*, p. 305; also *Democracy*, 1: 294.
26. Tocqueville, *Selected Letters*, p. 294.
27. Tocqueville, *Memoir*, 1: 245. (From "France before the Revolution.")

universal dependency everywhere, I ask myself if they will ever be much different from what they are."[28] So fundamental did Tocqueville regard mores that he set out to demonstrate, not simply to state, that customs and mores contributed more to the maintenance of freedom in the United States than did laws or the abundance of natural resources. He did this by comparing the United States with certain Latin American nations that shared a similar legal structure and a similar abundance of natural resources. Because none of these could boast of political freedom, he concluded that the customs or mores of the United States must be the major support of freedom. In *Democracy* he wrote, "The customs of the Americans of the United States are, then, the peculiar cause which renders that people the only one of the American nations that is able to support a democratic government. . . . Too much importance is attributed to legislation, too little to customs." After stating his conviction about the importance of mores, after presenting historical examples, after seeking to demonstrate its validity, Tocqueville still valued this proposition enough to insert a last, somewhat emotional appeal to the reader.

> The importance of customs is a common truth to which study and experience incessantly direct our attention. It may be regarded as a central point in the range of observation, and the common termination of all my inquiries. So seriously do I insist upon this head that, if I have hitherto failed in making the reader feel the important influence of the practical experience, the habits, the opinions, in short, of the customs of the Americans on the maintenance of their institutions, I have failed in the principal object of my work.[29]

As we have seen, mores and customs are essential to free government because they foster the habits and assumptions necessary for democratic freedom. Mores are also necessary because laws are not airtight. Balzac's Vautrin told Rastignac to "crawl through the holes that are left in the network of the code." In his *Persian Letters*, Montesquieu described a man who, to quench an "insatiable thirst for wealth," ruined a family, deprived the children of education, forced the father to die of grief and the mother of sadness, but still announced, "I did no more than is permitted under the law."[30] Halting moral or political decline with yet more laws trying to close yet more loopholes is like compressing a balloon in one's hands; wherever you

28. Tocqueville, *Selected Letters*, p. 308.
29. Tocqueville, *Democracy*, 1: 334 for this and the preceding quotation in the text.
30. Balzac, *Père Goriot* and *Eugénie Grandet*, p. 117; Baron de Montesquieu, *The Persian Letters*, ed. and trans. J. Robert Loy (New York, 1961), CXLVI.

press, it bulges out somewhere else. "There is no country in which everything can be provided for by the laws, or in which political institutions can prove a substitute for common sense and public morality."[31] The holes in the law must be filled by habits and personal morality. In his notebooks, Tocqueville wrote, "Ceremony of 4th July. . . . Perfect order that prevails. Silence. No police. Authority nowhere."[32] And yet clearly authority was somewhere; it had been internalized as a set of obligations and habits, making laws less important.

Just as the Roman was "enchained" by his oath,[33] the citizen of a free country internalizes restraints. The customs, mores, and habits of a free society form a popular culture that teaches people duties, restraint of passions and desires, and obligations. If modern democracies cannot embrace aristocratic culture in order to cultivate their abilities and control their desires, perhaps they can create the customs and mores of a democratic culture that lead to common sense, practical intelligence, and a sense of duty and restraint.

THE IMPORTANCE OF RELIGION

Tocqueville argued strongly that religion was essential to this internalized sense of duty. "Liberty regards religion as its companion in all its battles and its triumphs. . . . It considers religion as the safeguard of morality, and morality as the best security of law and the surest pledge of the duration of freedom." As the traditional ties of aristocratic society dissolved, as the hierarchical order that once inflexibly fixed individuals to assigned positions disappeared, an internal religious morality must supplant the coercive authority of the old regime. "How is it possible that society should escape destruction if the moral tie is not strengthened in proportion as the political tie is relaxed?"[34]

Tocqueville respected religion, not only because it was invaluable to political freedom, but also because it was useful to people in their private lives. Because "doubt has always seemed to me to be the most insupportable of all evils of this world," he maintained that people needed religion to answer persistent questions about God, moral

31. Tocqueville, *Democracy*, 1: 127.
32. Tocqueville, *Journey to America*, p. 125.
33. Montesquieu, *Considerations on the Causes of the Greatness of the Romans and Their Decline*, p. 97.
34. Tocqueville, *Democracy*, 1: 46, 318.

choice, and the meaning of life.[35] Religion fills a "void within," conforms to "man's natural instincts," and contributes mightily toward one's "peace of mind."[36] Quite possibly "men need *authority* in questions of religion," because they "go astray" when seeking to rely on "reason alone."[37]

Tocqueville was, of course, projecting on to the world much of his own personal torment. His letters and private notebooks return again and again to expressions of doubt, to his despair at not being capable of belief, and to his yearning for certainty. Again and again, he admitted, he was tormented by "the need for *infinity* and the sad experience of *finitude* that we meet at each step" in our lives.[38] In his notes for *Democracy in America*, we run across a single page with only this note to himself. "The only truth that I recognize as absolute is that there is no absolute truth. After having found this, do not weary yourself by searching for another truth, because it does not exist."[39] It is in a famous letter to Madame Swetchine in 1857, however, when he confessed that he had always been haunted by doubt, that Tocqueville offered the most dramatic testimony to his inability to find certainty. "The appearance of the problem of human existence preoccupies me incessantly and overpowers me incessantly. I can neither penetrate into this mystery, nor detach my eyes from it. . . . In this world, I find human life inexplicable and in the other world, frightening." As he continues the letter, the reader hears echoes of Tocqueville's own Romantic generation and perhaps even some sympathy for Goethe's Werther or Chateaubriand's René. Tocqueville dated his inability to believe to an episode of his youth when, driven by his "insatiable curiosity," he devoured so many books that he ended by hurling himself into "le doute universel" and "la mélancholie la plus noire," sentiments from which he admitted he never entirely escaped. "This is a sad and frightening illness, Madame, and I do not know if I have ever described it to anyone with as much force and unfortunately as much truth as I have described it to you. Happy are those who have never known this illness, or who no longer know it!"[40]

However much he may have been inflicted with doubt, Tocqueville thought religion was important for personal reasons; he also

---

35. Tocqueville, *Oeuvres* (M), vol. 15, pt. 2, *Correspondance . . . Corcelle*, p. 29. Elsewhere, Tocqueville ranked life's evils as illness, death, and doubt. (*Journey to America*, p. 155.)

36. Tocqueville, *The Old Regime*, pp. 149–50.

37. Tocqueville, *Journeys to England and Ireland*, p. 22.

38. Yale Tocqueville Collection, C.V.a., Paquet No. 8, p. 57.

39. Yale Tocqueville Collection, C.V.e.

40. Tocqueville, *Oeuvres* (M), vol. 15, *Correspondance . . . Swetchine*, pp. 314–15.

maintained that it was necessary for political freedom. Tocqueville never made this argument naively, however, because he recognized all the political dangers that accompany religion, all the dangers that concerned such thinkers as Machiavelli and Rousseau. He knew that religion had frequently been a central support to despotisms, even despotisms characterized by "terror." "On close inspection we shall find that religion and not fear has ever been the cause of the long-lived prosperity of an absolute government."[41] In addition, he consistently criticized religion whenever it fostered withdrawal or indifference to the affairs of this world, whenever it exhorted sequestration for purposes of salvation. "Ascetic works" that glorify a "claustral life" are frankly "dangerous," because in stressing the central importance of "private virtues," these teachings dissipate politically important "public virtues."[42] The European religions of the nineteenth century, Tocqueville argued, paid great attention to the duties of private life, especially the duties of the domestic household, but these religions cared little for the duties of the citizen. As a result, Christianity was making individuals "every day more and more indifferent to public virtue; so much so, that the great family of nations seems more corrupt, more base, and more tottering while every little family is better regulated."[43] Finally, like Machiavelli, Tocqueville despised religion that willingly promoted resignation and humility, weakening confidence and pride.

> Moralists are constantly complaining that the ruling vice of the present time is pride. This is true in one sense, for indeed everyone thinks that he is better than his neighbor or refuses to obey his superior; but it is extremely false in another, for the same man who cannot endure subordination or equality has so contemptible an opinion of himself that he thinks he is born only to indulge in vulgar pleasures. He willingly takes up with low desires without daring to embark on lofty enterprises, of which he scarcely dreams. . . . Humility is unwholesome to them; what they most want is, in my opinion, pride.[44]

Despite his awareness of religion's potential for undermining freedom, Tocqueville still thought that the proper religion was essential to freedom, and he confided to a friend that his chief dream in political life was to reconcile liberalism with Catholicism. "Man's true gran-

41. Tocqueville, *Democracy*, 1: 321, 97; *Oeuvres* (M), vol. 8, pt. 3, *Correspondance . . . Beaumont*, p. 435.
42. Tocqueville, *Oeuvres* (B), vol. 7, *Nouvelle correspondance*, p. 130.
43. Tocqueville, *Memoir*, 2: 317, 328.
44. Tocqueville, *Democracy*, 2: 261–62.

deur lies only in the harmony of the liberal sentiment and religious sentiment, both working simultaneously to animate and restrain souls, and [my] sole political passion for thirty years has been to bring this about."[45] Certainly Tocqueville was not urging a union of Church and State, for whenever religion tied itself to government, it relinquished all moral influence over the citizenry.[46]

Tocqueville argued that religion could foster and support political freedom in two different ways. First, it should help restrain passions, enabling individuals to master themselves, something we saw in his admiration for the "beauty of that rare, open struggle of the spirit against the ruling flesh."[47] Or, as he puts it in his notes, "as if one could have mores without religion and freedom without mores!"[48] But religion also curbs the passion for wealth, an obsessive desire that Tocqueville regarded as dangerous for democratic freedom. "We shall see that of all the passions which originate in or are fostered by equality, there is one which it renders peculiarly intense, and which it also infuses into the heart of every man; I mean the love of well-being. . . . The chief concern of religion is to purify, to regulate, and to restrain the excessive and exclusive taste for well-being. . . ."[49] Second, religion should teach people that morality is more valuable than mere physical pleasure, that the soul is more important than the body. "Christianity put the ultimate aim of human life beyond this world; it gave thus a finer, purer, less material, less interested, and higher character to morality."[50] Without religion, individuals forfeit "the use of [their] sublimest faculties," ultimately becoming like animals devoting their lives to consuming comforts and pleasures, instead of becoming human beings who, with eyes "towards heaven," seek higher purposes and ideals. After all, contended Tocqueville, Christianity bestowed upon the world the principles of "equality, unity, fraternity."[51]

Thus, the question with which we opened this chapter finds its answer. Although most citizens of a modern democracy, because they lack leisure and not because they lack innate ability, will be incapable of sharing the benefits of French aristocratic culture, they can still be fashioned for freedom by a commonly shared culture embodied in the mores and in religion. From mores and religion, individuals gain

45. Tocqueville, *Selected Letters*, p. 295.
46. Tocqueville, *Correspondence . . . Senior*, 1: 85.
47. Tocqueville, *The European Revolution and Correspondence with Gobineau*, p. 207.
48. Yale Tocqueville Collection, C.V.h., Paquet No. 3, Cahier No. 3, p. 113.
49. Tocqueville, *Democracy*, 2: 27.
50. Tocqueville, *The European Revolution and Correspondence with Gobineau*, p. 191.
51. Tocqueville, *Democracy*, 2: 154; *The European Revolution and Correspondence with Gobineau*, p. 191.

certain duties, a prism of perceptions through which they see the
political world, a socially enforced means of mastering their desires,
and a common fund of practical knowledge that enables them to
master their communities cooperatively. Left to themselves, individuals have only the independence to fall prey to their appetites.
Born into the proper culture, nourished by this fertile cultural soil,
individuals overcome mere desires and become what human beings
ought to be. If scattered at random, the seeds of oak trees may germi-
nate after a fashion, but if planted properly, they blossom mightily.

The Slow and Difficult Path to Political Regeneration

Yet another problem persists. If mores can nourish, can they not
just as easily stifle? If the mores of the United States enhanced freedom, did those of India or South America not give birth to servility
and subjection? Tocqueville answered yes to both these questions, and
in so doing, he broached the problem of generating, or regenerating,
freedom in an unfree society.

The United States, Tocqueville thought, established liberty with
the assistance of conditions perhaps never to be encountered again in
history. A people with relatively cohesive customs embodying English
notions of freedom, a people with neither a hereditary aristocracy to
vanquish nor an impoverished class to suppress, set foot on an abundantly fertile land that, after the American Indians had been deci-
mated and routed, was uninhabited. Borrowing from their heritage
and meeting the needs forced upon them by the wilderness, the colonial societies instilled self-reliance and the habits of self-government,
eventually creating the customs necessary for democratic freedom—
that is, the *"taste for, and practice of, provincial governments."* Because
free government emerged in the United States only with the assistance of this astounding combination of circumstances, "to imitate
it is absolutely impracticable without the pre-existing conditions. . . ."
From a conversation with a friend, Tocqueville noted: "How can a
man who has seen America imagine that one could transplant her
political laws to Europe and, especially, do so all at once. Since I have
seen this country, I cannot believe that M. de Lafayette held his theories in good faith; one could not deceive oneself so clumsily."[52]

52. Tocqueville, *Journey to America*, pp. 260, 261, 43 (from Tocqueville's conversation with his friend Francis Lieber).

Stendhal posed the question admirably when one of his characters asked, "Besides, how is one to establish a Republic without republicans?"[53] Tocqueville could only answer that a nation creates freedom simultaneously with the mores appropriate to freedom. Republican government, he said, "cannot be maintained without certain conditions of intelligence, of private morality, and of religious belief, that we, as a nation, have not reached, and that we must labor to attain before grasping their political results."[54] Although a slave can be granted independence by legal decree, he must, as we have seen, shoulder the "thoughts, the habits, and morals of a free man" before attaining freedom.[55] Tocqueville feared greatly that, although liberated from the ties of dependence that positioned them in the old aristocratic hierarchy, individuals will attain the independence of a democracy without the habits and customs necessary for freedom.

> Democracy [in Europe] has consequently been abandoned to its wild instincts, and it has grown up like those children who have no parental guidance, who receive their education in the public streets. . . . The result has been that the democratic revolution has taken place in the body of society without that concomitant change in the laws, ideas, customs, and morals which was necessary to render such a revolution beneficial. Thus we have a democracy without anything to lessen its vices and bring out its natural advantages.[56]

From a long chain of French political thinkers extending at least back to Montaigne, Tocqueville learned that, because one must alter the mores to alter society significantly, such changes simply cannot come suddenly. Far-reaching transformations of society are always gradual, nearly imperceptible. Montesquieu suggested that "politics is a smooth file, which cuts gradually, and attains its end by a slow progression"; de Maistre ridiculed those poor souls who claim "one can constitute nations with ink."[57] Both exemplify a tradition that included such diverse thinkers as Rousseau, Burke, Bonald, and Proudhon. Only those who think that a radical alteration of society can be enacted from above could declare, as Turgot once did, that one can profoundly transform a nation in ten years. In a letter written in 1853, Tocqueville confided that in his *Old Regime* he tried to show

---

53. Stendhal, *The Charterhouse of Parma*, p. 415.
54. Tocqueville, *Memoir*, 1: 377.
55. Drescher, ed., *Tocqueville and Beaumont on Social Reform*, p. 100.
56. Tocqueville, *Democracy*, 1: 8.
57. Montesquieu, *The Spirit of the Laws*, XIV, 13, 1: 232; de Maistre quoted in Leroy, *Histoire des idées sociales en France*, 2: 141.

that "the greatest revolutions do not change peoples as much as people pretend, and that the principal reason for what they are is always in what they have been."[58] When far-reaching change does occur, it is the consequence of strenuous efforts compelling incremental changes over many generations. As he said of the United States, "it is evident that nothing but a long series of events, all having the same tendency, could substitute for this combination of laws, opinions, and manners a mass of opposite opinions, manners, and laws."[59]

Besides being nearly impossible, attempts at sudden, dramatic change are destructive, because they invariably lead to centralization. Each class or group that seeks radical change harnesses itself to the power of the state in order to effect its purpose; since they all admire centralization because they regard the state as a vehicle for their own special journey, what was once a car becomes an omnibus.

> . . . the people endeavor to centralize the public administration in the hands of the government, in order to wrest the management of local affairs from the aristocracy. Towards the close of such a revolution, on the contrary, it is usually the conquered aristocracy that endeavors to make over the management of all affairs to the state, because such an aristocracy dreads the tyranny of a people that has become its equal and not infrequently its master. . . . As long as the democratic revolution lasts, there is always one class in the nation, powerful in numbers or in wealth, which is induced, by peculiar passions or interests, to centralize the public administration. . . .[60]

By contrast, the United States temporarily managed to avoid centralization, because it "had no aristocracy to combat." If by itself the struggle for power does not suffice for centralization, then the ensuing hatreds, conflicts of material interests, loss of belief, and inevitable exhaustion resulting from the struggle will foster a "most inordinate devotion to order."[61] Once begun, the attempt to alter society profoundly and rapidly serves to unleash hopes and desires that swiftly surpass any capability of satisfying them; only a more powerful government can restrain these resulting passions.[62] One can never impose new mores, habits, and customs without in turn becoming the master.

Convinced of this analysis, Tocqueville suggested that the only

58. Tocqueville, *Oeuvres* (B), vol. 7, *Nouvelle correspondance*, p. 305.
59. Tocqueville, *Democracy*, 1: 436.
60. Ibid., 2: 315–16.
61. Ibid., pp. 316, 318.
62. Tocqueville, *Recollections*, pp. 25–27.

conceivable way to regenerate a political order had to be long, slow, and deliberate. One simply cannot journey to a decentralized democracy in the vehicle of centralization. By encouraging decentralization, education, religion, morality, a sense of public purpose, and some restrictions on self-interest, France could proceed slowly but relentlessly to reshape its mores and customs so that they enhance freedom. "In America free morals have made free political institutions; in France it is for free political institutions to mould morals. This is the end towards which we must strive but without forgetting the point of departure."[63] France must "proceed slowly, with precaution, and with legality," extending "provincial liberties" until "the majority of the nation itself can be involved with its own affairs," that is, until almost all people take an active part in political life. After selecting its destination, France must march toward it deliberately. "I wish finally that people knew where they wanted to go, and that they advanced toward it prudently instead of proceeding aimlessly as they have been doing almost constantly for twenty years."[64]

Once more Tocqueville's proposals belie his own pessimism. In his analysis he suggested that modern industrial states (1) have inherent tendencies toward centralization that undermine participatory democracy, (2) become dominated by the commercial classes that use the state for their own purposes, (3) promote an acquisitive ethic that extolls personal self-interest rather than duties and public obligations, and (4) produce consumer societies suggesting in the long run that individuals not restrain passions but chase desires, comforts, and pleasures. From where will this force emerge that can make these slow but deliberate changes in the habits and mores of society?

Revolutions and governmental reforms instituted from above always fail. Tocqueville concluded that, despite all the difficulties, the only way to establish the proper conditions for freedom is for them to be cultivated by the populace itself—in particular, through the practical experience gained in decentralized participation. One cannot impose them or force them to grow; one can only prepare the soil and allow nature to do the rest.

63. Tocqueville, *Journey to America*, p. 149.
64. Tocqueville, *Selected Letters*, pp. 112–14.

10 Freedom as Overcoming Self-Interest: The Importance of a Sense of History

W hen Hobbes suggested that the goal of a political order should be gratifying the desires of individuals, he clashed dramatically with an ancient tradition that defined politics as the pursuit of the general good, not the satisfaction of private interests. Tacitus recorded that the Roman republic collapsed when "the public good was sacrificed to private interests"; Bodin assumed that a "commonwealth" necessarily addressed itself to "common concerns," not private ones.[1] A republic endured, Montesquieu asserted, only if it managed to teach a "constant preference of public to private interests" along with a "love of the public." Montesquieu's description of democracy, which borrows heavily from classical examples, would seem fanciful to thinkers like Locke and Mill. "The love of equality in a democracy," said Montesquieu, "limits ambition to the sole desire, to the sole happiness, of doing greater services to our country than the rest of our fellow citizens."[2] By using the example of a Spartan mother who thanked the gods for Sparta's victory, even though she lost five sons in battle, Rousseau also sought to demonstrate that a republic must sacrifice private interests in the general good.[3]

---

1. Tacitus, *Complete Works*, p. 205. (*Annals*, VI, 16.) Bodin, *Six Books of the Commonwealth*, I, 1–7, pp. 1ff.
2. Montesquieu, *The Spirit of the Laws*, IV, 5; XXIII, 7; V, 3; 1: 34, 2: 5, 1: 41.
3. Rousseau, *Émile*, p. 8.

TOCQUEVILLE'S DISLIKE OF A REPUBLIC FOUNDED ON PRIVATE INTEREST

When Tocqueville argued in a letter to Chabrol[4] and in a famous chapter in *Democracy in America*—passages frequently used to depict Tocqueville as an advocate of a pluralist politics based on group and individual interests[5]—that "the principle of self-interest rightly understood appears to me the best suited of all philosophical theories to the wants of men in our time . . ."[6] he seemed to sever himself from the political tradition that so strongly influenced him. In fact, he did not. Even in these passages, he never argued, with Mandeville or with Adam Smith, that the general good would result from the undirected action of each seeking his or her material interests. Nor did he argue, with Madison or modern pluralists, that the self-interested actions of groups and individuals would bring the general good because of the balancing of groups and interests along with a modicum of government intervention. Rather, Tocqueville suggested that individuals will be acting in their own interests, for their own happiness, if they "sacrifice themselves for their fellow creatures," a claim that reminds us of Montesquieu and Rousseau, not Smith and Madison. It is also a claim that should not be surprising in a chapter that followed twenty-two pages after he affirmed the pernicious consequences of individualism and fifteen pages before he described the restless dissatisfaction that accompanies the pursuit of material wealth.

The great undertaking of modern liberal thinkers—including Locke, Hume, Madison, and Mill—was the argument that, with a balancing of interests, one could have republican institutions without ancient republican virtue. Although Tocqueville was too experienced and too intelligent to reject this argument entirely, he was too indebted to the republican thinkers of eighteenth-century France to accept the argument wholeheartedly. Modern pluralists who seek to claim Tocqueville as one of their own need to explain how he could offer the following description of American democracy: "They therefore do not deny that every man may follow his own interest, but they endeavor to prove that it is the interest of every man to be virtuous."[7] In preparing to write *Democracy in America*, he decided that the United

4. Tocqueville, *Selected Letters*, pp. 37–41.
5. For example, Zetterbaum, *Tocqueville and the Problem of Democracy*, pp. 101–12, 122–37; Mayer, *Alexis de Tocqueville*, pp. 22, 24; Lerner, "Tocqueville's *Democracy in America*."
6. Tocqueville, *Democracy*, 2: 131; see also pp. 129–30.
7. Ibid., p. 130.

States did not offer an example, which would have refuted Montesquieu, of a republican world without republican virtue.

> Americans do not form a virtuous people, but nevertheless they are free. This does not prove absolutely that virtue, as Montesquieu thought of it, is not essential to the existence of republics. It is not necessary to take Montesquieu's idea in a narrow sense. . . . What he means by virtue is the moral power which each individual exercises on himself and which prevents him from violating the rights of others. . . . Montesquieu was therefore right, although he spoke of ancient virtue, and what he said of Greeks and Romans is still applicable to Americans.[8]

Tocqueville refused to see in the example of American democracy a justification for an ethic of self-interest instead of an ethic that reminded one of public duties. American citizens "show with complacency how an enlightened regard for themselves constantly prompts them to assist one another and inclines them willingly to sacrifice a portion of their time and property to the welfare of the state." Finally, he emphatically repudiated those who encouraged individuals to chase after only what is personally useful, allowing the general good to take care of itself. "Everybody I see about me seems bent on teaching his contemporaries, by precept and example, that what is useful is never wrong. Will nobody undertake to make them understand how what is right may be useful?"[9] Any detailed study of Tocqueville's letters and notebooks should cure the temptation to see Tocqueville as championing a politics based on interests. Once his concentration on American democracy had subsided—that is, once back in the company of Pascal, Montesquieu, and Rousseau—he wrote scarcely a word that would countenance any kind of politics based on self-interest. As he wrote to his friend Kergorlay in 1835, "How small, cold, and sad life would become if, beside this everyday world so full of egoism and cowardice, the human spirit could not construct another in which disinterestedness, courage, in a word, virtue, could breathe at ease!"[10] Or again, as he wrote to Madame Swetchine, praising the French soldiers fighting in the Crimean War, "Are you not astonished along with me, Madame, upon seeing spring from a nation that appears so devoid of public virtues, an army that demonstrates itself

8. Yale Tocqueville Collection, C.V.e., pp. 12–13.
9. Tocqueville, *Democracy*, 2: 130, 131–32. For a good discussion of Tocqueville's notion of self-interest and his wish for virtue, see Schleifer, *The Making of Tocqueville's "Democracy in America*," ch. 17.
10. Tocqueville, *Selected Letters*, p. 104.

to be full of virtue? So much egoism here, so much self-sacrifice there. . . ."[11] Once we have situated Tocqueville in his own time, we see that he does not write with the language of a twentieth-century pluralist.

This does not mean that Tocqueville either anticipated or hoped for perfect, selfless individuals. Unlike some of his French predecessors, he saw little realistic hope for ancient Roman virtue in this new industrial world. Responding to a friend's despair over the depravity of human beings, he said: "If to console you for having been born, you must meet with men whose most secret motives are always actuated by fine and elevated feelings, you need not wait, you may go and drown yourself immediately."[12] He readily acknowledged that people never conduct "political affairs" with "the scrupulous refinement of private life" and that "private interest which always plays a great part in political passions" is often "skillfully concealed under the veil of public interest."[13] He recognized that the modern world of politics reclined upon compromise, intrigues, and base interests, and he described the politics of his day as an "anthill of vices, baseness, and betrayals."[14]

Despite all this, he strove for a politics that, *as much as possible*, overcame mere interests, especially material interests, and converged on a dispute over political principles. When, as in 1789, nations seem to transcend private interest, in some way he thought that they redeemed a very fallible human race. In this, Tocqueville judged politics almost artistically, as if one or two beautiful examples vindicate all political efforts—like a gardener who has many flowers but one special rose that justifies all his labor and talent. Thus, in a curious way, the beauty of 1789 seemed to redeem, in Tocqueville's eyes, the pettiness and brutality of so many historical eras.

> I think no epoch of history has ever witnessed so large a number so passionately devoted to the public good, so honestly forgetful of themselves, so absorbed in the contemplation of the common interest, so resolved to risk everything they cherished in their private lives, so willing to overcome the small sentiments of their hearts. . . .
>
> The spectacle was short, but it was one of incomparable grandeur. It will never be effaced from the memory of mankind. All foreign nations witnessed it, applauded it, were moved by it.[15]

11. Tocqueville, *Oeuvres* (M), vol. 15, pt. 2, *Correspondance . . . Swetchine*, p. 263.
12. Tocqueville, *Memoir*, 1: 392–93.
13. Ibid., 2: 80; *Journey to America*, p. 171.
14. Tocqueville, *Oeuvres* (M), vol. 8, pt. 1, *Correspondance . . . Beaumont*, p. 207.
15. Tocqueville, *The European Revolution and Correspondence with Gobineau*, p. 86.

Suspended between such rare historical moments of grandeur, we must struggle to approach these standards and set examples for others.

Individuals must carry the maxims of morality with them into politics, at best adopting a "scrupulous conformity to religious morality in great affairs."[16] As he wrote to a friend, "it is evident that the most novel, the most honorable, and the most useful base that one could find for the creation of a new party is an energetic call to political morality."[17] When Tocqueville briefly outlined his "new" liberalism, religion and morality were among the most conspicuous ingredients. He did not want to be confused with those "friends of order," he said, who pretend to be liberals, but who are "indifferent to freedom and justice" as long as they can sleep safely at night. Nothing "great and lasting" will come from this kind of liberalism. "I hope to show so much respect for justice, such sincere love of order and law, such a deliberate attachment to morality and religion, that I cannot but believe that I shall be discovered to be a liberal of a new kind."[18] In the search for *grandes institutions nouvelles*,[19] morality and religion are cornerstones of the foundation.

As we saw in the previous chapter, Tocqueville felt it essential that citizens have a consistent, internalized political ethic. He despised Thiers, certainly because he thought Thiers traded in his most cherished political principles,[20] but also because Thiers altered his principles as his interests demanded. Thus, Tocqueville heartily enjoyed Beaumont's tale of how Thiers, during a single meal, changed his opinion three times *entre la soupe et le dessert*.[21] When politics revolves around the chase after interests, it brings forth ambitious people devoid of personal independence who, lacking in principles, become vulnerable to those who satisfy their interests for wealth or power. The Medicis of Florence, Tocqueville noted, controlled the city by forcing almost all citizens into their debt, and then "they could easily win nearly all the citizens one by one and hold them in their dependence."[22] Or, as

16. Tocqueville, *Democracy*, 2: 156.

17. Quoted in Pierre-Marcel, *Essai politique sur Alexis de Tocqueville*, p. 336.

18. Tocqueville, *Memoir*, 1: 381.

19. Tocqueville, *Oeuvres* (M), vol. 8, pt. 1, *Correspondance . . . Beaumont*, p. 474. For further discussion of the relation among religion, citizenship, and self-interest, see Doris S. Goldstein, *Trial of Faith: Religion and Politics in Tocqueville's Thought* (New York, 1975), pp. 88–97, 121–30.

20. Tocqueville, *Oeuvres* (M), vol. 8, pt. 1, *Correspondance . . . Beaumont*, p. 603; *Oeuvres* (M), vol. 11, *Correspondance . . . Royer-Collard . . . Ampère*, pp. 29–30.

21. Tocqueville, *Oeuvres* (M), vol. 8, pt. 2, *Correspondance . . . Beaumont*, pp. 353, 341.

22. Tocqueville, *Oeuvres* (B), vol. 8, *Mélanges, fragments*, p. 444.

Tocqueville said of a prominent contemporary, "Molé is always for sale. He is the dirtiest intriguer of the whole pack."[23] In Tocqueville's opinion, political freedom requires individuals to enter politics, not from personal interest, but from a wish to promote their individual vision of the general good. Because these people are not subject to the manipulation of those who can satisfy their interests, they can leave politics if their convictions so demand. "The power to quit the political arena without repining is, perhaps, the most essential qualification for acting independently and nobly."[24]

Citizens must view political questions from a general perspective, addressing themselves to the general needs of the nation. "What strikes me most is . . . the absence of every political idea and impression whatsoever. It is a nearly complete suspension of the collective and national life. Each is retired and as if buried in his private affairs. . . ."[25] Upon entering the public and political realm, citizens of free countries—as much as possible—leave behind private interests. If each "wants to consider public affairs from his single point of view," France will discover, Tocqueville warned the Chamber of Deputies, that it is by "acting in this manner that, in all centuries, people have lost their liberty."[26] Citizens must concern themselves with community needs more than individual needs, national ones more than community ones.

> It is said, it is repeated; all the organs of the press, from whatever side, say: local interests are becoming, in the mind of citizens, in the mind even of deputies, stronger than the general interest.
>
> What is that, Gentlemen, if not the greatest political demoralization which can exist in a country. . . . ?
>
> How do you expect that, in this fight between the general interest and the particular that will take place without cease in their hearts, the particular interest will not often be the stronger? Is that possible? And will they not soon lose the country from view in order to see only themselves?[27]

Although interests will never vanish, their influence can be minimized. In free countries, citizens enter the public realm to dispute principles, that is, ideas and convictions about the public good. Tocqueville's contemporaries, however, complacently existed "free"

23. Tocqueville, *Selected Letters,* p. 236.
24. Tocqueville, *Memoir,* 1: 390.
25. Tocqueville, *Oeuvres* (B), vol. 7, *Nouvelle correspondance,* p. 288.
26. Tocqueville, *Oeuvres* (B), vol. 9, *Études économiques, politiques,* pp. 376–77.
27. Ibid., pp. 385–86.

from principles,[28] and Tocqueville felt only "disgust" while "watching the public men of our day traffic, according to the smallest interests of the moment, in things as serious and sacred as principles."[29] The government reinforced, and reflected, this general tendency, because it approached individuals "by their interests rather than by their opinions . . . addressing itself to the small side of the human heart rather than the grand. . . ."[30] Tocqueville longed for a time when "there are fixed opinions and when men are rigorously classified, opposite one another, by these opinions."[31] Yet while he yearned for a politics in which principled individuals confronted one another in public debates that addressed the general good of the nation, he noted with dejection that "there are no longer opinions, but [only] individual interests."[32]

This kind of politics gives birth to disgust and instability, because freedom can find no firm and lasting foundation in interests. Many think, Tocqueville said, that while the love and respect that people formerly held for political authority is disappearing, one must devise a political order that more tightly controls citizens by means of their interests. Tocqueville maintained, however, that this would not work, that "what may appear to be a source of strength for a certain time will assuredly become, in the end, a great cause of embarrassment and weakness."[33] Why does a political system founded upon interests lack both durability and stability? Precisely because political authority will have lost legitimacy, government all moral authority, and laws all appearance of fairness. In his well-known speech of January 1848, the speech in which he predicted the forthcoming revolution, Tocqueville argued that "public mores are changing," because "private interests" now lurk behind every opinion about the common good. Slowly but surely an ethic had emerged that suggests individuals with political power have every right to use that power for their own private interests. "What is that," asked Tocqueville, "if not a deep and continuing degradation, a more and more complete corruption of public mores?" Once individuals perceive politics as an arena in which a plurality of interests compete for the means of satisfaction, political freedom is threatened because "interest has replaced disin-

---

28. Tocqueville, *Oeuvres* (M), vol. 11, *Correspondance . . . Royer-Collard . . . Ampère*, p. 20.

29. Tocqueville, *Selected Letters*, p. 129.

30. Tocqueville, *Oeuvres* (B), vol. 9, *Études économiques, politiques*, pp. 377–78.

31. Tocqueville, *Oeuvres* (M), vol. 8, pt. 1, *Correspondance . . . Beaumont*, p. 371.

32. Quoted in Pierre-Marcel, *Essai politique sur Alexis de Tocqueville*, p. 270. (From an unpublished note.)

33. Tocqueville, *Democracy*, 2: 264.

terested feelings in public life," greed will supplant all cooperation for the public good,[34] and citizens will mock all political decisions, seeing them not as a careful and principled choice for the general good, but as merely the victory by the strongest. It will no longer be a commonwealth but a chase after private wealth. "And besides, Gentlemen, are therefore so many words needed to prove that in substituting private interest for the general interest, one depraves society?"[35]

POLITICAL PARTIES AND THE RELATIONS BETWEEN CLASSES

In a speech before the Chamber of Deputies, Tocqueville lamented the impending destruction of what he called the "public spirit" of the nation. France, he suggested, was becoming *une troupe de soliciteurs,* an aggregation of individuals distinguished by no consistent views of the general good and incapable of forming parties or groups with distinct perspectives. "In substituting, as you are doing, private interest for general interest, individual passions for common passions, what is it that you are doing? You are undermining parties, you are enervating them, you are destroying them. Now, do you think, Gentlemen, that a free society can live without parties?"[36] When the France of the past witnessed parties—and Tocqueville thought of parties as groups with distinct and principled perspectives on political issues, not as organized election machines—politics had a certain grandeur and distinction. Tocqueville, for example, regarded the period of 1789 to 1830 as one long struggle between "the old feudal aristocracy and the middle class." Such a struggle gave birth to what he called great parties. "Between these two classes there was a longstanding separation of status, memories, interests, passions, and ideas. There had to be great parties—there were."[37]

Tocqueville made a fundamental distinction between "great parties" and "little parties." Great parties affirm or question the most fundamental political assumptions and values upon which a political culture rests. "What I call great political parties, those concerned with principles and not their consequences, with general questions and not with particular cases, with ideas and not with men, those parties generally have nobler traits, more generous passions, more real convic-

34. Tocqueville, "Speech of January 1848," in *Democracy in America*, ed. Mayer, p. 750.

35. Tocqueville, *Oeuvres* (B), vol. 9, *Études économiques, politiques*, pp. 380–82.

36. Ibid.

37. Drescher, ed., *Tocqueville and Beaumont on Social Reform*, p. 175.

tions, and a look of more frankness and boldness than the others."[38] Little parties, by contrast, busy themselves with quarreling about day-to-day material interests, and, "As they are not sustained or dignified by lofty purposes, they ostensibly display the selfishness of their character in their actions."[39] Although little parties avoid the potentially destructive turmoil of grand parties and produce a "great gain in happiness," Tocqueville doubted they produced a similar gain in morality. When he was in periods of personal despair about the future, he probably preferred to content himself with the stability offered by little parties. More often, however, he noted the absence of noble purpose in such parties, their character of "dishonourable selfishness," and the fact that they "do not rest upon principles, but upon material interests"; he embraced great political parties for their "generosity" and their quests for political greatness.[40] Only great parties bestow "power and brilliance to public life," engendering "variety, movement, fecundity, [and] life."[41] In one passage in his notes, Tocqueville listed "great parties" as one of several prerequisites for restoring freedom to France.[42]

If Tocqueville liked the principled clash of great political parties, he felt similarly about classes. Although he recognized that classes frequently use the powers of government to oppress one another, nevertheless a free society actually relies upon class competition, especially if over political principles, along with class cooperation for the common good. Freedom comes not from constructing a classless society, preeminently dull and sterile in Tocqueville's eyes, but from ensuring that no single class oppresses all others. Actually, Tocqueville walked a political tightrope in his analysis of classes. On the one hand, class hatred, by separating classes and undermining all class cooperation, promotes despotism. "Nothing serves despotism better than the mutual hatreds and jealousies of classes."[43] Thus, Tocqueville argued that class cooperation was important to freedom, and again he drew upon the French Middle Ages for an example. In the local, provincial, and national assemblies of the fourteenth century, class cooperation was essential. "Indeed, when we study such records of the proceedings of the Estates-General in the fourteenth century as

38. Tocqueville, *Journey to America*, p. 250.

39. Tocqueville, *Democracy*, 1: 182.

40. Tocqueville, *Journey to America*, pp. 251, 164; *Democracy*, 1: 184.

41. Drescher, ed., *Tocqueville and Beaumont on Social Reform*, p. 175.

42. Quoted in Pierre-Marcel, *Essai politique sur Alexis de Tocqueville*, p. 270. (From an unpublished note.)

43. Tocqueville, *The European Revolution and Correspondence with Gobineau*, p. 77.

have survived, we cannot fail to be struck by the place assigned to the Third Estate in these assemblies and the power it exercised."[44] On the other hand, a political system that lacks all class confrontation generates no grand ideas and passions, as under the July Monarchy when a "single class" dominated all power, creating a "singular homogeneity" and producing a "lull in the political world" by removing all principles from politics and leaving mere interests.[45]

> In a political world thus composed and led, what was most lacking, especially at the end, was political life itself. . . . As every matter was settled by the members of one class, in accordance with their interests and point of view, no battlefield could be found on which great parties might wage war. This peculiar homogeneity of position . . . deprived parliamentary debates of all originality, all reality, and so of all true passion.[46]

Because freedom cannot exist without competition among classes, or with extreme hatred and jealousy among classes, a delicate balance is necessary. Like Machiavelli who asserted that "in every republic there are two parties, that of the nobles and that of the people; and all the laws that are favorable to liberty result from the opposition of these parties to each other,"[47] Tocqueville argued that nations will always have rich and poor, that classes will never disappear, and that an aristocratic element will "be found amongst every people and at every period in history";[48] hence freedom requires a delicate balance that entails both competition over opinions about the general good and cooperation concerning the basic political structure of society. Tocqueville's admiration of the clash between great parties, and the classes they represent, meshes nicely with his advocacy of political turmoil, something we will see in the next chapter.

COMMERCIAL INTERESTS AS A DANGER TO POLITICAL FREEDOM

In Tocqueville's notebooks, one can find a famous passage, entered just after he left England, in which he suggested that commerce and freedom go hand in hand. "But I can find no example of a

44. Tocqueville, *The Old Regime*, pp. 85, 220.
45. Drescher, ed., *Tocqueville and Beaumont on Social Reform*, pp. 175–76.
46. Tocqueville, *Recollections*, pp. 11–12.
47. Machiavelli, *Discourses*, I, 4.
48. Tocqueville, *Memoir*, 1: 219–20, 230–31. (From "France before the Revolution.")

manufacturing and, above all, a trading people who have not been free. . . . So there must be a hidden relationship between those two words: *liberty* and *trade*."[49] Back on French soil, and nestled in his library of French and ancient authors, Tocqueville wrote scarcely another word to support this view of trade, and he often stated that the preoccupation with trade and wealth gives birth to certain tendencies that can undermine freedom. Again, he drew upon Montesquieu who also exhibited an ambivalence toward commerce. "We see that in countries where the people move only by the spirit of commerce, they make a traffic of all the humane, all the moral virtues; the most trifling things, those which humanity would demand, are there done, or there given, only for money." In addition, Montesquieu concurred with Cicero that a manufacturing people lacks greatness of purpose. "For this would, indeed, be to suppose that every individual in the state, and the whole state collectively, had their heads constantly filled with grand views, and at the same time with small ones; which is a contradiciton."[50] When private economic interest provides the state's reservoir of energy, as in the first society of Montesquieu's Troglodytes, concern for the public vanishes, and with it, free government.[51] "Commercial powers can continue in a state of mediocrity for a long time," Montesquieu wrote, "but their greatness is of short duration."[52]

In chapter 4 we saw Tocqueville's dislike for the pettiness and mediocrity of the new bourgeois order and in chapter 6 the way in which the new manufacturing society accelerated the process of centralization. Tocqueville now argued that excessive attention to material interests, by glorifying self-interest, enervates all public purpose. "The commercial spirit . . . has stifled all public spirit."[53] Tocqueville considered the political domination by the commercial classes to be "vulgar and corrupt," lacking in all "higher feelings"; it might ultimately render individuals indifferent to all "political affairs," to all literature, to anything but *bourse ou toilette*.[54] The American who asks only "how much money will it bring in," as Tocqueville said in a letter

49. Tocqueville, *Journeys to England and Ireland*, p. 105.

50. Montesquieu, *The Spirit of the Laws*, XX, 2; XX, 4; 1: 316–17, 1: 318.

51. Montesquieu, *The Persian Letters*, XI.

52. Montesquieu, *Considerations on the Causes of the Greatness of the Romans and Their Decline*, p. 47. Contrast to Richter who overstates the admiration that Montesquieu and Tocqueville had for commerce. See Richter, "The Uses of Theory: Tocqueville's Adaptation of Montesquieu," in Richter, ed., *Essays in Theory and History*, pp. 93–102.

53. Tocqueville, *Memoir*, 2: 81.

54. Tocqueville, *Correspondence . . . Senior*, 1: 32; *Oeuvres* (M), vol. 11, *Correspondance . . . Royer-Collard . . . Ampère*, p. 371.

to Chabrol, "trades in everything, not excluding even morality and religion."[55] This passion for wealth grows inexorably, finally extinguishing all political or public concerns. "The commercial fervour" and the "thirst for gain," said Tocqueville, eliminate all human passions but one: "the love of wealth."[56] When commercial passions devour political ones, a food sweetened by the comforts of wealth, one surrenders political liberty to the first master who promises order amidst abundance.

> Who among us doesn't see that human activity has changed its end, that the dominant passion, the *mother* passion, has changed? Instead of political it has become industrial. Who fails to see that our contemporaries are at present hardly concerned about liberties and government, and much more concerned about wealth and well-being?
> A man absorbed by the cares of making money has always been a timid or indifferent citizen.[57]

Whatever its benefits, however much it might bring prosperity, commerce also promotes an ethic devoted to material self-interest; this ethic has the potential of turning citizens into subjects. Free individuals dispute grand political principles and their application; politics must not be reduced to economic questions and a dispute over commercial interests. "I believe," said Tocqueville, "that there are political interests in favor of which it is wise to sacrifice, to a certain degree, industrial interests."[58]

POLITICS AND THE LEGAL SYSTEM

If political questions should not be reduced to commercial interests, neither should they become legal disputes. Ever since Rabelais' satire of lawyers, many French thinkers had warned against the process of transforming political issues into legal ones. "It is ridiculous," said Montesquieu, "to decide the rights of kingdoms, of nations, and of the whole globe by the same maxims on which (to make use of Cicero's expression) we should determine the right of a gutter between individuals."[59] Although Tocqueville admired lawyers for a methodical, conservative nature that helped mitigate the "ex-

55. Tocqueville, *Selected Letters*, p. 39; *Journey to America*, p. 364.
56. Tocqueville, *Journey to America*, p. 257.
57. Drescher, ed., *Tocqueville and Beaumont on Social Reform*, p. 195.
58. Tocqueville, *Oeuvres* (B), vol. 7, *Nouvelle correspondance*, p. 202.
59. Montesquieu, *The Spirit of the Laws*, XXVI, 16, 2: 75.

cesses of democracy," he regretted that lawyers—who, he said, loved "legality" more than "freedom"—hindered popular political action. By their "instinctive love of order and formalities," by their constant reference to precedents, lawyers do restrain the "tyranny of the majority," but at the same time they inhibit the energy and innovations of the majority.[60] When admiring the ever-present political action of the Americans, Tocqueville recorded a conversation in which he was informed that Americans "shake free from legal *technicalities* so as to get quickly to the bottom of things."[61] He also praised the American justice of the peace, because "he is not a slave to those legal superstitions which render judges unfit members of a government."[62] In fact, "the men of law in the United States are the enemies of change, the men of precedents," notably lacking in "general ideas."[63] "They participate in the same instinctive love of order and formalities [as an aristocracy]; and they entertain the same repugnance to the action of the multitude, and the same secret contempt of the government of the people."[64] Once a lawyer himself, Tocqueville quit the career because he found it constricting and stifling. "I am beginning to fear that with time I will become a law machine like most of my fellows, specialized people if ever there were any, as incapable of judging a great movement and of guiding a great undertaking as they are well-fitted . . . to finding analogies. . . ."[65]

Tocqueville believed that a free nation could boast of citizens who debated broad political principles and the most basic political questions, not subjects who yielded to the interests of those in the legal system. Free nations, while leaning heavily on the laws for protection of individual rights, cannot confuse political decisions with legal judgments. Lawyers will endeavor forcefully, if subtly, to declare that political action is no more than legal action, that lawyers alone are political actors while all other citizens are properly spectators. Swallowing grand movements in precedents and technicalities, lawyers will in fact narrow political questions to legal ones, ultimately fastening people to the political principles already embodied in the law. Whenever people make an attempt at popular political action, "they are checked and stopped by the almost invisible influence of their legal counselors. These secretly oppose their aristocratic propensities to the

60. Tocqueville, *Democracy*, 1: 283–85.
61. Tocqueville, *Journey to America*, p. 87.
62. Tocqueville, *Democracy*, 1: 77.
63. Tocqueville, *Journey to America*, p. 321.
64. Tocqueville, *Democracy*, 1: 284.
65. Tocqueville, *Selected Letters*, p. 34.

nation's democratic instincts, their superstitious attachments to what is old to its love of novelty, their narrow views to its immense designs. . . ."[66] The law must not become a reified entity that towers above citizens, an entity understood and interpreted by lawyers while mystifying everyone else. Laws are made, not found; in a free society, laws embody political principles selected by popular and representative political action. Lawyers, however, seek to replace democratic decision making and, in the end, attempt to merge their interests with the interests of the dominant power of a political order, snuffing out debate over political principles and hiding their interests under the guise of the supposed neutrality of law. "No one is ignorant of the immense influence that legalists of the Middle Ages, both the secular legalists and those of the Church, ultimately obtained on the destiny of their time." Armed with legal arguments about the divine right of kings and the power of sovereigns, lawyers promoted their own interests while they established the groundwork for the practice of absolute monarchy. "To carry this grand enterprise to its end, kings furnish material force, legalists the right."[67]

But how can a free nation make good use of judicial proceedings and still avoid both yielding to the interests of lawyers and transforming important political questions into legal bickering? Tocqueville thought this could be done by focusing a nation's gaze on goals it would like to achieve in the future.

The Importance of Some Vision of the Future

Burke and Marx had at least one conviction in common; liberalism was usually a philosophy that, by fastening people to the present consumption of goods and services, sought to sever individuals from both a familiarity with the past and a vision of the future. Tocqueville agreed heartily, arguing that free nations consciously address the future and create for themselves a purpose that embraces a grand political goal. In a letter to a friend, Tocqueville related his encounter with an old man who was just twenty-seven when the French Revolution began; seven decades later the man recalled those times.

> "Ah! Monsieur," he answered me, "I think I am dreaming when I recall the condition of minds in my youth, the vivacity, the sincerity of opinions, the respect for oneself and for public opinion, the disinterested-

66. Tocqueville, *Democracy*, 1: 289.
67. Tocqueville, *Oeuvres* (B), vol. 9, *Études économiques, politiques*, p. 70.

ness in political passion. Ah! Monsieur," he added, . . . "then people had a cause; now they have only interests. There were ties between men then; there are none any more. It is very sad, Monsieur, to outlive one's country!"[68]

Tocqueville regretted that France had shed itself of any cause, shouldering instead mere interests, and he angrily criticized the "tendency to treat with indifference all the ideas that can stir society, whether they are right or wrong, noble or base."[69] Arguing in the Chamber of Deputies that France was becoming indifferent to those very ideas— freedom and equality—that once constituted her greatness, Tocqueville declared that self-interest "harms not ourselves only but our principles and our cause; it harms that fatherland of the mind which I, for my part, as a Frenchman, value more than the physical and material fatherland which we see before our eyes."[70] By contrast, the American "confidently takes charge of the future" and has learned to "fashion the universe to please himself."[71] Tocqueville marveled that, while Europe groaned with absolute monarchies seventeenth-century colonists constructed a free polity whose conception had sprung from "the natural originality of men's imaginations"[72]—that is, a political order that in the past was a mere vision of the future, a grand purpose toward which citizens successfully marched.

Ideas, purposes, or principles offer a people a definition of itself and bestow upon this people a sense of pride in the historical task it has selected. As we shall see more fully in the next two chapters, without this sense of pride in the future—a pride derived from the excellence of the goal that is chosen—people perceive themselves as mere consumers of pleasure and remain content to pursue their self-interest. One of the first needs of a people is to be "proud of itself,"[73] proud of its importance and its purpose. For a nation to abandon its ideas and purposes is the first sign of decadence, and the first characteristic of decadence is the widespread assumption that individuals dwell on earth only to enjoy themselves. Thus, Tocqueville throughout his entire life sought to remind France of her ideas and principles and to revivify them. "Who spread those ideas of freedom and equality which

68. Tocqueville, *Selected Letters,* p. 371.

69. Ibid., p. 81.

70. Tocqueville, "Speech in January 1848," in *Democracy in America,* ed. Mayer, p. 752.

71. Tocqueville, *Journey to America,* p. 186.

72. Tocqueville, *Democracy,* 1: 44.

73. Tocqueville, *Oeuvres* (M), vol. 5, pt. 2, *Voyages en Angleterre, Irlande, Suisse et Algérie,* p. 184.

shatter and destroy servitude throughout the entire world? . . . We did, we ourselves." Will France now be the only European nation to condone slavery? If so, "let her surrender for good all claims to the great role that she had the arrogance to claim, but not the courage to carry out."[74] This intense yearning to breathe life into old ideas and principles explains Tocqueville's quarrel with Mill to which we referred in chapter 3.

> . . . one cannot let this nation take up easily the habit of sacrificing what it believes to be its grandeur to its repose, great matters to petty ones; it is not healthy to allow such a nation to believe that its place in the world is smaller, that it is fallen from the level on which its ancestors had put it, but that it must console itself by making railroads. . . .[75]

Once a nation discards an inspiring purpose, it forfeits its conception of itself as an influence on the world and becomes content with being a consumer of "material enjoyments and small pleasures," consoling itself with prosperity.

POLITICAL PASSION

In our analysis, we have wound our way back to the word *passion*. Tocqueville, who condemned passions for pleasures and wealth, sought to harness other passions to transport people to a higher purpose. Nonetheless, he worried that people would lose all capacity to become impassioned for noble purposes, that human energy would be swallowed in calculation.[76] In his own time, "one hardly ever finds a true passion except for a man's self."[77] To Royer-Collard he wrote, "Has there never been a political world in which, I do not say virtue, but great passions have reigned and which was led by considerations other than miserable day-to-day interests?"[78] To Ampère Tocqueville described his wish to witness grand passions, despite the fact that France no longer knew how to "want, or love, or hate." Indeed, lack of passion had made France "incapable of all things, of great evil as well as great good."[79] Napoleon's entire secret, suggested Tocque-

74. Drescher, ed., *Tocqueville and Beaumont on Social Reform*, pp. 148–49.
75. Tocqueville, *Selected Letters*, pp. 151–52.
76. Gargan, *Alexis de Tocqueville*, p. 6.
77. Tocqueville, *Recollections*, p. 28.
78. Tocqueville, *Selected Letters*, p. 118; see also *Oeuvres* (M), vol. 15, pt. 1, *Correspondance . . . Corcelle*, pp. 139, 141.
79. Tocqueville, *Selected Letters*, p. 153.

ville, was the knowledge that great passion is necessary for the accomplishment of a great political purpose; Napoleon managed "to suppress every great passion of the human heart for the sake of one, that one which makes people die in battle."[80] Political passion, notwithstanding all its dangers, is one way in which nations manage to transcend self-interest.

A passionate commitment to a vision of the future is an essential, if not sufficient, ingredient to all successful political action. The working class insurgents of 1848 were dangerous, Tocqueville believed, precisely because "they sincerely believed that society was founded on injustice."[81] Like a good Romantic, Tocqueville argued that passion leads to action, reason to political paralysis.[82] Acting comes from transforming probabilities into certainties, instinctively recognizing that it is better to act vigorously, even if sometimes mistakenly, than to paralyze oneself forever by equivocation.[83] Only passion, only purposeful and grand passion, triumphs over uncertainty and pushes people toward great political effort. To act boldly, individuals require "ephemeral convictions" that extinguish all doubt, convictions that blind one to alternatives and bind one to a course of action.[84] "A man on the point of taking a side is like a mathematician who is making a long addition. One counts numbers, the other reasons. The irresolute man recommences the addition without cease; the determined man abides entirely by the first total sum."[85] The most energetic action will arise from seasoning noble passions with a touch of self-interest, and, for this reason, Tocqueville criticized the leaders of 1848 for not recalling that the men of 1789 had offered the peasantry very tangible benefits for joining the revolution.[86] When interest is wedded to a grand purpose, the human potential for extraordinary action emerges. "Add to passions born of self-interest the aim to change the face of the world and to regenerate the human race; only then will you see what men are really capable of."[87]

Only the people and aristocracies, only democracies and monarchies, can act with grandeur; the middle class distinguishes itself with

80. Tocqueville, *The European Revolution and Correspondence with Gobineau*, p. 150.

81. Tocqueville, *Selected Letters*, p. 216.

82. Tocqueville, *Oeuvres* (M), vol. 11, *Correspondance . . . Royer-Collard . . . Ampère*, p. 109.

83. Tocqueville, *Oeuvres* (B), vol. 7, *Nouvelle correspondance*, p. 83.

84. Tocqueville, *Recollections*, p. 106.

85. Tocqueville, *Oeuvres* (B), vol. 8, *Mélanges, fragments*, p. 485.

86. Tocqueville, *Recollections*, p. 122; *The European Revolution and Correspondence with Gobineau*, p. 135.

87. Tocqueville, *The European Revolution and Correspondence with Gobineau*, p. 172.

"weakness and egoism."[88] Tocqueville claimed that the people by themselves, lacking the requisite enlightenment, cannot make a revolution, and they must unite themselves with members of an enlightened class.[89] Speaking of a fourteenth-century attempt by the poor of Florence to found a new government, Tocqueville said, "The poor who made the revolution of 1378 were too isolated from the upper classes, too bereft of aristocracy to be able to conserve the government. The democratic element can never found anything."[90] But only the people can furnish the passionate boldness that infuses energy and durability into a political movement, and Tocqueville ridiculed the bourgeoisie that, in the French Revolution, summoned the peasants to its aid, only to be overwhelmed by the force it had unleashed. "It was only after [the bourgeois] had put arms in [the peasants'] hands that he realized he had kindled passions such as he had never dreamed of, passions which he could neither restrain nor guide, and of which, after being their promoter, he was to be the victim."[91] His respect for the military might of the people, a respect derived of course from Napoleon's marches the length of Europe, led him to declare that England might subdue the *governments* of China or India, but once aroused, "a people, however miserable and corrupt, is invincible on its own territory, if it be supported and impelled by common and violent passions."[92]

If we reflect on what has been argued in the last three chapters, we see Tocqueville contending that a nation can be free only if it manages to live in the present, in the past, and in the future. People must democratically control their present political world, but in doing so they depend upon tools inherited from a rich culture and from mores and customs created and bequeathed by past generations. In addition, only a vision of the future gives people a definition of themselves, enables them to sustain their political and moral principles, and prevents them from perceiving themselves as mere consumers. In an unfree state, however, people lose that acute awareness of past and future, and they content themselves with the petty pleasures and worries of the present. Thus, Tocqueville lamented, France was fastened to the present without memories of the past or hope for the future. His generation "interests [itself] in nothing that has preceded

88. Tocqueville, *Oeuvres* (M), vol. 6, pt. 1, *Correspondance anglaise*, p. 335.
89. Tocqueville, *Oeuvres* (M), vol. 8, pt. 3, *Correspondance . . . Beaumont*, p. 544.
90. Tocqueville, *Oeuvres* (B), vol. 8, *Mélanges, fragments*, p. 442.
91. Tocqueville, *The Old Regime*, p. 136.
92. Tocqueville, *Correspondence . . . Senior*, 2: 156.

and in little of what is to follow."[93] Again, this threat to freedom is peculiar to times of equality, for in aristocracies, "a man almost always knows his forefathers and respects them; he thinks he already sees his remote descendants and he loves them. He willingly imposes duties on himself towards the former and the latter, and he will frequently sacrifice his personal gratifications to those who went before and to those who will come after him." By contrast, in democracies,

> Those who went before are soon forgotten; of those who will come after, no one has any idea: the interest of man is confined to those in close propinquity to himself. . . . Thus not only does democracy make every man forget his ancestors, but it hides his descendants and separates his contemporaries from him; it throws him back forever upon himself alone and threatens in the end to confine him entirely within the solitude of his own heart.[94]

Free men and women must learn to cherish and, if necessary, to alter the heritage of the past but also to imbibe "that love of the future with which religion and the state of society no longer inspire them."[95] Out of this love of the future will circulate a common purpose, encouraging finally a deemphasis of the self-interest that would otherwise threaten freedom.

93. Tocqueville, *Oeuvres* (M), vol. 8, pt. 3, *Correspondance . . . Beaumont*, pp. 52, 350–51.
94. Tocqueville, *Democracy*, 2: 104–5, 105–6.
95. Ibid., p. 160.

11 The Relation of Freedom to Glory, Nationalism, and Turmoil

When Tocqueville suggested that individuals in a free nation must define themselves by a grand purpose, he revealed a modest contempt for what he called *mere* happiness, a contempt predictably found in many French thinkers who preceded him and a contempt that fostered his dislike for English utilitarianism, that is, a science of making people happy. Fénelon stated that "glory is due to those only who dare to associate with pain, and have trampled pleasure under their feet"; Diderot declared that, without virtue, people would deteriorate into a "vile herd of happy beings."[1] Similarly, happiness, in Tocqueville's writings, always seems to be the possession of servants, of people whose aspirations in life are constricted until attainable. For example, Tocqueville said he envied his servant, because his servant had the capacity to attain everything he wished for. "I have all my life been striving at things, not one of which I shall completely obtain. In becoming a thoroughly good servant, he has done all that he wishes to do."[2] In another example, the medieval serf whose limited desires corresponded to his limited powers, and whose subsistence was assured, "enjoyed a kind of vegetative happiness" with a certain "charm" difficult for the "very civilized man" to comprehend.[3] Tocqueville openly admitted, however, that some

---

1. Fénelon, *The Adventures of Telemachus*, p. 6; Diderot quoted in Lester G. Crocker, *The Embattled Philosopher* (East Lansing, Mich., 1954), p. 132.
2. Tocqueville, *Correspondence . . . Senior*, 1: 139–40.
3. Drescher, ed., *Tocqueville and Beaumont on Social Reform*, p. 6.

things were of more value than happiness. In a letter to a very unhappy friend, he wrote:

> Like you, like all men, I feel within me an ardent passion that carries me away toward limitless happiness, and makes me consider the absence of that happiness to be the greatest misfortune. . . . But that, you can be sure, is a foolish passion that must be fought. The feeling is not manly and cannot produce anything that is. Life is neither a pleasure nor a sorrow; it is a serious affair with which we are charged, and toward which our duty is to acquit ourselves as well as possible.[4]

Happiness is valuable, but only if one can obtain it without "delivering too strong a blow to human morality."[5]

The Importance of Virtue, Glory, and Duty

Tocqueville's attitude toward happiness typified his general conviction that one should measure the value of a political order, at least in part, by the sacrifices and the efforts toward excellence made by its citizens. *Virtue, dignity, duty, grandeur,* and *glory* were words that sprinkled Tocqueville's political vocabulary, and—to take just one— virtue entailed by definition some sacrifice of one's interests and perhaps happiness. "The principle of the republics of antiquity was to sacrifice private interests to the general good. In that sense one could say that they were *virtuous.*"[6] Those who argue that Tocqueville advocated the orchestration of individual self-interest as the foundation of a free society, ignore his enthusiastic presentation in 1847 of the French Academy's awards for "virtue," awards given in order to furnish examples of self-sacrifice for the French people to emulate.[7] Only virtue did Tocqueville cherish as much as freedom, but like Montesquieu, he assumed the two were interconnected. "Freedom is, in truth, a *sacred* thing. There is only one thing else that better deserves the name: that is virtue. But what is virtue if not the *free* choice of what is good?"[8] Virtue is a moral imperative that constitutes, again in an Aristotelian sense, the end proper to human beings. It is frankly

4. Tocqueville, *Selected Letters*, p. 63.
5. Quoted in Gargan, *Alexis de Tocqueville*, p. 7. (From an unpublished letter.)
6. Tocqueville, *Journey to America*, pp. 217–18.
7. Tocqueville, *Oeuvres* (B), vol. 9, *Études économiques, politiques*, pp. 34–50, passim.
8. Tocqueville, *Journeys to England and Ireland*, p. 106. In his wish to reconcile virtue with republican freedom, Tocqueville had not entirely passed beyond what Pocock calls "the Machiavellian moment." See J.G.A. Pocock, *The Machiavellian Moment* (Princeton, 1975).

false and undignified, Tocqueville thought, for human beings to perceive themselves as selfish consumers of goods and pleasures. Virtue, honor, and nobility were all important to Tocqueville, and he believed that they all emerged in moments of glory and grand political action. In this, his political lexicon resembled less the commercial, calculating utilitarianism of Bentham, and more the praise of virtue and glory found in the ancient Roman republic and in the writings of eighteenth-century Frenchmen who longed to be republicans of ancient Rome.

The image of Tocqueville as a bookish man, floundering in the political world while content only in reading dusty books in libraries and archives, leaves out the fact that, in his friend Royer-Collard's words, "literary glory" could never satisfy Tocqueville's hunger for "political glory."[9] Tocqueville, in fact, exhibited an urge for excitement, passions, and powerful emotions. "When I return to regular habits, the monotony is fatal to me; I am possessed by an internal restlessness. I must have bodily or mental excitement, even at the risk of my life. The desire for strong emotions becomes irresistible. . . ."[10] Tocqueville involved himself in the political world: he served in the Chamber of Deputies for nine years, and he edited *Le Commerce* with an avowed purpose of restoring grandeur to France. Yearning for grand political events, he helped direct the fighting in the streets in 1848 (after which his father said, "Alexis does not know what fear is"), and as Foreign Minister, he despaired that France enjoyed the memory of greatness without recognizing its limited power to reattain it.[11] To Beaumont he confided, "You know what a taste I have for great events and how tired I am of our little democratic and bourgeois pot of soup." In the midst of the 1848 Revolution, he said, "Perhaps a moment will come in which the action we will undertake can be glorious." To Kergorlay he confessed a wish for noble action. "Oh! How I wish that Providence would present me with an opportunity to use, in order to accomplish good and grand things, whatever dangers Providence might attach to them, this internal flame I feel within me that does not know where to find what feeds it."[12]

9. Tocqueville, *Oeuvres* (M), vol. 11, *Correspondance . . . Royer-Collard . . . Ampère*, p. 110.

10. Tocqueville, *Memoir*, 1: 373.

11. Tocqueville, *Oeuvres* (M), vol. 8, pt. 1, *Correspondance . . . Beaumont*, p. 538; ibid., pt. 2, p. 13; *Recollections*, pp. 169–206, passim; *Correspondence . . . Senior*, 1: 63; *Oeuvres* (M), vol. 8, pt. 2, *Correspondance . . . Beaumont*, p. 201.

12. Tocqueville, *Selected Letters*, pp. 143, 210, 105. Richter rightly points out Tocqueville's obvious dislike of Bonapartism but fails to account for his admiration for Napoleon himself and even for Napoleon's foreign conquests. Melvin Richter, "Toward a Concept of Political Illegitimacy: Bonapartist Dictatorship and Democratic Legitimacy." *Political Theory* 10 (May 1982): 185–214.

This wish for glory explains Tocqueville's esteem for nation-states that encourage individuals of ambition to climb to acclaim and reputation. Although he once acknowledged that "vast empires" are harmful to freedom, he suggested that these empires foster "love of glory" and promote "the increase of knowledge and the advance of civilization" more than do small nations.[13] Most often, he saw no conflict between nations seeking glory and nations seeking freedom. Indeed, Tocqueville embraced freedom because it gave birth to grandeur and nobility of purpose, because it generated "manly virtues and great actions." "I have loved liberty instinctively," he wrote, "and the more I reflect, the more convinced am I that neither political nor moral greatness can long subsist without it."[14]

TOCQUEVILLE'S NATIONALISM

But greatness meant national greatness for Tocqueville, and he was preeminently a nationalist, contending that although patriotism would seem to be a "false and narrow passion" which one should supplant by a general concern for humankind, in fact patriotism is the best we can do. "I am convinced that the interests of the human race are better served by giving every man a particular fatherland than by trying to inflame his passions for the whole of humanity."[15] Even though despondent under the suffocation of the Second Empire, he still admitted that national integrity outweighed his beloved freedom, that if some external force truly threatened France, "nationality must be considered even before liberty."[16] Tocqueville's pride in and love of France are abundantly evident. For example, he said of 1789, "I venture to say that there is but one people on this earth which could have staged such a spectacle. . . . There are enterprises which only the French nation can conceive; there are magnanimous resolutions which this nation alone dares to take."[17] Tocqueville concurred with Montesquieu who said that "virtue in a republic is a most simple thing; it is love of the republic."[18]

Notwithstanding his claim in *Democracy* that "nothing is more opposed to the well-being and the freedom of men than vast empires,"[19]

13. Tocqueville, *Democracy*, 1: 167.
14. Tocqueville, *Memoir*, 2: 305, 1: 380.
15. Tocqueville, *The European Revolution and Correspondence with Gobineau*, p. 170.
16. Tocqueville, *Oeuvres* (B), vol. 7, *Nouvelle correspondance*, p. 320.
17. Tocqueville, *The European Revolution and Correspondence with Gobineau*, p. 87.
18. Montesquieu, *The Spirit of the Laws*, V, 2, 1: 40.
19. Tocqueville, *Democracy*, 1: 167.

Tocqueville supported European colonization throughout the world. Although he consistently and ardently demanded that both England and France treat their apologetics about "civilization" seriously, he could not hide his delight at the touch of national glory in these conquests. "Nothing under the sun is so wonderful as the conquest and still more the government of India by the English."[20] In another letter, after rebuking the British for an excessively harsh suppression of a rebellion in India, he added, "Your title to govern these savages is that you are better than they are. You ought to punish them, not to imitate them."[21] What is even more upsetting to modern sensibilities, he declared that France was doing "grand things" in Algeria; he became a staunch advocate for French domination there (and even for brutal methods of doing so—burning crops and villages, seizing women and children[22]) and exclaimed that colonizing and civilizing Algeria would constitute a "great monument to the glory of our homeland."[23] "The European population has come; the civilized and Christian society has been founded." In 1840, critical of what he regarded as Guizot's dishonorable appeasement, Tocqueville wrote, "I do not believe that France can seriously think of leaving Algeria. Such a withdrawal would be in the eyes of the world the certain announcement of her decadence. . . ."[24]

Despite this heartfelt push for empire, Tocqueville consistently maintained that nations must act honorably in foreign relations. He exhibited an aristocratic paternalism toward Algeria, sincerely believing that France could treat the Algerian population fairly by establishing schools, allowing freedom of religion, intermixing the French and Algerian people, educating some Algerians thoroughly, and seizing

20. Tocqueville, *Memoir*, 2: 387. Tocqueville contradicted this opinion in his unfinished work *L'Inde*, where he asserted that England was plundering and oppressing India, rendering the country more sterile than it was before England's arrival. Despite all that England had accomplished in India (an end to wars, an end to cruel customs, the establishment of a sense of law and justice, etc.) to which Tocqueville gave credit, "nevertheless the primary effects of their domination have been to augment destitution, unrest, the number of crimes." (*L'Inde*, in *Oeuvres* (M), vol. 3, *Écrits et discours politiques*, pp. 457, 478–80, 494–95, 505.) One should remember that *L'Inde* was an unfinished work, never published by Tocqueville, and written in the early 1840s when he was most hostile toward the British.

21. Tocqueville, *Memoir*, 2: 389.

22. Tocqueville, *L'Algérie*, in *Oeuvres* (M), vol. 3, *Écrits et discours politiques*, pp. 226–30.

23. Tocqueville, *Memoir*, 2: 63; *L'Algérie*, in *Oeuvres* (M), vol. 3, *Écrits et discours politiques*, p. 151.

24. Tocqueville, *L'Algérie*, in *Oeuvres* (M), vol. 3, *Écrits et discours politiques*, pp. 310, 213–14. For an excellent discussion of Tocqueville's attitude toward colonialism, see Jardin, *Alexis de Tocqueville*, ch. 18; also Drescher, *Dilemmas of Democracy*, pp. 191–95.

lands only rarely and, in those cases, paying full indemnities.[25] He wisely warned that, if France ignored these measures, a tragedy resembling the decimation of North American Indians would take place.

> . . . if we surrounded their populations, not in order to elevate them in our arms toward well-being and enlightenment, but in order to extinguish them and smother them, the question of life or death would pose itself between the two races. Algeria would become, sooner or later, you may believe it, a closed field, a walled arena, in which the two peoples would have to fight without mercy, and in which one of the two would have to die. May God divert us, Gentlemen, from such a destiny![26]

Later, when Tocqueville felt that France had violated its obligations to the Algerian people, he energetically censured French policy in Algeria without ever suggesting, of course, that France withdraw. "We have rendered the Islamic society much more miserable, more disordered, more ignorant, and more barbaric than it was before we knew it." In a public dispute with the Minister of War in 1847, he castigated France for reducing the population of Algiers to a "condition of misery impossible to describe."

Tocqueville's approach to foreign policy always had a moral hue, because just as individuals distinguish themselves by a code of honor, so do nations. Accordingly, there are certain things that decent and honorable nations simply do not do. For example, as Foreign Minister in 1849, Tocqueville threatened the Pope, unless the Pope promised both to treat his prisoners decently and to grant popular reforms.[27] Similarly, he stopped Baden from executing political prisoners, and he berated Russia for not allowing political prisoners to emigrate.[28] These instances illustrate his conviction that nations must maintain a principled stance, adhering to their ideals even in matters of foreign policy; otherwise, their principles will fade domestically. If England did not condemn Louis Napoleon's coup, Tocqueville said in his famous letter smuggled at significant personal risk to the London *Times*,

25. Tocqueville, *L'Algérie*, in *Oeuvres* (M), vol. 3, *Écrits et discours politiques*, pp. 151, 320–25, 419–25.

26. Ibid., p. 329; see also pp. 323, 420–23, and passim for the quotations that follow in the text.

27. Tocqueville, *Correspondence . . . Senior*, 1: 234–39. To Tocqueville's great regret, his predecessor as Foreign Minister had sent French troops into Rome to extinguish a popular revolt.

28. Tocqueville, *Recollections*, pp. 300–301; *Oeuvres* (M), vol. 8, pt. 2, *Correspondance . . . Beaumont*, pp. 182–227, passim; *Recollections*, pp. 317–27.

"I shall mourn for you and for ourselves, and for the sacred cause of legal liberty. . . ."[29]

Reputation, glory, virtue, honor, the grandeur of one's nation—again a political vocabulary reminding one of aristocratic France. But Tocqueville embraced all these attributes because they continually command the individual citizen's attention, compelling the realization that certain public concerns transcend private interests, and because they revivify a public or national purpose. These attributes also bind themselves snugly to Tocqueville's notion that freedom lies in control of one's political world. Yet because Tocqueville sought virtue, glory, and greatness, he had no deep yearning for a continually tranquil state; the attributes he sought emerged from incessant political action and quite often from turmoil.

THE OCCASIONAL USEFULNESS OF WAR AND POLITICAL TURMOIL

Once more we discover how Tocqueville differed from the liberals of his era who, beginning with Condorcet, hoped that the commercial spirit would pervade the world, enabling trade to supplant conquest, peace to replace war. Although Tocqueville never urged war for its own sake, although he agreed that the commercial spirit weakened the military spirit,[30] he cautiously but persistently pointed to the dangers of tranquillity. Certainly he disliked war: war centralizes governments, war is especially harmful to republics because even an ordinary man (e.g., Jackson) by winning an ordinary battle (e.g., New Orleans) gains general admiration and power, war brings harmful political habits of unreflecting obedience, and of course war is murderously destructive (at one point Tocqueville defined man as "the animal . . . best endowed with the power of destroying his fellow-creatures").[31] Tranquillity, however, is sometimes a greater political danger than war.

Nowhere is Tocqueville's aristocratic heritage more apparent. As calamitous as he believed war to be, he thought that from war could spring noble actions and sacrifices that show a wondrous side to the human character. To a friend, Tocqueville wrote of the Crimean war, "What gigantic efforts! What energy, what manly and heroic virtues come spontaneously from the breast of these societies that seemed to

29. Tocqueville, *Selected Letters*, pp. 276–77.
30. Tocqueville, *Oeuvres* (M), vol. 6, pt. 1, *Correspondance anglaise*, p. 322.
31. Tocqueville, *Democracy*, 2: 284, 1: 299; *Journey to America*, pp. 158, 183; *Oeuvres* (B), vol. 9, *Études économiques, politiques*, p. 563; *Memoir*, 2: 419.

sleep in well-being. . . ."[32] Again, "except for the soldier who has rediscovered grandeur . . . what is not visibly declining and becoming enervated around us?"[33] And finally, in *Democracy,* he claimed:

> I do not wish to speak ill of war: war almost always enlarges the mind of a people and raises their character. In some cases it is the only check to the excessive growth of certain propensities that naturally spring out of the equality of conditions, and it must be considered as a necessary corrective to certain inveterate diseases to which democratic communities are liable.[34]

Tocqueville did not, of course, seek war for the advantages it might bring, but he did, like so many of his philosophical predecessors, seek a certain tension or political agitation. Montesquieu claimed that liberty arose from the "fires of discord and sedition," and he once defined a "free government" as "a government constantly subject to agitation."[35] Montesquieu had almost certainly borrowed from Machiavelli, who had contended that the very class struggles of the Roman Republic had assured its liberty.

> I maintain that those who blame the quarrels of the Senate and the people of Rome condemn that which was the very origin of liberty, and that they were probably more impressed by the cries and noise than by the good effect which they produced. . . . For good examples are the result of good education, and good education is due to good laws; and good laws in their turn spring from those very agitations which have been so inconsiderately condemned by many.[36]

Montesquieu's argument was clearly similar. "We hear in the authors only of the dissensions that ruined Rome, without seeing that these dissensions were necessary to it. . . . And, as a general rule, whenever we see everyone tranquil in a state that calls itself a republic, we can be sure that liberty does not exist there."[37] Similarly, Helvétius called for a "mild fermentation that renders the [body politic] sound and robust, and calls forth every virtue and every talent"; Mably wanted

32. Tocqueville, *Oeuvres* (M), vol. 6, pt. 1, *Correspondance anglaise,* p. 148.

33. Tocqueville, *Oeuvres* (B), vol. 7, *Nouvelle correspondance,* p. 347.

34. Tocqueville, *Democracy,* 2: 283.

35. Montesquieu, *The Persian Letters,* CXXXVI; Montesquieu, *Considerations on the Causes of the Greatness of the Romans and Their Decline,* p. 88.

36. Niccolò Machiavelli, *The Prince* and *The Discourses,* trans. Luigi Ricci and E.R.P. Vincent (*The Prince*), and Christian E. Detmold (*The Discourses*) (New York, 1950), from *The Discourses,* I, 4.

37. Montesquieu, *Considerations on the Causes of the Greatness of the Romans and Their Decline,* pp. 93–94.

"continual revolutions" in a democracy; and Rousseau announced that "tranquillity and freedom appear to me incompatible."[38] Suggesting that contentment can be dangerous, Pascal praised what Mesnard has labeled a "healthy disquiet" that keeps a soul longing for "moral truth."[39]

Tocqueville applied this notion of a "healthy disquiet" to the political world, asserting that the "turmoil of freedom" denoted a healthy political system, whereas repose often signaled danger. "Men who are possessed by the passion for physical gratification generally find out that the turmoil of freedom disturbs their welfare before they discover how freedom itself serves to promote it . . . they are always ready to fling away their freedom at the first disturbance. I readily admit that public tranquillity is a great good, but at the same time I cannot forget that all nations have been enslaved by being kept in good order." Indeed, agitation may "strengthen the state," for "quarrelling and passionate discussion belong to the very essence of a free country."[40] Freedom, he argued, "is generally established with difficulty in the midst of storms; it is perfected by civil discord. . . ."[41] Certainly freedom must never permit a sleepy boredom; in an 1848 letter he wrote, "I was so wearied by the monotony of the previous period that I have no right to complain of the stormy variety of this."[42] He admiringly quoted an Afghan leader who declared, "We resign ourselves to living in discord, apprehension and blood, but we would never resign ourselves to living under a master."[43]

The democracy of the United States, Tocqueville stated, displayed a "constant agitation" and a "love [of] change for its own sake." In fact, the "perpetual change" works to "keep the minds of the people in a perpetual feverish agitation, which admirably invigorates their exertions and keeps them, so to speak, above the ordinary level of humanity. The whole life of an American is passed like a game of chance, a revolutionary crisis, or a battle."[44] Turmoil, if not extended to the most fundamental principles of society and if not characterized by armed revolt,[45] actually plays a healthy role in establishing and maintaining freedom as well as in nourishing the attributes of virtue

38. Helvétius, *De L'Esprit*, p. 319; Mably quoted in Maxime Leroy, *Histoire des idées sociales en France*, vol. 1, *De Montesquieu à Robespierre* (Paris, 1946), p. 100; Rousseau, *Considérations sur le gouvernement de Pologne*, p. 420.

39. Mesnard, *Pascal: His Life and Works*, p. 101.

40. Tocqueville, *Democracy*, 2: 149–50, 126; *Memoir*, 1: 338.

41. Tocqueville, *Democracy*, 1: 256.

42. Tocqueville, *Memoir*, 2: 94.

43. Tocqueville, *L'Inde*, in *Oeuvres* (M), vol. 3, *Écrits et discours politiques*, p. 499.

44. Tocqueville, *Democracy*, 2: 69, 1: 443.

45. Tocqueville, *Oeuvres* (M), vol. 6, pt. 1, *Correspondance anglaise*, p. 326.

and self-sacrifice so cherished by Tocqueville. One might readily accept an argument that turmoil always accompanies a free nation—because freedom militates against a passive and docile citizenry—but how can turmoil be healthy? How can turmoil enhance freedom?

TOCQUEVILLE'S REASONING ABOUT POLITICAL TURMOIL

When one examines the reasoning for Tocqueville's approval of occasional political turmoil one can see, perhaps on this more than any other issue, that Tocqueville's idea of freedom is in large part a response to the concerns of his generation. Political turmoil helps alleviate the problems with which we are so familiar: (1) isolation, (2) powerlessness, (3) the disappearance of great individuals, (4) politics reduced to mere quarrels about self-interest, (5) the lack of public participation, (6) the decline of great intellectual accomplishment, (7) the tendency of European society, in Baudelaire's words, to fall asleep on a heap of riches, and so on.

First of all, Tocqueville thought that turmoil creates a public tension that mitigates the tendency to selfishness, the tendency to perceive oneself as a consumer of pleasures, and the tendency to withdraw into a private world. If, as Valéry said, comfort isolates, then adversity unites. When Machiavelli argued that the surrounding walls of a republic are harmful,[46] he was suggesting that the absence of walls generates a tension that forces citizens to rely on each other, to see themselves as interdependent. Not walls, but only the strength born of popular energy can defend a republic adequately. Similarly, Flaubert said of 1848, "anxiety and curiosity brought everybody out in the streets."[47] With public turmoil, citizens rush from their private worlds in an attempt to overcome their anxiety by uniting with others and ending their powerlessness, just as, if the lights go out in a hotel, each leaves the darkness of a private room in order to find companionship. "Revolutionary times," Tocqueville said, "have the advantage that they do not permit indifference and egoism in politics."[48] During the 1848 Revolution, each hastened from his private circle to engage in public affairs.

> . . . in the country all the landowners, whatever their origin, antecedents, education, or means, had come together and seemed to form a single unit: all the old political hatreds and rivalries of caste and wealth had vanished. Neither jealousy nor pride separated the peasant from

46. Machiavelli, *Discourses*, II, 24.
47. Flaubert, *Sentimental Education*, p. 293.
48. Tocqueville, *Oeuvres* (M), vol. 8, pt. 2, *Correspondance . . . Beaumont*, p. 274.

the rich man any longer, or the bourgeois from the gentleman; instead there was mutual confidence, respect, and goodwill . . . fear had acted upon them as a physical pressure might on very hard substances, forcing them to hold together while the compression continued, but leaving them to fall apart when it was relaxed.[49]

But even in an 1842 speech, Tocqueville rebuked the Chamber of Deputies for fearing "disorder" more than the ubiquitous, "frightening" tendency of each to "retire into himself and isolate himself."[50]

Second, the debates issuing from public turmoil in a free state force citizens to return to and reaffirm the fundamental principles of freedom and morality. Montesquieu, for example, maintained that the tension resulting from external threats united the Romans and perpetuated their habits of freedom. "Carthage and Rome were alarmed and strengthened by each other. Strange, that the greater security those states enjoyed the more, like stagnated waters, they were subject to corruption!"[51] Freedom and morality need tension to keep them alive. Tocqueville argued that, in the United States, equality was so fundamental to the society that time could bring inequality "only by long and laborious efforts" that changed habits, mores, laws, and basic beliefs. But, said Tocqueville, the United States could lose freedom more easily. "Political liberty is more easily lost; to neglect to hold it fast is to allow it to escape . . . Men cannot enjoy political liberty unpurchased by some sacrifices, and they never obtain it without great exertions."[52] As one labors tirelessly at the bellows to keep a fire going, so a nation must ceaselessly reaffirm the principles and habits of freedom; otherwise, it will begin to expire. Tocqueville suggested that turmoil, by pushing people into a concern for public affairs, encourages citizens to revivify the principles and habits of freedom.

Third, times of discord and tension bring forward individuals of lofty ambition, individuals who are seeking fame and are inspired by grand ideals. "During civil wars great men are often produced," Montesquieu argued, and Tocqueville agreed.[53] In times of turmoil, the scope of ambition, broadened from petty interests to grand ideals, attracts individuals of great ability. Tocqueville wrote in *Democracy*, "All revolutions enlarge the ambition of men. This is more peculiarly true of those revolutions which overthrow an aristocracy. . . . In this first burst of triumph nothing seems impossible to anyone." In a

49. Tocqueville, *Recollections*, p. 109.
50. Tocqueville, *Oeuvres* (B), vol. 9, *Études économiques, politiques*, pp. 375–76.
51. Montesquieu, *The Spirit of the Laws*, VIII, 5, 1: 113.
52. Tocqueville, *Democracy*, 2: 101–2.
53. Montesquieu, *Considerations on the Causes of the Greatness of the Romans and Their Decline*, p. 107; Tocqueville, *Democracy*, 2: 293.

startling passage, he suggested that leaders actually expose their nations to moments of danger in order to raise ambition and to elevate the citizens' perceptions of themselves. "I think, then, that the leaders of modern society would be wrong to seek to lull the community by a state of too uniform and too peaceful happiness, and that it is well to expose it from time to time to matters of difficulty and danger in order to raise ambition and give it a field of action." Times of danger and turmoil can create confidence and pride, much needed attributes in a world where a man "has so contemptible an opinion of himself that he thinks he is born only to indulge in vulgar pleasures."[54]

Fourth, agitation militates against an instinctive awe of political power, an awe that always tends to foster mere obedience.[55] "Passive obedience," as we have seen, merely resembles the "base compliances of the slave."[56] The tendency to such docility flourishes everywhere, however, because people are born into a world already constructed, and they invariably find themselves confronted by authorities, commands, customs, habits, and demands. The men and women of every new generation must learn to struggle for a mastery of their world. As they seek to learn this lesson, agitation can be one of several teachers, because it provides the spectacle of men and women cooperatively and publicly challenging established powers and asserting their right to order their surroundings. Thus, disorder helps overcome an instinctive inertia, one of democracy's most formidable enemies. In extreme cases, it prepares people to use their right to "justifiable resistance and legitimate rebellion."[57]

Finally, turmoil and agitation inject energy into the entire body politic, stimulating ideas, commerce, and political efforts. Turgot said, "It is not wars and revolutions which retard the progress of governments; it is softness, stubbornness, routine, and everything that leads to inaction."[58] De Staël claimed that "war, despite all its disasters, has often extended the empire of enlightenment," and "I can truthfully affirm that society has never been so brilliant and so serious altogether as it was during the first three or four years of the revolution, counting from 1788 to the end of 1791."[59] Tocqueville cherished the energy imparted by turmoil to all social spheres; tur-

54. For the preceding quotations in the text, see Tocqueville, *Democracy*, 2: 256, 261–62.
55. Tocqueville, *L'Algérie*, in *Oeuvres* (M), vol. 3, *Écrits et discours politiques*, p. 146.
56. Tocqueville, *Memoir*, 1: 247 (from "France before the Revolution"); *Correspondence . . . Senior*, 2: 102.
57. Tocqueville, *Democracy*, 2: 346.
58. Quoted in Manuel, *The Prophets of Paris*, p. 25.
59. Madame de Staël, *De la littérature considérée dans ses rapports avec les institutions sociales* (Paris, 1887), p. 116; quoted in Larg, *Madame de Staël*, p. 119.

moil can breathe life into a nation. "When a violent revolution occurs among a highly civilized people, it cannot fail to give a sudden impulse to their feelings and ideas."[60] After describing the violence of medieval and renaissance Florence, Tocqueville said:

> Another general remark on these three epochs: in the middle of these political passions and of these revolutions the grandeur and the riches of Florence increased without cease; the human spirit took an extraordinary stride there; arts, sciences, and letters reached a surprising degree of perfection. To such an extent is liberty a powerful agent, even when one knows only incompletely how to use it!
>
> Since Florence has become peaceful and servile, its powers, its riches, its scope and its enlightenment have, on the contrary, not ceased to diminish.[61]

Indeed, Tocqueville assumed that eras of revolution and disorder generate grand ideas, and although he usually condemned revolutions, he always admired the excitement they produced. He noted, by contrast, the comparative intellectual sterility of the "glorious reigns" of Louis XI and Louis XIV when domestic tranquillity was predominant. "It seems as if tyranny were worse than civil war." Revolutionary efforts, and by extension political turmoil, ripple an energy throughout an entire nation.

> It must be confessed, however, that this revolutionary regimen does not suit us ill. Every interval of convulsion has been succeeded by one of increased prosperity. Old prejudices are weakened, the experience of years is gained in months, and the most acute intellects and the most decided wills assume power. . . .
>
> Experience, indeed, teaches us that every revolution changes many positions, develops many wants, rouses many desires, and excites great animation and activity in every mind. When calm is once more restored to the political world, all this agitation does not at once cease—but its object changes; it passes into the industrial and commercial world, and induces greater efforts and bolder schemes than would have been the case had the tranquillity of society remained undisturbed.[62]

Mill praised Tocqueville for persuasively demonstrating that democracy's vigilance should be focused not on "anarchy or love of change, but Chinese stagnation [and] immobility."[63] China and India, the

---

60. Tocqueville, *Democracy*, 2: 43–44.
61. Tocqueville, *Oeuvres* (B), vol. 8, *Mélanges, fragments*, p. 443.
62. Tocqueville, *Correspondence . . . Senior*, 2: 77, 1: 81–82.
63. Tocqueville, *Oeuvres* (M), vol. 6, pt. 1, *Correspondance anglaise*, p. 328.

former distinguished by "immobility" and the latter "petrified," emerged as Tocqueville's preliminary models for the dangers of stagnation in modern democracies.[64] Indeed, he had only contempt for "these men who prefer a sort of social paralysis that despotism gives to the agitation and grand emotions of freedom."[65]

Tocqueville began to think that political collapse would arise, not from external threats or from internal agitation and turmoil, but from routine, habit, tranquillity, and unquestioned assumptions about political authority.

> Because the civilization of ancient Rome perished in consequence of the invasion of the Barbarians, we are perhaps too apt to think that civilization cannot perish in any other manner. If the light by which we are guided is ever extinguished, it will dwindle by degrees and expire of itself. . . .

> The Chinese, in following the track of their forefathers, had forgotten the reasons by which the latter had been guided. . . . The Chinese, then, had lost the power of change; for them improvement was impossible.[66]

The obsession with prosperity and tranquillity, a fear of agitation and turmoil, a loss of any vision about the future—all, according to Tocqueville, foster political decline. The new despotism that the modern industrial world has to fear will not descend upon nations from without; rather, it will grow from certain tendencies that necessarily accompany democratic society and threaten to smother political freedom.

64. Ibid., p. 58; *Democracy*, 1: 94; *L'Inde*, in *Oeuvres* (M), vol. 3, *Écrits et discours politiques*, p. 509.

65. Yale Tocqueville Collection, C.V.a., Paquet No. 8, p. 56.

66. Tocqueville, *Democracy*, 2: 48–49. In suggesting that the new commercial world of Europe was in danger of collapsing into a suffocating and motionless Asiatic despotism, Tocqueville was closely following his mentor Montesquieu who had used a similar analysis, and caricature, of the dangers of Asiatic stagnation in order to criticize the abuses of the French monarchy.

PART THREE

Despotism: Tocqueville's Fear

12 The New Despotism

With a Newtonian view of the political world, Madison and others offered a mechanical notion of political freedom in which free political institutions, once set in motion and properly balanced, continued to function almost by themselves. By contrast, Tocqueville pictured freedom as if he still agreed with Aristotle's theory that said objects stay in motion only if continually propelled by some force external to the object. In a marvelous passage, Montesquieu suggested why freedom is so precarious. "What makes free states last a shorter time than others is that both the misfortunes and the successes they encounter almost always cause them to lose their freedom. In a state where the people are held in subjection, however, successes and misfortunes alike confirm their servitude."[1]

Tocqueville argued in a similar fashion. Equality, he said, was the "generating principle" of modern democracy, the fundamental principle upon which the habits, the culture, and the institutions of modern democracies rested. As such, a culture can eliminate equality "only by long and laborious efforts" over a period of many generations. But if equality can weather most modern storms by itself, freedom must be nursed even through fair weather. "Political liberty is more easily lost; to neglect to hold it fast is to allow it to escape."[2] As a consequence, almost any development, good or bad, tends to weaken

1. Montesquieu, *Considerations on the Causes of the Greatness of the Romans and Their Decline*, p. 92.
2. Tocqueville, *Journey to America*, p. 170; *Democracy*, 2: 101.

freedom: successful wars centralize the government, unsuccessful ones destroy it; prosperity enfeebles public virtue, poverty foments class hatred; good leaders foster a sense of security, bad leaders corrupt; pleasures breed passivity, misery makes citizens anxious for revolt.

Moreover, a threat to freedom rarely strides toward us forthrightly, but it ambles and sidles until, just when we have concluded that it is an intruder that will never arrive, we find that it has already entered our house noiselessly. "Political institutions are like religions," said Tocqueville, "in that observances for a long time survive faith."[3] Or as Montesquieu said of Rome's method of subjugating others: the nation became "a subject people without anyone being able to say when its subjection began."[4] While Tocqueville clearly hoped that certain tendencies in modern democracies might lead to freedom, he grew increasingly pessimistic, believing more and more that other tendencies accompanying this new commercial world might escort modern democracies to a "new" despotism.

> I think, then, that the species of oppression by which democratic nations are menaced is unlike anything that ever before existed in the world; our contemporaries will find no prototype of it in their memories. I seek in vain for an expression that will accurately convey the whole of the idea I have formed of it; the old words *despotism* and *tyranny* are inappropriate: the thing itself is new, and since I cannot name it, I must attempt to describe it.[5]

Of course Tocqueville never said this new despotism was inevitable; it was only a possible outcome of his worst fears.

ORIGINS OF THE NEW DESPOTISM

Bourgeois Roots of the New Despotism

When reading the descriptions of despotism offered by Boulanger, Holbach, Diderot, and Condorcet, one notices that their models of despotism assumed the spectre of their enemies, of those political actors these men perceived as threatening: namely, kings and

---

3. Tocqueville, *The European Revolution and Correspondence with Gobineau,* p. 127.
4. Montesquieu, *Considerations on the Causes of the Greatness of the Romans and Their Decline,* p. 75.
5. Tocqueville, *Democracy,* 2: 336. (I have translated the word *définir* as "describe" rather than "define"; it has the sense of depicting something by drawing it.)

priests.[6] Similarly, the tendencies of modern industrial democracies that Tocqueville disliked were indelible characteristics of the class he feared. Like so many of the writers of his generation, he blamed the bourgeoisie for many of the ills of the age; in this case he argued that the despotism he dreaded would ride on the back of this class's race for predominance. It is well known that Tocqueville used the word *democracy* in a variety of ways, not all of them consistent. He used it to mean an irresistible tendency to equality, or majority rule, or the absence of fixed classes, or more equal opportunities for political participation. Nevertheless, Guizot's analysis of recent French history as chiefly the rise of the middle class to political and economic power remained persuasive for Tocqueville.[7] Consequently, the word *democracy* frequently means *middle-class society,* and when he wrote of his anxiety about democratic despotism, he was speaking of a despotism originating in bourgeois society.

Tocqueville did not come immediately to this conclusion that the new despotism will emerge rather naturally from the new commercial world, but instead, in his unpublished notes, he considered two other possible forms of despotism. First, he considered a tyranny of the lower classes, perhaps some all-powerful state that would rule in the name of the working classes, a state that would emerge from anarchy, since "despotism is the party of anarchy."[8] Clearly Tocqueville the aristocrat feared the new urban masses. "The barbarians are already at our gates. . . . They are around us, in the bosoms of our cities."[9] Second, probably thinking of Julius Caesar and Napoleon, Tocqueville considered a military tyranny, and he wondered in his notes if he should not simply adopt "the ancient idea of the military despotism" in his analysis of the future.[10] Long before he wrote his famous chapter on the new aristocracy of manufacturers, he considered the pos-

6. N. A. Boulanger, *Oeuvres,* vol. 3, *Recherches sur l'origine du despotisme* (Geneva, 1971), pp. 19, 100–105, 155–61; Irving Louis Horowitz, *Claude Helvétius* (New York, 1954), p. 58; Arthur Wilson, *Diderot,* 2 vols. in one (New York, 1972), p. 379; Antoine-Nicolas de Condorcet, *Sketch for a Historical Picture of the Progress of the Human Mind,* trans. June Barraclough (London, 1955), pp. 31–38.

7. For a good discussion of the varied meanings Tocqueville gave to the word *democracy,* see Schleifer, *The Making of Tocqueville's "Democracy in America,"* ch. 19. Lamberti illustrates quite well that Tocqueville's fears for the future of democracy relate to his mistrust of the bourgeoisie. Lamberti, *Tocqueville et les deux démocraties,* pp. 47–54, 189–98, 288–89.

8. Yale Tocqueville Collection, C.V.c., Paquet No. 5, p. 18.

9. Ibid., C.V.b. Paquet No. 13, p. 29.

10. For this and the following quotations in the text, see ibid., C.V.c., Paquet No. 5, pp. 16, 26, 14. See also pp. 2–4, 10–11, 15.

sibility of a new aristocracy of warriors. "When I said that an aristocracy was no longer possible, I was wrong, because one could still have an aristocracy of men of war." Even though he still maintained that war is sometimes good for "the hygiene of a democratic people," he admitted that war easily creates "a central power" that is "very energetic and nearly tyrannical"; hence war is a useful friend to all those who aim for despotism. "Even if I were allowed to lift the veil that hides us from the future, I would not dare to do so. I would be afraid to see the entire society in the hands of soldiers. A *military* and *bureaucratic* organization, the soldier and the clerk. Symbols of the future society. . . ."[11]

Yet Tocqueville ultimately abandoned both these early sketches of despotism. Although he still feared a bureaucratic world of clerks, he concluded that such a world would result, not from the violence either of the working classes or of the military, but from the predictable, inevitable, and perhaps ineradicable characteristics of the new bourgeois society. On one page of his notes about this new despotism, he wrote: "Centralization. Individualism. Material Enjoyments."[12] All these concerns, as we have seen, were held by his generation, and to Tocqueville, they quite logically accompanied the new commercial world. In the end, he perceived the greatest danger to be neither working-class irrationality nor military adventurism, but rather fundamental, yet frightening, characteristics of bourgeois society. "Commerce," he wrote, "has made man lowly."[13]

Tocqueville blamed the bourgeoisie only in private. In a letter to his father written from the United States, he mentioned his wish to write a book on the United States, but only if he could use it to comment on France, and only if he could find an indirect way to say everything he truly thought. "It is not good to announce every truth."[14] In published writings and public speeches, Tocqueville retreated from pointedly criticizing the bourgeoisie, even though in his letters and in his *Recollections,* which he did not originally intend for publication, he declared that the bourgeoisie of the July Monarchy was "the most selfish and grasping of plutocracies" and "treated government like a private business."[15] In public pronouncements he moved carefully and indirectly in his criticisms of the commercial classes, but how could he be expected to act otherwise? The small

11. Ibid., C.V.a., Paquet No. 8, p. 50.
12. Ibid., C.V.c., Paquet No. 5, p. 32.
13. Ibid., C.V.a., Paquet No. 8, p. 5.
14. Tocqueville, *Oeuvres* (B), vol. 7, *Nouvelle correspondance,* p. 110.
15. Tocqueville, *Correspondence . . . Senior,* 1: 134; *Recollections,* p. 6.

electorate under the July Monarchy was composed mainly of land-owners who had accumulated wealth, for the most part, in commerce and industry. Tocqueville said repeatedly that the electoral laws excluded both the great majority of ordinary people and the old aristocracy; he saw the electorate, perhaps not with complete accuracy, as overwhelmingly bourgeois. In pursuing his political ambitions, he certainly could not openly attack this class. In fact, he worked diligently to bury the issue of his own aristocratic heritage, to overcome the fact that his great-grandfather had defended Louis xvi; still he lost his first election because of hostility toward his class background. "When I first was a candidate I failed not because I was not personally popular, but because I was *gentilhomme*. I was met everywhere by the proverb: 'Cats seize mice.'"[16] If he openly castigated the bourgeoisie, he would be dismissed as just another royalist. Thus, he contented himself with depicting the dangers of "democracy."

Tocqueville's contempt for the bourgeoisie, however, was evident in the opening pages of *Democracy*. "Can it be believed that the democracy [which in this case he equated with equality] which has overthrown the feudal system and vanquished kings will retreat before tradesmen and capitalists?"[17] Tocqueville clung to—but masked—an instinctive, aristocratic dislike for the middle class. (When Voltaire said "the people," he meant lawyers, scientists, laborers, merchants, and mechanics; when the Duc de St. Simon said "the common people," he meant the middle class.[18]) For example, throughout his works, Tocqueville suggested that commerce threatened personal liberty, whereas landed property was invaluable to freedom. "The division of the land into small independent properties" is most conducive to "perfect freedom" and individual independence. By contrast, the individual engaged in business must bend to the desires of others, "is exposed to every vicissitude in the commercial or industrial condition of his country," and receives from this bustle of the business climate "disorder into his ideas and instability into his tastes."[19] In a letter to Senior disputing the claim that the French peasant was poorer than the English peasant, Tocqueville asked, even if we admitted "that the poor man temporarily makes more from cultivating the land of another rather than his own, do you think that there are not political,

16. Tocqueville, *Correspondence . . . Senior*, 1: 102.
17. Tocqueville, *Democracy*, 1: 6.
18. Voltaire, *The Portable Voltaire*, trans. H. I. Woolf et al., ed. Ben Ray Redman (New York, 1963), p. 518 (from *The English Letters*); W. H. Lewis, *The Splendid Century* (Garden City, N.Y., 1957), p. 62.
19. Tocqueville, *Memoir*, 1: 230–31. (From "France before the Revolution.")

moral, intellectual benefits attached to the possession of the earth, and which more than compensate, and above all in a permanent manner, for the disadvantage that you point out?"[20] The French peasant in Canada was superior in heart to the American farmer, because he manifested none of that *"mercantile* spirit which obtrudes in all the actions and sayings of an American."[21] Indeed, Tocqueville consistently displayed an aristocratic, if sometimes paternalistic, fondness for the peasantry, writing late in his life, "I have always thought that, after all, the peasantry were superior to all other classes in France."[22] A close reading of his *Old Regime* reveals a persistent attempt to vindicate the peasantry against the arrogance and abuses of other classes.[23]

If Tocqueville admired those who owned their own land, he had great misgivings about those engaged in commerce or industry, and yet these classes he virtually identified with the word *democracy.* Every nation, he said, has had industry and commerce, but in the United States, "what never occurred elsewhere, the whole community is simultaneously engaged in productive industry and commerce."[24] Indeed, he referred to the American republics as "companies of merchants formed to make a business that will prosper."[25] American democracy, he suggested, demonstrated once and for all that "the middle classes can govern a state" with "practical intelligence," but this is "in spite of their petty passions, their incomplete education and their vulgar manners."[26] Once more we see not only his conviction that democracy means middle-class rule but also his contempt for the middle class.

> Up to now it seems to me that [the United States] illustrates the most complete external development of the middle classes, or rather that the whole of society seems to have turned into one middle class. No one

---

20. Tocqueville, *Selected Letters,* p. 97.
21. Tocqueville, *Journey to America,* p. 192.
22. Tocqueville, *Correspondence . . . Senior,* 2: 126.
23. Tocqueville, *The Old Regime,* pp. 128–31, 281. If he admired the aristocracy of his ancestors, he had only contempt for those who dreamed, rather pathetically, that they could maintain an ancient aristocracy in the new world of industry and commerce. "In their obscene repose, they no longer cultivate the intellectual tastes that used to embellish their leisure. But they complain in their crass well-being and console themselves, with horses and dogs, for no longer being able to govern the state." (Yale Tocqueville Collection, C.V.d., Paquet No. 6, p. 54.)
24. Tocqueville, *Democracy,* 2: 37.
25. Yale Tocqueville Collection, C.V.h., Paquet No. 3, Cahier No. 4, p. 23.
26. Tocqueville, *Journey to America,* p. 271.

seems to have the elegant manners and refined politeness of the upper classes in Europe. On the contrary one is at once struck by something vulgar, and a disagreeable casualness of behavior.[27]

This analysis extended from the United States across the Atlantic to France as well. The French government' of his time, something he once called the "bourgeois state,"[28] exhibited a "narrow atmosphere of bourgeois and shopkeeper's aristocracy whose egoism and corruption equalled the lack of enlightenment."[29] In an 1847 letter he wrote of France, "The system of administration that has been practiced for seventeen years has so perverted the middle class, by making a constant appeal to the individual cupidities of its members, that this class is becoming little by little, for the rest of the nation, a little corrupt and vulgar aristocracy, by which it seems shameful to let oneself be led."[30] In fact, Tocqueville pointedly suggested that the ruling middle classes of the United States and France were remarkably similar.[31]

When Tocqueville identified democracy with middle-class rule, he was again borrowing from Guizot's analysis of class struggle in European history since the Middle Ages. For Tocqueville, the decline of aristocracy and the rise to power of the industrial classes was in fact the very phenomenon he called democracy. We find the following passage in his notebooks, and off to the side he wondered whether he "ought" to include this in *Democracy in America*.

> I have shown in this chapter how democracy serves the development of industry. I should be able to show equally how industry, in its turn, hastens the developments of democracy, because these two things are connected and react upon each other. Democracy gives birth to the taste for material enjoyment, which pushes men toward industry, and industry creates a multitude of medium-sized fortunes and constitutes, even in the bosom of aristocratic nations, a class apart where the ranks are badly defined and badly preserved. . . . This class forms over the long run, even in the bosom of aristocratic nations, a sort of small democracy that has its separate instincts, opinions, and laws. To the extent that a people extends its commerce and its industry, this democratic class becomes more numerous and more influential, little by little it passes its opinions into the mores and its ideas into the laws, until

27. Ibid., p. 290.

28. Tocqueville, *The European Revolution and Correspondence with Gobineau*, p. 152.

29. Quoted in Pierre-Marcel, *Essai politique sur Alexis de Tocqueville*, p. 369. (From unpublished notes.)

30. Tocqueville, *Selected Letters*, p. 188.

31. Tocqueville, *Oeuvres* (M), vol. 6, pt. 1, *Correspondance anglaise*, pp. 320–21.

finally it has become preponderant and, so to speak, unique, it takes hold of power and directs all things as it pleases, and founds democracy.[32]

Although Tocqueville's distaste for rule by the middle classes comes from his aristocratic heritage and from the concerns of his generation, as we saw in chapter 4, his analysis of how this class came to power reminds us of Marx, another political thinker who acknowledged a debt to Guizot's historical and class analyses.

It is worthwhile to emphasize, however, that Tocqueville's critique of the bourgeoisie was most emphatically not a Marxist one, nor was it a nostalgic longing for the Old Regime. Rather, as should be amply clear by now, his critique sprang from the anxieties and aspirations of his own generation, whereas his political convictions—especially about the idea of freedom—had deep roots in the French tradition of political thought and in the political ideas of ancient authors. If Tocqueville disliked the middle class, he certainly did not transfer his faith to some new working-class world, as we indicated in chapter 5. Tocqueville feared working-class rebellion, and he feared that the laboring classes might couple their strength with misguided aspirations for socialism, "a new form of servitude." Yet whenever he described socialism, he gave it characteristics that he always contended entered the world with the bourgeoisie. Socialism, Tocqueville said, is an "energetic continuous appeal to man's material passions," a political goal that foments "greedy, envious desires"; the prototypical socialist dreams of "unlimited consumption for everybody."[33] But the obsession with consuming goods, as Tocqueville said so frequently, was a "natural instinct" of the bourgeoisie, because in the absence of hereditary distinctions, money established itself as the "natural test to measure men's merit."[34] Indeed, "all men who live in democratic times more or less contract the ways of thinking of the manufacturing and trading classes," and the general motivation of these classes is, Tocqueville claimed, profit. "The love of wealth is therefore to be traced, as either a principal or an accessory motive, at the bottom of all that Americans do." Thus, the ethic of greed, acquisition, and envy, which in Tocqueville's eyes made working-class movements so dangerous to freedom, was bequeathed to the working classes by the bourgeoisie. "The passion for physical comforts is essentially a pas-

32. Yale Tocqueville Collection, C.V.j., Paquet No. 2, Cahier No. 2, pp. 16–17.
33. Drescher, ed., *Tocqueville and Beaumont on Social Reform*, pp. 183, 182; *Recollections*, p. 205.
34. Tocqueville, *Recollections*, p. 6; *Journey to America*, p. 274.

sion of the middle classes; with those classes it grows and spreads, with them it is preponderant. *From them it mounts into the higher orders of society and descends into the mass of the people.*"[35] Tocqueville might well have described socialism as Flaubert did democracy, that is, as an attempt to "elevate the proletariat to the level of stupidity of the bourgeoisie."[36] Because of the acquisitive ethic, because of the centralized government needed to watch over the economy, "it would seem as if despotism lurked within [the manufacturing classes] and naturally grew with their growth."[37]

Equality: Prerequisite for Freedom, Prerequisite for Despotism

Tocqueville suggested that although people in modern democracies tend to admire freedom, they cling stubbornly and passionately to equality, even if it means forfeiting this freedom.

> I think that democratic communities have a natural taste for freedom; left to themselves, they will seek it, cherish it, and view any privation of it with regret. But for equality their passion is ardent, insatiable, incessant, invincible; they call for equality in freedom; and if they cannot obtain that, they still call for equality in slavery. They will endure poverty, servitude, barbarism, but they will not endure aristocracy.[38]

Thus, the most important prerequisite of despotism in modern times must be the reduction of the state to a condition of equality. "The foremost or indeed the sole condition required in order to succeed in centralizing the supreme power in a democratic community is to love equality, or to get men to believe you love it."

One cannot conclude from this, as some authors have done, that Tocqueville wanted to find a new elite or new forms of inequality to curb the dangers of equality and so-called "mass" society. For example, Tocqueville thought in terms of equality under the law, equality of both economic and political opportunity, and equality of power in the decision-making process, at least at the local levels of governance. In this sense, equality was not dangerous; it was indispensable to freedom. As a consequence, Tocqueville never urged that the modern world abandon a quest for equality; instead he thought it must seek to reconcile equality with freedom. "I love liberty by taste, equality by instinct and by reason."[39] All aristocracies have assumed that

35. Tocqueville, *Democracy*, 2: 219, 239–40, 137–38 (my emphasis).
36. Quoted in Levin, *The Gates of Horn*, p. 287.
37. Tocqueville, *Democracy*, 2: 328–29.
38. Ibid., 102–3. See pp. 319–20 for the quotation that follows in the text.
39. Tocqueville, *Selected Letters*, p. 100.

"inequality of condition" was a right, but such assumptions, said Tocqueville, are no longer valid in a modern democratic world.[40]

One might legitimately wonder why those who comment on Tocqueville's ideas stress the potential tension between freedom and equality and not their compatibility.[41] What is at stake here? Many seem to see in Tocqueville's analysis an argument that the laboring classes will advance beyond a demand for legal and political equality to do battle for economic equality. In other words, these commentators understand Tocqueville to be suggesting that the primary danger to modern democracy lies in the irrational masses, motivated by what Nietzsche called envy or *ressentiment*, demanding equality of condition, even if the condition is servitude. In fact, Tocqueville probably did harbor that fear. "Democratic institutions develop to a very high degree the sentiment of envy in the human heart."[42] Yet Tocqueville always thought that the *origin* of working-class envy lay in the ethic that accompanied the bourgeoisie to power, an ethic of self-interest and obsession with consuming goods and pleasures. As a consequence, Tocqueville's fear of the working classes could not lead him to defend the privileges of the middle class, or what he called a new industrial aristocracy. Some commentators, forgetting Tocqueville's analysis of the origin of working-class greed and his powerful reservations about the commercial classes, have seized upon his argument to justify the privileges of inequality and property as well as a pluralist political system boasting of a new elite composed of the very commercial classes Tocqueville blamed the most.

CHARACTERISTICS OF THE NEW DESPOTISM

The Prison as Tocqueville's Model for Despotism

Once we have seen the roots of the new despotism, how can we approach its surface shape? Tocqueville's model for this despotism was quite possibly the prison he found in Philadelphia.[43] In describ-

---

40. Tocqueville, *Oeuvres* (M), vol. 3, *Écrits et discours politiques*, p. 117. (From *Abolition de l'esclavage.*)

41. See Zetterbaum, *Tocqueville and the Problem of Democracy*, pp. 69–73; Mayer, *Alexis de Tocqueville*, pp. 34–38; Lively, *The Social and Political Thought of Alexis de Tocqueville*, pp. 21–22, 89–90; Lipset, *Political Man;* Bendix, *Nation-Building and Citizenship.* For a very good discussion of the relation between freedom and equality in Tocqueville's thought, see Lamberti, *Tocqueville et les deux démocraties*, ch. 2.

42. Yale Tocqueville Collection, C.V.h., Paquet No. 3, Cahier No. 4, p. 36.

43. Boesche, "The Prison: Tocqueville's Model for Despotism."

ing this prison, which Tocqueville called the "most complete des-potism,"[44] we can obtain a quick overview of Tocqueville's analysis of the possible new despotism.

The three fundamental principles of the Philadelphia prison, founded as a matter of fact by Quaker reformers, were equality, isolation, and powerlessness. First, the prisoners ate the same bread, wore the same clothes, performed the same manual work and oc-cupied identical cells. Second, the Philadelphia reformers regarded the isolation of prisoners, architecturally quite expensive, as the one indispensable ingredient to rehabilitation. Each new convict was led to his cell with a cloth over his head, in order to prohibit any contact or recognition among prisoners. The convicts then remained in their cells all day and night, emerging only to a private, separated court-yard for fresh air and moderate exercise. Third, the prisoners were carried—through isolation—to a sense of helplessness and utter de-spair. Many, if not most, of the prisoners Tocqueville interviewed described a tremendous terror that seized them upon first being left in solitary confinement. After gradually triumphing "over the terrors which almost surrendered him to insanity or despair," the prisoner was "tamed and forever submissive to the rules of the prison."[45] "It is impossible that a regime especially designed to make a sharp impres-sion on a great number of minds, does not push some of them to-wards madness."[46]

Tocqueville and the Philadelphia reformers considered isolation not as mere punishment but as a powerful instrument for bringing genuine reform of the prisoner. Isolated from one another, the pris-oners found themselves powerless to communicate and hence com-pletely unable to act in concert against prison authority. In fact, Sing Sing was built by the nine hundred prisoners at Auburn who were constrained by a strict silence enforced by whips—all out in the open and watched by only thirty guards. As Beaumont explained, the pris-oners were "isolated one from the other. All strength is born of asso-ciation; and 30 individuals united through personal communication, by ideas, by plans in common, by concerted schemes, have more real power than 900 whose isolation makes them weak."[47] If the isolation among prisoners ever dissolved, they would be able to resist reform.

44. Tocqueville, *On the Penitentiary System*, p. 47.

45. Ibid., pp. 32, 187–98, 40.

46. Tocqueville, *Oeuvres* (B), vol. 9, *Études économiques, politiques*, p. 341; *On the Penitentiary System*, pp. 5–7.

47. Quoted in Pierson, *Tocqueville and Beaumont in America*, p. 101.

As Tocqueville said, once inmates formed an "association," they could no longer be manipulated individually.[48]

If isolation and powerlessness remained intact, however, the prisoner was vulnerable to manipulation. The warden, priests, and other upright citizens visited the prisoner regularly, attempting to reform him morally and impress upon him the benefits of rehabilitation. This meant, of course, that the isolation was not quite complete; indeed, Tocqueville wrote, complete isolation "destroys the criminal without intermission and without pity; it does not reform, it kills."[49] Through this aperture in his cell, the prevailing values embodied in the dominant culture rushed into the prisoner's private world. Isolation and powerlessness constituted a despotism that brought rehabilitation; the prisoner listened to and accepted the moral lessons of the priest and rushed to adopt an ethic of hard work as a central diversion from the fears of solitude.

> The necessity of labour which overcomes his disposition to idleness; the obligation of silence which makes him reflect; the isolation which places him alone in the presence of his crime and his suffering; the religious instruction which enlightens and comforts him; the obedience of every moment to inflexible rules; the regularity of a uniform life; in a word, all the circumstances belonging to this severe system are calculated to produce a deep impression upon his mind.[50]

Because it endeavored to control more than mere behavior, as past prisons managed to do, this system of isolation aspired to remold the very nature of the prisoner. If rehabilitation were successful, it would manage "to inculcate in him totally new sentiments, to change profoundly the nature of his habits, to destroy his instincts, to make in a word a virtuous man out of a great criminal."[51] In such a case, the prison "would cause so great and so salutary a revolution in the mind of man" and recast "the instincts of a bad nature or the propensities to which a bad education has given birth."[52]

Thus, for Tocqueville, the despotism of the prison was a powerful instrument for good, insofar as the individual criminal was like a caterpillar, hastened by prison processes into the proper state of a butterfly, grateful to the administrative despotism of the prison for

48. Tocqueville, *Oeuvres* (B), vol. 9, *Études économiques, politiques*, pp. 321–22, 329.

49. Tocqueville, *On the Penitentiary System*, p. 5.

50. Ibid., p. 58.

51. Tocqueville, *Oeuvres* (B), vol. 9, *Études économiques, politiques*, pp. 320–21.

52. Drescher, ed., *Tocqueville and Beaumont on Social Reform*, p. 84; Tocqueville, *Oeuvres* (B), vol. 9, *Études économiques, politiques*, p. 365.

transforming him into a new state of moral rectitude. If this microscopic despotism were ever writ large in society as a whole, however, it would have the capacity to alter the thoughts and habits of ordinary men and women in terrifying ways. The butterfly might regress to being a caterpillar.

Isolation

When Tocqueville discussed despotism more directly, isolation was the fulcrum on which he thought the new despotism would balance itself. Isolation was axiomatic, however, even in ancient theories of despotism, as in Tacitus, or in Bodin—who said, "the tyrant tries to eradicate [associations] altogether, knowing full well that unity and bonds of friendship among his subjects spell his inevitable ruin."[53] Similarly, Montesquieu asserted that "in despotic states, each house is a separate government"; Rousseau declared that "it is only the fiercest despotism which is alarmed at the sight of seven or eight men assembled."[54] Tocqueville merely followed his mentors in arguing that despotism endeavored to separate citizens. "Despotism, which by its nature is suspicious, sees in the separation among men the surest guarantee of its continuance, and it usually makes every effort to keep them separate."[55]

Although Tocqueville certainly borrowed from a time-honored analysis of despotism, he also added much to it. Ancient despotisms relied on fear to enforce separation among citizens and to dissolve all groups or associations; the isolation of the new despotism originated in the dissolution of the old ties and groups characterizing aristocratic society. Thus, as we saw in chapter 2, modern isolation eliminated all natural intermediaries between the individual and the state. Never in the past, Tocqueville maintained, could this new despotism have existed, because never before had isolation, its central precondition, flourished so widely. "No sovereign ever lived in former ages so absolute or so powerful as to undertake to administer by his own agency, and without the assistance of intermediate powers, all the parts of a great empire." In fact, even if a former despot such as the so-called absolutist Louis XIV had wanted to control and to direct every community and every individual, it would have been impossible because of

53. Tacitus, *The Complete Works*, p. 206. (*Annals*, VI, 19.) Bodin, *Six Books of the Commonwealth*, III, 7, p. 106.

54. Montesquieu, *The Spirit of the Laws*, IV, 3, 1: 32; Rousseau, *Politics and the Arts*, p. 108.

55. Tocqueville, *Democracy*, 2: 109.

poor means of communication, an imperfect administrative system, and the recalcitrance of intermediate associations that have always appeared whenever there has been an "inequality of condition."[56] Only in this modern, urbanized world of industry and commerce does each individual—deprived of groups, trade corporations, classes, parishes, extended families, and associations—dwell isolated and alone in the shadow of all-powerful government.

Middle-class society, Tocqueville felt, rushed to make modern isolation its undetachable companion; it befriended this isolation while celebrating the demise of aristocratic society, and like a good chum, it lent a hand by disseminating the passion for wealth and private enjoyment. Eventually citizens of the new middle-class world might surrender public affairs and political concern to whatever government will labor to secure their pleasures.

> I seek to trace the novel features under which despotism may appear in the world. The first thing that strikes the observation is an innumerable multitude of men, all equal and alike, incessantly endeavoring to procure the petty and paltry pleasures with which they glut their lives. Each of them, living apart, is as a stranger to the fate of all the rest; his children and his private friends constitute to him the whole of mankind. As for the rest of his fellow citizens, he is close to them, but does not see them; he touches them, but he does not feel them; he exists only in himself and for himself alone; and if his kindred still remain to him, he may be said at any rate to have lost his country.
>
> Above this race of men stands an immense and tutelary power, which takes upon itself alone to secure their gratifications and to watch over their fate.[57]

Tocqueville generally depicted this new despotism as faceless and without identifiable despots, like Kafka's world in which everyone is entangled but no one does the tangling; occasionally Tocqueville thought that a faction of the manufacturing class might direct this despotism. "When the bulk of the community are engrossed by private concerns, the smallest parties need not despair of getting the upper hand in public affairs . . . they alone are in action, while all others are stationary; they regulate everything by their own caprice."[58]

The most fundamental characteristics of bourgeois society—individualism, private business and private profit, the accumulation of wealth, and self-interest—become the indispensable conditions for

56. Ibid., p. 334.
57. Ibid., p. 336.
58. Ibid., p. 150.

the new despotism to stage its alluring and awesome spectacle. Once again, however, the chief element of the drama is personal isolation.

> For in a community in which the ties of family, of caste, of class, and craft fraternities no longer exist, people are far too much disposed to think exclusively of their own interests, to become self-seekers practicing a narrow individualism and caring nothing for the public good. Far from trying to counteract such tendencies despotism encourages them, depriving the governed of any sense of solidarity and interdependence; of good-neighborly feelings and a desire to further the welfare of the community at large. It immures them, so to speak, each in his private life and, taking advantage of the tendency they already have to keep apart, it estranges them still more. Their feelings toward each other were already growing cold; despotism freezes them.
>
> Since in such communities nothing is stable, each man is haunted by a fear of sinking to a lower social level and by a restless urge to better his condition. And since money has not only become the sole criterion of a man's social status but has also acquired an extreme mobility—that is to say it changes hands incessantly, raising or lowering the prestige of individuals and families—everybody is feverishly intent on making money or, if already rich, on keeping wealth intact. Love of gain, a fondness for business careers, the desire to get rich at all costs, a craving for material comfort and easy living quickly become ruling passions under a despotic government. . . . It is in the nature of despotism that it should foster such desires and propagate their havoc.[59]

This passage from the introduction to his *Old Regime* is among Tocqueville's last systematic descriptions of the despotism he feared. When he linked "interests," "narrow individualism," "private life," "love of gain," and "business careers," he revealed even to the most casual reader his conviction that the isolation of the new despotism had its roots in the soil of bourgeois society.

One cannot overstress the importance of this point. Tocqueville argued clearly and forcefully that bourgeois society, if not despotic at its inception, slowly and relentlessly unfolds the preconditions of this new despotism. The seed of despotism was planted by the bourgeoisie, it germinated with isolation and the collapse of the ties and the groups of aristocratic society, it sprouted with the praise of self-interest, and it might blossom fearfully if the world immerses itself in an obsessive, private pursuit of wealth. "Thus the vices which despotism produces are precisely those which equality fosters. These two things perniciously complete and assist each other. Equality places

59. Tocqueville, *The Old Regime*, p. xiii.

men side by side, unconnected by any common tie; despotism raises barriers to keep them asunder; the former predisposes them not to consider their fellow creatures, the latter makes general indifference a sort of public virtue."[60] Although Tocqueville never foresaw the murderous character of Stalin's Russia or Hitler's Germany, he was correct in seeing isolation as the requisite foundation, something we can see in a passage from Arendt:

> [Himmler] proved his supreme ability for organizing the masses into total domination by assuming that most people are neither bohemians, fanatics, adventurers, sex maniacs, crackpots, nor social failures, but first and foremost job holders and good family men.
>
> The philistine's retirement into private life, his single-minded devotion to matters of family and career was the last, and already degenerated, product of the bourgeoisie's belief in the primacy of private interest. The philistine is the bourgeois isolated from his own class, the atomized individual who is produced by the breakdown of the bourgeois class itself. The mass man whom Himmler organized for the greatest mass crimes ever committed in history bore the features of the philistine rather than of the mob man, and was the bourgeois who in the midst of the ruins of his world worried about nothing so much as his private security, was ready to sacrifice everything—belief, honor, dignity—on the slightest provocation. Nothing proved easier to destroy than the privacy and private morality of people who thought of nothing but safeguarding their private lives. After a few years of power and systematic co-ordination, the Nazis could rightly announce: "The only person who is still a private individual in Germany is somebody who is asleep."[61]

Powerlessness and the Absence of Political Action

The new despotism would rob individuals of the ability, the desire, and the forum for political action. Isolated and concentrating on increasing their own fortune, people would feel helpless outside their private worlds. As Tocqueville said of the individual who is isolated from fellow citizens, "when he comes to survey the totality of his fellows and to place himself in contrast with so huge a body, he is instantly overwhelmed by the sense of his own insignificance and weakness." Furthermore, as we have seen, people engrossed in private affairs do not gather to act publicly; a political inertia accompanies their quest for accumulating greater goods and pleasures in

60. Tocqueville, *Democracy*, 2: 109.
61. Arendt, *The Origins of Totalitarianism*, pp. 338–39.

their personal lives. Every American, Tocqueville said, was constantly engaged in private pursuits designed to improve his or her economic position, and the long-term result of this might be indifference to any political action whatsoever. "Do not talk to him of the interest and rights of mankind; this small domestic concern absorbs for the time all his thoughts and inclines him to defer political agitation to some other season." If a society offers a host of private gains such as wealth and pleasure—whereby desires are only increased rather than satisfied by temporary gratification—it enfeebles all inclination for public involvement and political action. "Political passions" for "momentous undertakings" have "but little hold on those who have devoted all their faculties to the pursuit of their well-being." Tocqueville suggested that great political movements designed to effect far-reaching change would become less and less likely in modern commercial societies. Even if an individual with great energy, high ideals, and staggering charisma appeared, the person would have to drag an entire population that wanted only to be left alone with its private concerns.

> They will not struggle energetically against him, sometimes they will even applaud him; but they do not follow him. To his vehemence they secretly oppose their inertia, to his revolutionary tendencies their conservative interests, their homely tastes to his adventurous passions, their good sense to the flights of his genius, to his poetry their prose. . . . He strains himself to rouse the indifferent and distracted multitude and finds at last that he is reduced to impotence, not because he is conquered, but because he is alone.[67]

Under the new despotism, Tocqueville suggested, each individual would become a consumer not a citizen, an observer not a participant. The proliferation of entertainment and the cult of enjoyment (the modern sense of the word *fun* entered the English language in the late eighteenth and early nineteenth centuries) would sap people's energies, lulling them into a vicarious enjoyment of adventures that were not political and often not their own. Rousseau's critique of the theater argued this well. "In giving our tears to these fictions, we have satisfied all the rights of humanity without having to give anything more of ourselves." Theaters and entertainment teach people, in Rousseau's words, to see life "only on the stage," not to live it.[63] Thus, in entertainment, we win battles, rescue the unfortunate, vanquish

---

62. Tocqueville, *Democracy*, 2: 11, 269, for this and the preceding quotations in the text.

63. Rousseau, *Politics and the Arts*, pp. 25, 48.

political corruption, save the hungry, and feel self-satisfied, even though the entire action is fiction. Tocqueville agreed emphatically.

> I read [no novels] that end ill. Why should one voluntarily subject oneself to painful emotions? To emotions created by an imaginary cause and therefore impelling you to no action. I like vivid emotions, but I seek them in real life, in society, in travelling, in business, but above all in political business. There is no happiness comparable to political success. . . . Having enjoyed that, I am ashamed of being excited by the visionary sorrows of heroes and heroines.[64]

The new despotism will replace actors on a political stage with an arena full of spectators.

Despotism with the Appearance of Freedom

Most pernicious and most deceptive, the new despotism will announce itself in the name of freedom, and in fact, the very ideology designed to buttress the despotism will ostensibly embrace freedom as its most basic value, until those in servitude believe themselves to be free. While sparkling with the glitter of diamonds, the gems will merely be glass, for "the secret slave of tyranny may be the professed lover of freedom."[65]

Retaining the form of freedom has always helped conceal the fact that the substance has been drained. "Every student of history knows that this phenomenon is a common one; rulers who destroy men's freedom commonly begin by trying to retain its forms—and so it has been from the reign of Augustus to the present day."[66] Tocqueville even argued that the new despotism might well be an elected one that, however preferable that might be to nonelective government, would not change the despotic character of society. In his notes, Tocqueville wrote that if he were a friend to despotism, he would allow "the deputies of the country [to deliberate] freely about peace and war, about the nation's finances, about its prosperity, its industries, its life. But I would avoid agreeing, at any price, that the representatives of a village had the right to assemble peacefully to discuss among themselves repairs for their church and the plan for their parsonage."[67] In the absence of municipal freedom, the debates of a national legislature offer only the appearance of freedom, as the Senate did under

64. Tocqueville, *Correspondence . . . Senior*, 2: 206–7.
65. Tocqueville, *Democracy*, 1: 100.
66. Tocqueville, *The Old Regime*, p. 45.
67. Yale Tocqueville Collection, C.V.c., Paquet No. 5, p. 50.

the Roman Empire. Tocqueville labeled this "theatrical representation." Elections procure only the illusion that individuals have control over their lives, allowing them to hasten back within their private walls, close the door, and pretend that they are free. As we have seen, Tocqueville did not equate freedom, as did Constant, with the preservation of an independent and private place in which one can do as one pleases; rather for him, free citizens participate in decision making. The new despotism, even if benevolent and elected, would slowly but relentlessly corrupt people until they could neither act nor think for themselves.

> Our contemporaries are constantly excited by two conflicting passions: they want to be led, and they wish to remain free. As they cannot destroy either the one or the other of these contrary propensities, they strive to satisfy them both at once. They devise a sole, tutelary, and all-powerful form of government, but elected by the people . . . they console themselves for being in tutelage by the reflection that they have chosen their own guardians. . . .
>
> By this system the people shake off their state of dependence just long enough to select their master and then relapse into it again. . . .
>
> It is in vain to summon a people who have been rendered so dependent on the central power to choose from time to time the representatives of that power; this rare and brief exercise of their free choice, however important it may be, will not prevent them from gradually losing the faculties of thinking, feeling, and acting for themselves, and thus gradually falling below the level of humanity.[68]

The new despotism will summon apologists who will help retain the appearance of freedom without the reality, and lawyers in particular will rush to legitimize the new despotism. Tocqueville, who did appreciate the protection laws can offer, also thought that laws were efficient tools invariably used by despots, because they created the twin illusions of consensus and civility. Whereas the Spanish "pursued the Indians with bloodhounds, like wild beasts," the Americans managed to do it legally and, to appearances, morally. "It is impossible to destroy men with more respect for the laws of humanity."[69] Despots can always find "a lawyer ready to prove the lawfulness of their acts—to establish learnedly that violence was just, and that the oppressed were in the wrong."[70] More important, perhaps, Tocqueville claimed

68. Tocqueville, *Democracy*, 2: 337, 339.
69. Ibid., 1: 368–69.
70. Tocqueville, *The Old Regime*, pp. 223–24.

that lawyers attempt to substitute legal questions for political ones, legal quarrels for popular political activity, rules for movements. Laws confine quarrels to legal disputes over property and rights but obscure questions of general interest. Indeed, the entire legal vocabulary, focusing on individual rights and the protection of property, will convince people that a private, self-interested pursuit of goods and pleasures is both necessary and sufficient for freedom.

The blame for legitimizing despotism with the banner of freedom, however, does not lie with lawyers alone. As we will see in the next section, the whole ideology of society—created by newspapers, schools, intellectuals, and public opinion—threatens any diversity of thought.

The Eclipse of Both the Private World and Independence of Thought

Montaigne suggested that, in a harsh and unstable world, one could protect one's personal freedom by private withdrawl. As we saw in chapter 5, Stendhal continued this argument two centuries later when his characters found freedom and security from a threatening world in private rooms and prison cells. Tocqueville maintained that this alternative of a private, independent existence, an alternative that was once probably attainable under past despotisms, would no longer be feasible in the despotism of the new industrial world. Rousseau had been one of the first to suggest that a new despotism might control not just public behavior but private life and thought. "Do you think it is so easy to find a place where you can always live like an honest man? . . . beware lest an unjust government, a persecuting religion, and evil habits should disturb you in your home."[71]

Tacitus had declared that men and women in the Roman Empire had lived in anxiety and suspicion even in their homes—"the very roofs and walls were eyed with suspicion"[72]—but this was the ordinary fear of violence, falling heavily on those with threatening influence but leaving the bulk of the population alone. Tocqueville suggested that every private sphere would be invaded, only rarely by police, but instead by a uniformity of ideas, habits, and tastes. The new despotism will quietly influence our most private thoughts, and if not forestalled will permeate every home; and even those drawing rooms that once witnessed frank and free thought will resemble "one

---

71. Rousseau, *Émile*, pp. 420–21; also p. 436.
72. Tacitus, *The Complete Works*, p. 185. (*Annals*, IV, 69–70.)

of those low, close, and gloomy abodes where the light which breaks in from without soon faints and fades away."[73] Not only is this despotism the "absolute master of public life," it also "penetrates from all sides into private life."[74] Confronted by powerless individuals who live as hostile strangers to one another, the new government will seep into each home and invade "the domain heretofore reserved to private independence . . . it gains a firmer footing every day about, above, and around all private persons, to assist, to advise, and to coerce them."[75] Not contenting itself with destroying public life, the new despotism will exert control over the private habits and thoughts of citizens. Once more, Tocqueville foresaw the basis, if not the violent character, of Hitler's Germany and Stalin's Soviet Union.

> Totalitarian government, like all tyrannies, certainly could not exist without destroying the public realm of life, that is, without destroying, by isolating men, their political capacities. But totalitarian domination as a form of government is new in that it is not content with this isolation and destroys private life as well. It bases itself on loneliness, on the experience of not belonging to the world at all, which is among the most radical and desperate experiences of man.[76]

How is it that despotism, which had once contented itself with controlling behavior, has found a new way to insinuate itself into the minds of its subjects? How could Tocqueville argue that, in the "tyranny of democratic republics," the "body is left free, and the soul is enslaved"? The process should be familiar by now. Individuals left to themselves simply accept without question the predominant opinion of society, because only as active participants in groups and communities can one sustain a diversity of opinion in the modern world. "The multitude require no laws to coerce those who do not think like themselves: public disapprobation is enough; a sense of their loneliness and impotence overtakes them and drives them to despair."[77] By the second part of *Democracy*, Tocqueville had refined his notion of tyranny of the majority, because it was quite possible that virtually no dissenters would exist to be tyrannized and that all would embrace, or be enveloped by, the dominant opinions.

Tocqueville recognized that individual beliefs had been controlled before, especially by religions (Louis xiv deferred to Church leaders

---

73. Tocqueville, *Democracy*, 2: 39.
74. Yale Tocqueville Collection, C.V.c., Paquet No. 5, p. 4.
75. Tocqueville, *Democracy*, 2: 323–24.
76. Arendt, *The Origins of Totalitarianism*, p. 475.
77. Tocqueville, *Democracy*, 1: 274, 2: 275.

"in order that they might aid him in ruling over the minds of the people"[78]); but, he suggested, the manner and the extent of this rule would become historically unique under this possible new despotism. Dissenting intellectuals, for example, might write what they wish, because few would read them and their thoughts would hardly damage the predominant ideas of the age. Under Louis Napoleon's dictatorship, he said, "Montalembert, or Guizot, or Falloux, or I may publish what we like. We are not read by the soldier or by the proletarian."[79] The dominant ideas—reinforced by intellectuals, churches, and schools—would reach into every home largely by means of the press. Before the enormous new capacities of the electronic age, Tocqueville worried about newspapers that "can drop the same thought into a thousand minds at the same moment."[80] The press managed to "set the public mind" and "to [form] political questions."[81] When concentrated, the influence of the press is "unbounded."[82] Tocqueville was not afraid simply of straightforward government censorship; he also feared its eventual control of the mind. Even a press independent of government control, he suggested, might embrace a subtle self-censorship, unconsciously reflecting the dominant values and repeating them ceaselessly until no one ever dreamed of questioning them.

The Pleasures of Servitude

Although in one passage Tocqueville feared "a yoke heavier than any that has galled mankind since the fall of the Roman Empire," he generally argued that the new despotism would be distinguished by its "sweetness."[83] The despotism that Tocqueville envisioned would rarely use violence—only "at certain periods of extreme effervescence or of great danger."[84] Its strength would derive not from force but from the material enjoyments it could provide; not from fear, but bribery. "Civilization, instead of preparing men to live without any master except themselves, seems to have been useful only for sugar-

78. Tocqueville, *Memoir*, 1: 205. (From "France before the Revolution.")
79. Tocqueville, *Correspondence . . . Senior*, 2: 160.
80. Tocqueville, *Democracy*, 2: 119.
81. See Tocqueville, *Oeuvres* (M), vol. 8, *Correspondance . . . Beaumont*, pt. 2, p. 24; pt. 1, p. 564.
82. Tocqueville, *Democracy*, 1: 193.
83. Tocqueville, *Memoir*, 1: 377; *Oeuvres* (M), vol. 8, pt. 3, *Correspondance . . . Beaumont*, p. 228.
84. Tocqueville, *Democracy*, 2: 335.

coating and legitimizing their servitude."[85] Not only will the despotism refrain from cruelty, it will seek to please, but all the while degrading its subjects. Tacitus described this well: "Step by step [the Britons] were led to things which dispose to vice, the lounge, the bath, the elegant banquet. All this in their ignorance, they called civilization, when it was but a part of their servitude."[86] In Montesquieu's *Persian Letters,* a eunuch wrote to his master, "you are more absolute when you caress than when you threaten."[87] Similarly, Tocqueville said:

> Above this race of men stands an immense and tutelary power, which takes upon itself alone to secure their gratifications and to watch over their fate. That power is absolute, minute, regular, provident, and mild. It would be like the authority of a parent if, like that authority, its object was to prepare men for manhood, but it seeks, on the contrary, to keep them in perpetual childhood: it is well content that the people should enjoy themselves, provided they think of nothing but enjoyment. For their happiness such a government willingly labors, but it chooses to be the sole arbiter of that happiness; it provides for their security, foresees and supplies their necessities, facilitates their pleasures, manages their principal concerns, directs their industry, regulates the descent of property, and subdivides their inheritances: what remains, but to spare them all the care of thinking and all the trouble of living?[88]

This condition "degrades men without tormenting them," for it transforms human beings who might be active makers of history into gratified beasts.

> The will of man is not shattered, but softened, bent, and guided; men are seldom forced by it to act, but they are constantly restrained from acting. Such a power does not destroy, but it prevents existence; it does not tyrannize, but it compresses, enervates, extinguishes, and stupefies a people, till each nation is reduced to nothing better than a flock of timid and industrious animals, of which the government is the shepherd.[89]

In the end, "that mighty human intelligence which has so often stirred the world" busies itself with satiation.

85. Tocqueville in Richard Laurin Hawkins, ed., *Newly Discovered French Letters of the Seventeenth, Eighteenth, and Nineteenth Centuries* (Cambridge, Mass., 1933), p. 199.
86. Tacitus, *The Complete Works,* p. 690. (*Agricola,* 21.)
87. Montesquieu, *The Persian Letters,* XCVI.
88. Tocqueville, *Democracy,* 2: 336; see also p. 335.
89. Ibid., 337; see also p. 168.

Just as the Roman people wept at the death of their own tyrants,[90] the subjects of the new despotism might eventually enjoy their degradation. Stendhal explored this idea in *The Charterhouse of Parma* when the prisoners in Parma, confined to "dungeons three feet high," grew to love their jailers.[91] Similarly, Tocqueville argued that people often learn to love and respect their oppressors, "for nothing is more customary in man than to recognize superior wisdom in the person of his oppressor." His premier example was probably the servant of the Old Regime who, Tocqueville suggested, abandoned his own personality and lived vicariously through the activities of his master.

> Servants sometimes identify themselves with the person of the master, so that they become an appendage to him in their own eyes as well as in his. . . .
>
> In this predicament the servant ultimately detaches his notion of interest from his own person; he deserts himself as it were, or rather he transports himself into the character of his master and thus assumes an imaginary personality. He complacently invests himself with the wealth of those who command him; he shares their fame, exalts himself by their rank, and feeds his mind with borrowed greatness. . . .[92]

People will cherish and revere their new servitude, because it is built, buttressed, and guarded by the practice of granting satisfactions. Some of Tocqueville's French predecessors had already argued that despotism maintained its rule by disseminating the material goods, pleasures, and sometimes security that were accorded a servant. Montesquieu argued that great wealth signaled the downfall of republics, but "in despotic governments . . . the principle motive of actions is the hope of the conveniences of life."[93] In the seraglio of Montesquieu's *Persian Letters*—probably an important source for Tocqueville's theory of despotism—each woman eagerly busied herself with prolonging and perfecting her submission, simply because she felt a "dreadful need" for the rewards bestowed for good behavior. "We note that the more women we have under our eyes, the less trouble they give us. A more stringent need to please, less opportunity to band together, more examples of submissive obedience—all of this forges chains for them."[94] This idea of a despotism that caresses also

90. See Montesquieu, *Considerations on the Causes of the Greatness of the Romans and Their Decline*, pp. 132–33.
91. Stendhal, *The Charterhouse of Parma*, pp. 374–75.
92. Tocqueville, *Democracy*, 2: 12, 189–90.
93. Montesquieu, *The Spirit of the Laws*, V, 18, 1: 66.
94. Montesquieu, *The Persian Letters*, XCVI.

appears in Rousseau's claim that people "forge themselves chains of gold, not as a mark of slavery, but as an ornament of pride"; likewise in a remark by Balzac's character Vautrin, who whispered that you can control others if you manage to "engineer dreadful needs."[95]

Tocqueville argued this point far more systematically. Human beings, he suggested, were created with comparatively few needs, but needs multiplied with the development of civilization. "Man is born with needs, and he creates needs for himself . . . but in proportion as life's pleasures have become more numerous, they have become habits. These in turn have finally become almost as necessary as life itself."[96] As these needs proliferate and as what used to be "superfluities" (a word dear to Fénelon) become necessities, people succeed in fastening their chains with their pleasures. So sensitive was Tocqueville to the seductive power of pleasures and comforts that he *advocated* the conscious proliferation of material pleasures as a means of bringing the Cabyles of Algeria into submission. The French must engender an *envie*, he said, quelling the rebelliousness of the Cabyles and capturing them by their desires. "The great passion of the Cabyle is the love of material enjoyments, and it is by this that one can and one must seize him."[97] Individuals obsessed with the accumulation of wealth and pleasure both reinforce their isolation and powerlessness and become more willing to submit to any order that promises them the security of ownership. "Thus men are following two separate roads to servitude; the taste for their own well-being withholds them from taking a part in the government, and their love of that well-being forces them to closer and closer dependence upon those who govern."[98]

Abundance, Doubt, and Nihilism

In his notebooks from North America, Tocqueville made the following cryptic entry: "This commercial movement will for America still further delay the moment of *plenitude,* which is so much to be feared, and will put off the century of revolutions."[99] Why is the "moment of *plenitude*" to be feared? Once more Montesquieu can

---

95. Rousseau, *Eloisa,* 4: 116; Balzac, *A Harlot High and Low,* p. 191.

96. Drescher, ed., *Tocqueville and Beaumont on Social Reform,* pp. 9–10; see also p. 5.

97. Tocqueville, *Oeuvres* (M), vol. 3, *Écrits et discours politiques,* pp. 291, 146. (From *L'Algérie.*)

98. Tocqueville, *Democracy,* 2: 325.

99. Tocqueville, *Journey to America,* p. 249.

assist us. First, as we have seen, comfort isolates and adversity unites; when citizens create wealth slowly and laboriously, they must rely on each other, but when wealth is excessive, people tend to withdraw and confine themselves to enjoyment. As Montesquieu said, land that is too fertile destroys a republic, whereas the "barrenness of the earth renders men industrious, sober, inured to hardship, and fit for war," all while fostering republican institutions.[100] Second, plenitude, or abundant wealth, corrupts. Tocqueville was suggesting that Americans, for whom wealth was available in the nation's early decades only on condition of hard work, would for a while maintain an ethic of self-denial, self-discipline, frugality, morality, and moderation needed to extract this wealth from the continent. When wealth came easily and abundance dispersed throughout the population, then desires would proliferate uncontrollably, self-interest would surface as the predominant virtue, and the republic—which demands austerity—would vanish. As Montesquieu said, the spirit of commerce is compatible with democracy for a while, because "the spirit of commerce is naturally attended with that of frugality, economy, moderation, labor. . . ." The difficulty, he added, arises "when excessive wealth destroys the spirit of commerce," because then this abundance destroys the very ethic needed for a workable democracy.[101]

Last of all, the abundance brought by the productivity of the industrial world will increase both the goods and the desires for these goods, but along with this will come a sense of doubt and even nihilism. With the emergence of equality, and of course the new world of commerce and industry, people "are plunged" into "uncertainty," and they know "neither the extent of their duties, nor that of their rights."[102] Tocqueville thought that the anxiety and despair, discussed in chapters 1–4, emanated from the sense of isolation and powerlessness inherent in bourgeois society; but at the moment of abundance the anxiety would transform itself into serious doubt about any certain belief. Despotism, said Tocqueville, "confounds the notions of good and evil."[103] The obsession with material comforts would become a feeble substitute, always accompanied by anxiety, for what Tocqueville regarded as genuine human needs—participation in the control over one's world, a sense of purpose, membership in a community, and so forth. Thus we return to the first chapters of this book. Tocqueville answered that the anxiety of his generation sprang

100. Montesquieu, *The Spirit of the Laws*, XVIII, 4, 1: 273.
101. Ibid., V, 6, 1: 46.
102. Yale Tocqueville Collection, C.V.e., p. 4.
103. Yale Tocqueville Collection, C.V.b., Paquet No. 13, p. 30.

from a society that ignored genuine needs and tried to substitute spurious satisfactions. The argument was Pascal's.

> Nothing is so insufferable to man as to be completely at rest, without passions, without business, without diversion, without study. He then feels his nothingness, his forlornness, his insufficiency, his dependence, his weakness, his emptiness. There will immediately arise from the depth of his heart weariness, gloom, sadness, fretfulness, vexation, despair. . . . I have discovered that all the unhappiness of men arises from one single fact, that they cannot stay quietly in their own chamber.[104]

So disconcerting is this realization, Pascal said, that people spend (an apt verb) their time trying to banish it from their minds. "The only thing which consoles us for our miseries is diversion, and yet this is the greatest of our miseries."[105]

Similarly, Tocqueville argued that the isolation of individuals would bring a sense of insignificance, and with this would come indifference to all belief and then doubt about the validity of any belief whatsoever. "It was not only the isolation of minds that was to be dreaded, but their uncertainty and their indifference; each searching in his way for the truth, many were to arrive at doubt, and with doubt, the taste for material enjoyments, that taste so fatal to liberty and so dear to those who want to ravish men, penetrated naturally into these souls."[106] It is a circular argument, but still important. People obsessed with accumulating goods become anxious and restless, but people who are anxious and restless try to overcome anxiety by accumulating goods. Eventually disillusion, doubt, and uncertainty about *any* ideals set in, and people perceive themselves as mere consumers. Each "has so contemptible an opinion of himself that he thinks he is born only to indulge in vulgar pleasures. He willingly takes up with low desires without daring to embark on lofty enterprises, of which he scarcely dreams."[107] A despotism in which "the people may amuse itself, as long as it dreams only of amusing itself" and in which the people may "have pleasure, even if it has no happiness"[108] paints a desperate picture.

104. Pascal, *Pensées* (Br), 131, 139; see also Mesnard, *Pascal: His Life and Work*, pp. 188–89.

105. Pascal, *Pensées* (Br), 171, also 146.

106. Tocqueville, *Oeuvres* (B), vol. 9, *Études économiques, politiques*, p. 11.

107. Tocqueville, *Democracy*, 2: 262. Pierre Manent also notes Tocqueville's use of Pascal's ideas in describing the relation between the obsession with wealth and pervasive doubt. See his *Tocqueville et la nature de la démocratie* (Paris, 1982), pp. 82–91.

108. Yale Tocqueville Collection, C.V.c., Paquet No. 5, p. 14.

A World without a Future: A People Fastened to the Present

As we saw in chapter 10, people who are bereft of any historical purpose fasten themselves to the pleasures and interests of the present; as Balzac said, "Misers do not believe in a life hereafter: the present is everything for them. This throws a horrible light on the present day, when more than at any other time, money controls law, politics, and morals."[109] Societies without a future, Tocqueville said, "dissolve."[110] We saw several reasons for this; a sense of the future gives people a definition of themselves, a grand goal that affirms their political ideas and principles, a public interest that militates against self-interest and even hedonism. If people accepted Gobineau's fatalism, if they had no vision of the future at all, they might act like Boccaccio's Florentines who faced the plague and "think of nothing else but to sample all the possible pleasures before this inevitable end."[111] Members of an aristocracy who no longer believe in a religious future can degenerate into consumers of pleasure who "require sumptuous depravity and splendid corruption."[112] Whenever people close themselves off in their private homes, trying to be content with petty pleasures and comforts, the blame, according to Tocqueville, must descend upon the political world, for people who derive no sense of purpose from society at large will try to construct goals in their private lives. "When no opinions are looked upon as certain, men cling to the mere instincts and material interests of their position, which are naturally more tangible, definite, and permanent than any opinions in the world."[113]

People immersed in the consumption of goods and pleasures and tied to enjoyment of the present surrender all ability to build a future. As a result, Tocqueville thought that a free political order manages to inspire citizens with a love of the future, with a love of some goal that they might achieve.

> There exist more family ties than are supposed between political passions and religious passions. On both sides general goods, immaterial to a certain degree, are in sight; on both sides an ideal of society is pursued, a certain perfecting of the human species, the picture of which raises souls above contemplation of private interests and carries them

109. Balzac, *Père Goriot* and *Eugénie Grandet*, p. 381.
110. Tocqueville, *Oeuvres* (M), vol. 3, *Écrits et discours politiques*, p. 120. (From *Abolition de l'esclavage*.)
111. Tocqueville, *The European Revolution and Correspondence with Gobineau*, p. 292.
112. Tocqueville, *Democracy*, 2: 139.
113. Ibid., 1: 197; see also *Oeuvres* (M), vol. 11, *Correspondance . . . Royer-Collard . . . Ampère*, p. 112.

away. For my part, I more easily understand a man animated at the same time [by both] religious passion and political passion than [by] political passion and the passion for well-being, for example. The first two can hold together and be embraced in the same soul, but not the second two.114

Tocqueville thought that religion was extremely important in forcing one's gaze on the future, often enabling a person to act with principle and even nobility. This is just one more reason he thought that doubt and disbelief were so useful to despotism; once religious faith declines, people "lapse into that complete and brutal indifference to futurity" and "seek to gratify without delay their smallest desires." The new despotism, however, will welcome subjects who give no thought to the future and have no wish for political movements that will disturb the present.

> Amid the ruins which surround me shall I dare to say that revolutions are not what I most fear for coming generations? . . . I dread, and I confess it, lest they should at last so entirely give way to a cowardly love of present enjoyment as to lose sight of the interests of their future selves and those of their descendants and prefer to glide along the easy current of life rather than to make, when it is necessary, a strong and sudden effort to a higher purpose.115

In his notes, we find a passage that Tocqueville eventually decided not to use and crossed out, but it illustrates his distaste of a world out of touch with its past and indifferent to its future. "For the American, the past is in some way like the future: it does not exist."116

At bottom Tocqueville's fear of a new despotism was a rejuvenated, even if far more elaborate and analytical, expression of the ancient conviction that luxury induces decadence and destroys popular government. As Montesquieu said, "with possessions beyond the needs of private life it was difficult to be a good citizen."117 Montesquieu was in fact restating the maxim of many of the great Roman historians that "the less luxury there is in a republic, the more it is perfect"—a maxim that led to the belief that the early Roman Republic multiplied its strength with its poverty, while Carthage dissi-

114. Tocqueville, *Selected Letters*, p. 192.
115. Tocqueville, *Democracy*, 2: 158–59, 277.
116. Yale Tocqueville Collection, C.V.h., Paquet No. 3, Cahier No. 2, p. 47.
117. Montesquieu, *Considerations on the Causes of the Greatness of the Romans and Their Decline*, p. 98.

pated its virtues with its opulence.[118] But from monarchists like Fénelon to radicals like Rousseau, Montesquieu was only one among many of Tocqueville's French predecessors who held this view.[119] Diderot, for example, gave an ironic warning to the fledgling United States that it must "prevent the enormous increase and unequal distribution of wealth and luxury" and "bear in mind that it is neither gold, nor even by the multitude of arms, that a state is upheld, but by morals."[120]

In fact, until the end of the eighteenth century, few in the French tradition questioned the belief that republican government rested on a foundation of public virtue that scorned luxury. Conservatives followed Bossuet and Fénelon in asserting as much, and everyone in eighteenth-century France who might merit being called a political radical—for example, d'Argenson, Meslier, Mably, and Morelly—insisted on republican virtue and an end to luxury. Only with thinkers like Condorcet—who belittled asceticism, lauded the productive power of the commercial classes, and promised "each successive generation will have larger possessions"—did this axiom about republican government vanish.[121] In the nineteenth century both liberals such as Guizot and Constant, who enjoyed their position in the new commercial world, and radicals such as Saint-Simon, Comte, and Marx, who sought to harness the new productive powers of industry to an historical carriage that would transport working people to a new age, discarded this time-honored critique of luxury—a critique that rapidly became an oddity of earlier times.

Tocqueville, however, still had one foot in the past and was too fond of his French mentors. Although he certainly never advocated an ascetic, subsistence-level existence, he did warn that the unchecked luxury that seemed to be the inseparable companion of bourgeois society might very well bring a new despotism rather than a golden age. The very prosperity that accompanied bourgeois society might, in Tocqueville's opinion, give birth to the conditions that make this

118. Montesquieu, *The Spirit of the Laws*, VII, 2, 1: 96; *Considerations on the Causes of the Greatness of the Romans and Their Decline*, p. 45. Lamberti notes the passages in which Montesquieu praised commerce, but he fails to see how Montesquieu was frequently critical of its political and moral effects. He does point out how Tocqueville feared the deleterious effects of commerce and of an obsessive love of material well-being. See Lamberti, *Tocqueville et les deux démocraties*, pp. 237–38.

119. Fénelon, *The Adventures of Telemachus*, pp. 368–69; Rousseau, *The Government of Poland*, p. 18.

120. Quoted in Crocker, *The Embattled Philosopher*, pp. 399–400.

121. Condorcet, *Sketch for a Historical Picture of the Progress of the Human Mind*, pp. 180–81, 32, 130, 187–88.

new despotism possible, like a plant whose flowering moment also signals its demise. "One must take care," wrote Tocqueville, "not to confuse political liberty with certain effects it sometimes produces." Political liberty leads to prosperity, but prosperity leads to "the taste for material well-being" and to a "passion for making fortunes"; these in turn threaten to "extinguish" the very political liberty that gave them birth.[122]

122. Tocqueville, *Oeuvres* (M), vol. 13, pt. 2, *Correspondance . . . Kergorlay,* p. 211.

Conclusion

Consider the characteristics Tocqueville gave to the new despotism that he feared: (1) equality of condition, (2) isolation resulting from a collapse of community and tradition, (3) powerlessness, (4) an ethic of self-interest, (5) obsession with accumulating wealth, (6) apathy, or indifference to political participation, (7) centralization of government, (8) uncertain faith or belief in ideals, and (9) no sense of either past or future. As we saw in chapters 1–5, he and his contemporaries shared an anxiety about exactly these characteristics of the emerging industrial world.

A PHILOSOPHY OF AMBIVALENCE

Tocqueville did not predict that this new despotism was inescapable, but rather he suggested it was merely one possibility. He remained fundamentally ambivalent, tossed between his hopes and his fears, unable either to have confidence in human ability to secure political freedom or to embrace entirely the occasional pessimism of his own analysis. On the one hand, Tocqueville attacked any fatalism that condemned Europe to inevitable decline; for example, he detested Gobineau's racial theories for reinforcing French feelings of powerlessness, because a determined France, he said, could certainly have some control over its destiny.[1] One finds, sprinkled throughout

1. Tocqueville, *Selected Letters*, pp. 302–5.

his writings, bursts of confidence and exhortations about the future possibilities of democracy. In one passage he announced that we must "strive to work out that species of greatness and happiness which is our own," and elsewhere he suggested that new generations with the energy of new ideals might push democracy in the correct directions. "Let it not be said that it is too late to make the experiment; for nations do not grow old as men do, and every fresh generation is a new people." At times he even maintained that, whatever its difficulties, democracy might naturally produce the cure for its ills. "I admire [equality] because it lodges in the very depths of each man's mind and heart that indefinable feeling, the instinctive inclination for political independence, and thus prepares the remedy for the ill it engenders."[2]

This cautious optimism formed perhaps the central reason he wrote *Democracy in America*—to instruct European leaders as to how they might avoid the "evils" of democracy while taking advantage of the "benefits it may confer."[3] This in itself suggests confidence that Europeans might be able to act directly and consciously to protect freedom in the midst of a new and changing commercial society. Indeed, if we look at Part Two of this book, we can discover a number of suggestions Tocqueville might well make to political actors and legislators intent on checking a march toward despotism. First, fortify the judicial process and all constitutional protections for individual freedom. Second, broadly decentralize and disperse power, beginning with the power concentrated in both government and industry. Third, combat isolation by devising ways of bringing citizens together on a regular basis in associations and communities. Fourth, educate people; for Tocqueville this would mean acquainting people with a rich cultural heritage from which they would learn freedom of thought and personal discipline of desires as well as the habits of political participation. Fifth, ensure that neither the government nor a single class monopolizes access to ideas and information and that a sharp competition of political perspectives is fostered in each community. Sixth, strengthen religious conviction. Seventh, establish a national purpose—a reinvigoration of democracy, a war on poverty— that will give citizens some goal for the future beyond an increasingly materialistic standard of living. Eighth, address the real needs of citizens to help them overcome a sense of powerlessness, loneliness, and purposelessness.

2. Tocqueville, *Democracy*, 2: 352, 1: 97, 2: 305.
3. Ibid., 1: 8.

Such a list is easy to make and could extend much further. The point is simple; when Tocqueville was hopeful, he offered a wide range of concrete suggestions for reform, and he refused to surrender to anyone's fatalism, even his own. On the other hand, if Tocqueville escaped fatalism, he did not escape a pessimism about reforms such as the ones listed above. Tocqueville's ambivalence about the future arose, in part, not because he lacked ideas but because he could find neither groups nor political movements with tangible interests and opportunities to initiate these reforms. Had he known Marx's writings, he would have envied Marx for finding a historical hero in the working class, a class that would feel an "unembellishable need" to transform the world. Put simply, Tocqueville wanted to go from point A to point B, but he could find no means of transportation. Time and again his analysis of the problems of democracy is so persuasive that, in the reader's eyes, it seems to leave all optimism unwarranted. Consider three examples. First, against a detailed analysis of all the forces contributing to centralization of both political and economic power, he offers only the hope of voluntarily joining associations that would help disperse that power. Second, against a careful examination of the reasons the modern world will become obsessed with acquiring goods and pleasures, he merely warns us that the accumulation of goods should not have such a central place in the life of the nation. Finally, after analyzing the reasons for indifference, apathy, and withdrawal, he tells us that all political transformations demand great political passions and commitment. "After all, gentlemen, there is but one real secret to making men do great things—by appealing to great feelings."[4]

Over and over, his penetrating but pessimistic analysis seems to outrun even his mild optimism. What, we want to ask, can possibly push an apathetic people into effective associations? How can a nation so enamored with accumulating wealth heed the warnings about the dangers of this practice? Tocqueville knew that his proposed reforms frequently remained empty exhortations, because he could point to no possible group or class or political movement to take him from point A to point B. He must have felt very much like Weber looking for a political party that might combat bureaucracy, finally arguing that all successful political parties become bureaucratized. Tocqueville leaves his readers not simply with pessimism but with ambivalence. His suggested reforms are too widespread to allow for a complete pessimism, but his pessimism is too well-argued to allow for

4. Drescher, ed., *Tocqueville and Beaumont on Social Reform*, p. 184.

complete belief in his suggestions. Tocqueville had no wish to offer the hope of an ideal world, and indeed, he asserted that a yearning for such a world was simply the result of the hopes and wishes of individual men and women in their powerlessness. To Mill he wrote, "You know that I am not exaggerating the final result of the great Democratic Revolution that is taking place at this moment in the world; I do not regard it in the same light as the Israelites saw the Promised Land. But, on the whole, I believe it to be useful and necessary, and I work toward it resolutely. . . ."[5] In fact, he wanted a politics of pessimism, but one that took realistic advantage of the limited possibilities of action, not one that paralyzed action. He offered a politics for those willing to see both the potential for great danger in the future and only limited possibilities for improvement.

Tocqueville offers ambivalence and uncertainty because, he thought, that is what the political world has always offered. In his conception of the world, one can uncover none of the classical harmony of Plato or the modern harmony of Marx, both of whom assumed that the good things of this world—happiness, justice, freedom, peace, excellence, creativity—are ultimately compatible. Tocqueville had no such confidence. For example, he argued that democracy, by dispersing happiness and security to greater numbers, might in fact contribute to justice but not to excellence, grandeur, or art. Similarly, people rightly abhor war as the greatest of all evils, but it engenders noble virtues and sacrifices; people cherish peace, but it lulls nations to sleep preparing the way for servitude; abundance can generate despotism, poverty can nourish nobility; order can destroy freedom, turmoil can enhance it; passions for material goods and pleasures can weaken freedom, but people without passions cannot defend it; freedom promotes prosperity, but prosperity can kill freedom; happy people are often servile, but free men and women are often anxious. In short, Tocqueville refused to offer a philosophy of fatalism that might give anyone an excuse to avoid choice and political participation, yet he also refused to offer another nineteenth-century panorama of progress that might give reassurance and consolation.

THE STRANGE LIBERALISM OF ALEXIS DE TOCQUEVILLE

Although Tocqueville gives us neither convenient excuse nor soothing consolation, he does offer us his insight and analysis into

5. Tocqueville, *Selected Letters*, p. 102.

many of the political problems facing the new commercial world; if his political questions arise from the concerns of his generation, his answers and analysis of these questions set him apart. One must be content, however, to read Tocqueville for his deep understanding and astute analysis, for he offers no easily adaptable solutions.

Perhaps the richness of Tocqueville's work is related directly to the fact that his political thought frustrates all attempts to categorize it. On the one hand, so many can claim Tocqueville as an ally, because he has something to offer everyone, and his readers can find in his writings whatever they wish to find. On the other hand, Tocqueville's ideas are exciting and full of insight, precisely because he defies classification. As was said in the Introduction, Tocqueville was reacting to familiar problems, even our own problems, since they are a product of this new industrial, urban world, but he was responding without our categories of political thought. His categories were mainly those of Montesquieu, Rousseau, Chateaubriand, and Guizot, although to a lesser extent he borrowed from classical thinking. He speaks to us and to our problems, but not with our language and not with our vocabulary; this is precisely what makes him such an enticing and original thinker.

If pressed, I would classify Tocqueville as a liberal, although such labels help us little to understand him. Clearly he feared concentrations of political power, and he borrowed from the liberal tradition to defend aggressively the rights of individuals vis-à-vis the state. In addition, he upheld the right to property, echoed Montesquieu's admiration for a legal and judiciary system that would defend the individual, advocated limited and constitutional government, and argued for such traditionally liberal rights as free speech, trial by jury, and the right to form groups or associations.

And yet Tocqueville was a liberal who was an aristocrat by birth and by taste, a democrat by political conviction, and thus deeply disenchanted with the age of liberalism. He was a liberal who worried about the collapse of traditional, even paternal, ties among people—a worry shared not nearly so much by the liberals of his time as by radicals such as Fourier and Comte and by reactionaries such as Bonald and de Maistre. He was a liberal who spoke, not like Locke but instead like Rousseau, of one attaining individuality from within a political community, by means of participation and even cooperation. He was a liberal who, like conservatives such as Chateaubriand and Balzac, harbored a deep distaste for the middle classes, commerce, and industry. He was a liberal who objected, as did Marx nearly a decade later, to certain miseries of the new industrial world, especially to the crippling effects of the stultifying division of labor. He was a liberal who despised a politics founded on self-interest, preferring to talk of Roman virtue, as described to him by Montesquieu and Rousseau, or national—even military—glory, showing his debt both to the new age of empire and to his ancestral nobility. He was a liberal who regarded the preoccupation with prosperity as a disturbingly petty endeavor, and thus he occasionally longed for a turmoil that might bring political greatness, an idea that betrays his admiration for the ancient French nobility, the French Revolution, and even Napoleon. He was a liberal who, plagued by his own doubts, borrowed from French royalist thinkers such as Bossuet and Fénelon to argue for the usefulness of religion in producing self-discipline and self-control; he even wondered whether God might not be working His will through history. He was a liberal who, unlike the liberal Madison and more like the conservative Burke, had comparatively little confidence in the effectiveness of laws, but much more confidence in habits, customs, and mores. He was a liberal who bemoaned the propensity to focus on the gratifications of the present, preferring instead, like Burke, to look to the past, and, like Saint-Simon, to imagine the future. Finally, he was a liberal who worried that perhaps the very ethic of liberalism might form the foundation for a new and dangerous despotism.

Such characteristics indeed make for a strange liberalism; in reality, we can feel free in calling Tocqueville a liberal only if we see in his thought a strange mixture of the "liberalism" of Constant, the "conservatism" of Chateaubriand, and the radical, "democratic" thought of Rousseau. But this only makes our encounter with Tocqueville more exciting, because through him we see our own world anew, with fresh eyes.

Bibliography

PRIMARY SOURCES

Available English Translations

Where possible, I have used primary sources available in English translation. These include the following:

Correspondence and Conversations of Alexis de Tocqueville with Nassau William Senior, From 1834 to 1859. Ed. M.C.M. Simpson. 2 vols. in one, 2d ed. New York: Augustus M. Kelley, 1968. (Reprint of 1872 ed.)

Democracy in America. Ed. Phillips Bradley. Trans. Henry Reeve, Francis Bowen, and Phillips Bradley. 2 vols. New York: Vintage Books (Alfred A. Knopf, Inc., 1945).

The European Revolution and Correspondence with Gobineau. Trans. and ed. John Lukacs. Gloucester, Mass.: Peter Smith, 1968.

Journey to America. Ed. J. P. Mayer. Trans. George Lawrence. Rev. ed. in collaboration with A. P. Kerr. Garden City, N.Y.: Doubleday, 1971.

Journeys to England and Ireland. Ed. J. P. Mayer. Trans. George Lawrence and K. P. Mayer. Garden City, N.Y.: Doubleday, 1968.

Memoir, Letters, and Remains. No. trans. given. 2 vols. Boston: Ticknor and Fields, 1862. The first volume includes Beaumont's *Memoir* and Tocqueville's article "France before the Revolution," trans. John Stuart Mill. When this article first appeared in the *London and Westminster Review* in April 1836, it was titled "Political and Social Condition of France." (These two volumes are a translation of *Oeuvres et correspondance inédites*, ed. Gustave de Beaumont. Paris: Michel Lévy Frères, 1861. Eventually they were included as Volumes 5 and 6 in *Oeuvres complètes d'Alexis de Tocqueville*, ed. Gustave de Beaumont. Paris: Michel Lévy Frères, 1860–66. This edition of Tocqueville's works is discussed below.)

The Old Regime and the French Revolution. Trans. Stuart Gilbert. Garden City, N.Y.: Doubleday, 1955.

On the Penitentiary System in the United States and Its Application in France. Written with Gustave de Beaumont. Trans. Francis Lieber. New York: Augustus M. Kelley, 1970.

Recollections. Ed. J. P. Mayer and A. P. Kerr. Trans. George Lawrence. Garden City, N.Y.: Doubleday, 1971.

"Report Given Before the Academy of Moral and Political Sciences on January 15, 1848, On the Subject of M. Cherbuliez' Book Entitled *On Democracy in Switzerland.*" Appendix 2 to Tocqueville's *Democracy in America.* Ed. J. P. Mayer. Trans. George Lawrence. Garden City, N.Y.: Doubleday, 1969.

Selected Letters on Politics and Society. Ed. Roger Boesche. Trans. James Toupin and Roger Boesche. Berkeley: University of California Press, 1985.

"Speech Pronounced in the Chamber of Deputies on January 27, 1848, During the Proposed Answer to the Speech from the Throne." Appendix 3 to Tocqueville's *Democracy in America.* Ed. J. P. Mayer. Trans. George Lawrence. Garden City, N.Y.: Doubleday, 1969.

Tocqueville and Beaumont on Social Reform. Essays selected, ed. and trans. Seymour Drescher. New York: Harper & Row, 1968.

The Beaumont Edition of Tocqueville's Complete Works

There are two editions of Tocqueville's "complete" works, neither of which is complete. The first was published by Madame de Tocqueville and edited by Gustave de Beaumont. 9 vols. (*Oeuvres complètes d'Alexis de Tocqueville.* Paris: Michel Lévy Frères, 1860–66.) Throughout the book, this edition has been referred to as *Oeuvres* (B). The first three volumes contained *De la démocratie en Amérique,* the fourth *L'Ancien Régime et la Révolution,* and the fifth and sixth contained letters that are available in the English translation listed previously. I have used volumes 7, 8, and 9, as listed below:

7. *Nouvelle correspondance entièrement inédite d'Alexis de Tocqueville* (1866).
8. *Mélanges, fragments historiques et notes sur l'Ancien Régime, la Révolution et l'Empire: voyages, pensées entièrement inédits* (1865).
9. *Études économiques, politiques, et littéraires* (1866).

The Mayer Edition of Tocqueville's Complete Works

The second edition of Tocqueville's "complete" works is in the process of publication under the general direction of J. P. Mayer (*Oeuvres complètes.* Paris: Gallimard, 1951–   .) Throughout the book, this edition has been referred to as *Oeuvres* (M). The first volume contains *De la démocratie en Amérique,* and the second volume contains *L'Ancien Régime et la Révolution,* as well as notes about the French Revolution and the First Empire. The twelfth volume contains Tocqueville's *Souvenirs.* For all of these, I have used available English translations, as indicated above. In this book, I have referred to the volumes listed below, all of the volumes—other than Volumes 1, 2, and 12—published to date.

3. *Écrits et discours politiques* (1962), ed. André Jardin. (This includes works under the subheadings of *Abolition de l'esclavage, L'Algérie,* and *L'Inde;* references in the text have included these subheadings, where appropriate.)

5, pt. 1. *Voyages en Sicile et aux États-Unis* (1957), ed. J. P. Mayer.

5, pt. 2. *Voyages en Angleterre, Irlande, Suisse et Algérie* (1958), ed. J. P. Mayer and André Jardin.

6, pt. 1. *Correspondance anglaise: Correspondance d'Alexis de Tocqueville avec Henry Reeve et John Stuart Mill* (1954), ed. J. P. Mayer and Gustave Rundler.

8, 3 pts. *Correspondance d'Alexis de Tocqueville et de Gustave de Beaumont* (1967), ed. André Jardin.

9. *Correspondance d'Alexis de Tocqueville et d'Arthur de Gobineau* (1959), ed. M. Degros.

11. *Correspondance d'Alexis de Tocqueville et de Pierre-Paul Royer-Collard: Correspondance d'Alexis de Tocqueville et de Jean-Jacques Ampère* (1970), ed. André Jardin.

13, 2 pts. *Correspondance d'Alexis de Tocqueville et de Louis de Kergorlay* (1977), ed. André Jardin.

15, 2 pts. *Correspondance d'Alexis de Tocqueville et de Francisque de Corcelle et correspondance d'Alexis de Tocqueville et de Madame Swetchine* (1983), ed. Pierre Gibert.

18. *Correspondance d'Alexis de Tocqueville avec Adolph de Circourt et avec Madame de Circourt* (1983), ed. A. P. Kerr.

Unpublished Sources

Over the last several decades, Yale University has acquired large numbers of manuscripts, notes, and letters relating to Tocqueville's journey to North America. These are available to scholars in the Beinecke Rare Book and Manuscript Library at Yale. In footnotes, I have referred to this material as "Yale Tocqueville Collection."

Miscellaneous Primary Sources

Alexis de Tocqueville als Abgeordneter: Briefe an Seinen Wahlagenten Paul Clamorgan, 1837–1851. Hamburg: Ernst Hauswedell, 1972.

"The Art and Science of Politics," *Encounter* 36 (January 1971): 27–35.

"How Democracy Influences Preaching: A Previously Unpublished Fragment From Tocqueville's *Democracy in America,*" James T. Schleifer, *The Yale University Library Gazette* 52, no. 2 (October 1977): 75–79.

Letters in Richmond Laurin Hawkins, ed., *Newly Discovered French Letters of the Seventeenth, Eighteenth, and Nineteenth Centuries.* Cambridge, Mass.: Harvard University Press, 1933. (Reprinted by Kraus Reprint Corporation, New York, 1966.)

Letters in *The Romanic Review* 19 (1928) and 20 (1929).

"Tocqueville and American Literature: A Newly Acquired Letter," James T.

Schleifer, *The Yale University Library Gazette* 54, no. 3 (January 1980): 129–34.

"Tocqueville and Centralization: Four Previously Unpublished Manuscripts," James T. Schleifer, *The Yale University Library Gazette*, 58, nos. 1–2 (October 1983): 29–39.

RELATED PRIMARY AND SECONDARY SOURCES

Adams, Herbert B. *Jared Sparks and Alexis de Tocqueville.* Johns Hopkins Studies in Historical and Political Science. Series 16, no. 12. Baltimore: Johns Hopkins Press, 1898.

D'Alembert, Jean Le Rond. *Preliminary Discourse to the Encyclopedia of Diderot.* Trans. Richard N. Schwab and Walter E. Rex. New York: Bobbs-Merrill, 1963.

Alexis de Tocqueville: Livre du centenaire, 1859–1959. Paris: Éditions du Centre national de la recherche scientifique, 1960.

Arendt, Hannah. *The Origins of Totalitarianism.* 2d rev. ed. New York: World, 1958.

Aristotle. *The Basic Works of Aristotle.* Ed. Richard McKeon. New York: Random House, 1941.

Aron, Raymond. "La Définition libérale de la liberté, II: Alexis de Tocqueville et Karl Marx." *Archives européennes de sociologie* 5, no. 2 (1964): 159–89.

————. *Main Currents in Sociological Thought*, Vol. 1, *Montesquieu, Comte, Marx, Tocqueville*, and *The Sociologists and the Revolution of 1848.* Trans. Richard Howard and Helen Weaver. Garden City, N.Y.: Doubleday, 1968.

Artz, Frederick B. *Reaction and Revolution, 1814–1832.* New York: Harper & Row, 1934.

Arvin, Neil Cole. *Eugene Scribe and the French Theatre, 1815–1860.* Cambridge, Mass.: Harvard University Press, 1924.

Balzac, Honoré de. *Cousin Bette.* Trans. Marion Ayton Crawford. Baltimore: Penguin, 1965.

————. *Cousin Pons.* Trans. Herbert J. Hunt. Baltimore: Penguin, 1968.

————. *A Harlot High and Low.* Trans. Rayner Heppenstall. Baltimore: Penguin, 1970.

————. *Lost Illusions.* Trans. Herbert J. Hunt. Baltimore: Penguin, 1971.

————. *A Murky Business.* Trans. Herbert J. Hunt. Baltimore: Penguin, 1972.

————. *Père Goriot* and *Eugénie Grandet.* Trans. E. K. Brown, Dorothea Walter, and John Watkins. New York: Modern Library, 1950.

Barzun, Jacques. *Berlioz and His Century: An Introduction to the Age of Romanticism.* New York: Meridian, 1956.

Baudelaire, Charles. *Flowers of Evil: A Selection.* Trans. Jackson Mathews et al. Ed. Marthiel Mathews and Jackson Mathews. New York: New Directions, 1955.

————. *Selected Writings on Art and Artists.* Trans. P. E. Charvet. Baltimore: Penguin, 1972.

Bayle, Francis. *Les Idées politiques de Joseph de Maistre.* Montchrestien: Éditions Domat, 1945.

Beaumont, Gustave de. *Ireland: Social, Political, and Religious.* No trans. given. 2 vols. London: n.p., 1839.

————. *Marie, or Slavery in the United States.* Trans. Barbara Chapman. Stanford: Stanford University Press, 1958.

Becker, Carl. *The Heavenly City of the Eighteenth-Century Philosophers.* New Haven: Yale University Press, 1932.

Bendix, Reinhard. *Nation-Building and Citizenship.* Garden City, N.Y.: Doubleday, 1969.

Benjamin, Walter. *Charles Baudelaire: A Lyric Poet in the Era of High Capitalism.* No trans. given. London: n.p., 1973.

————. *Illuminations.* Ed. Hannah Arendt. Trans. Harry Zohn. New York: Schocken, 1969.

Biddiss, Michael D. "Prophecy and Pragmatism: Gobineau's Confrontation with Tocqueville." *The Historical Journal* 13 (December 1970): 611–33.

Bird, C. Wesley. *Alfred de Vigny's Chatterton: A Contribution to the Study of Its Genesis and Sources.* Los Angeles: Lyman House, 1941.

Bloch, Marc. *Feudal Society.* Trans. L. A. Manyon. 2 vols. Chicago: University of Chicago Press, 1961.

Bodin, Jean. *Method for the Easy Comprehension of History.* Ed. and trans. Beatrice Reynolds. New York: Norton, 1969.

————. *Six Books of the Commonwealth.* Trans. and abridged by M. J. Tooley. New York: Barnes & Noble, 1967.

Boesche, Roger. "Hedonism and Nihilism: The Predictions of Tocqueville and Nietzsche." *The Tocqueville Review,* forthcoming 1987.

————. "The Prison: Tocqueville's Model for Despotism." *Western Political Quarterly* 33 (December 1980): 550–63.

————. "The Strange Liberalism of Alexis de Tocqueville." *History of Political Thought* 2 (Winter 1981): 495–524.

————. "Tocqueville and *Le Commerce:* A Newspaper Expressing His Unusual Liberalism." *Journal of the History of Ideas* 44 (April–June 1983): 277–92.

————. "Why Could Tocqueville Predict So Well?" *Political Theory* 11 (February 1983): 79–104.

Bonald, Louis Gabriel Ambroise, Vicomte de. *Oeuvres complètes,* Vol. 2, *Économie sociale et oeuvres politiques.* Migne: n.p., 1859.

Bossuet, Abbé. *Extraits des oeuvres diverses.* Paris: Librairie Ch. Delagrave, 1899.

Boulanger, N. A. *Oeuvres,* Vol. 3, *Recherches sur l'origine du despotisme.* Geneva: Skatkine Reprints, 1971. (Réimpression de l'Édition d'Amsterdam, 1794.)

Bradley, Phillips. "A Historical Essay." Appendix 2 in Tocqueville's *Democracy in America.* Ed. Phillips Bradley. Trans. Henry Reeve, Francis Bowen, and Phillips Bradley. 2 vols. New York: Vintage Books, Knopf, 1945.

Brandes, Georg. *Revolution and Reaction in Nineteenth Century French Literature.* New York: Russell & Russell, n.d.

Brereton, Geoffrey. *An Introduction to the French Poets: Villon to the Present Day.* London: Methuen, 1957.

Brogan, Hugh. "Alexis de Tocqueville and the Liberal Moment." *The Historical Journal* 14 (June 1971): 289–303.

————. *Tocqueville*. London: Fontana, 1973.

Brombert, Victor. *The Novels of Flaubert*. Princeton: Princeton University Press, 1966.

————. *Stendhal: Fiction and the Themes of Freedom*. New York: Random House, 1968.

————, ed. *Stendhal*. Englewood Cliffs, N.J.: Prentice-Hall, 1962.

Bryce, James. *The Predictions of Hamilton and de Tocqueville*. Selections printed in William Ebenstein, ed., *Political Thought in Perspective*. New York: McGraw-Hill, 1957.

Carlyle, Thomas. *Selected Writings*. Ed. Alan Shelston. Baltimore: Penguin, 1971.

Cassirer, Ernst. *The Philosophy of the Enlightenment*. Trans. Fritz C. A. Koelln and James P. Pettegrove. Boston: Beacon, 1955.

————. *The Question of Jean-Jacques Rousseau*. Trans. Peter Gay. Bloomington: Indiana University Press, 1963.

Ceaser, James. "Alexis de Tocqueville on Political Science, Political Culture, and the Role of the Intellectual." *American Political Science Review* 79 (September 1985): 656–72.

Chateaubriand, François-René de. *Atala* and *René*. Trans. Walter J. Cobb. New York: Signet Books, 1962.

————. *The Memoirs of Chateaubriand*. Ed. and trans. Robert Baldick. New York: Knopf, 1961.

Clapham, J. H. *The Economic Development of France and Germany, 1815–1914*. 4th ed. Cambridge: Cambridge University Press, 1936.

Clark, Barrett H., ed. *European Theories of the Drama*. Rev. ed. New York: Crown, 1947.

Clark, Robert T., Jr. *Herder: His Life and Thought*. Berkeley: University of California Press, 1955.

Clement, N. H. *Romanticism in France*. New York: Modern Language Association of America, 1939.

Cobban, Alfred. *A History of Modern France*, Vol. 2, *From the First Empire to the Second Empire, 1799–1871*. 2d ed. Baltimore: Penguin, 1965.

Collins, Irene. *The Government and the Newspaper Press in France, 1814–1881*. Oxford: Oxford University Press, 1959.

Comte, Auguste. *A General View of Positivism*. Trans. J. H. Bridges. Stanford, Calif.: Academic Reprints, n.d.

Conder, Alan, ed. and trans. *A Treasury of French Poetry*. New York: Harper, n.d.

Condillac, E. B. de. *Treatise on the Sensations*. Trans. Geraldine Carr. Los Angeles: University of Southern California Press, 1930.

Condorcet, Antoine-Nicolas de. *Sketch for a Historical Picture of the Progress of the Human Mind*. Trans. June Barraclough. London: Weidenfeld & Nicolson, 1955.

Constant de Rebecque, Henri Benjamin. *Benjamin Constant: Choix de textes politiques*. Ed. Olivier Pozzo di Borgo. Paris: J. J. Pauvert, 1965.

Craig, Gordon A. *Europe, 1815–1914*. 2d ed. New York: Holt, Rinehart & Winston, 1966.

Crocker, Lester G. *The Embattled Philosopher: A Biography of Denis Diderot*. [East Lansing, Mich.]: Michigan State College Press, 1954.

Delacroix, Eugène. *The Journal of Eugène Delacroix.* Trans. Walter Pach. New York: Viking, 1972.

Denommé, Robert T. *Nineteenth Century French Romantic Poets.* Carbondale, Ill.: Southern Illinois University Press, 1969.

Diderot, Denis. *Rameau's Nephew and Other Works.* Trans. Jacques Barzun and Ralph H. Bowen. New York: Bobbs-Merrill, 1964.

Dishman, Robert B., ed. *Burke and Paine on Revolution and the Rights of Man.* New York: Scribner's, 1971.

Doolittle, Dorothy. "The Relations between Literature and Mediaeval Studies in France From 1820 to 1860." Ph.D. dissertation, Bryn Mawr College, 1933.

Draper, Frederick William Marsden. *The Rise and Fall of the French Romantic Drama.* London: Constable, 1923.

Drescher, Seymour. *Dilemmas of Democracy: Tocqueville and Modernization.* Pittsburgh: University of Pittsburgh Press, 1968.

———. *Tocqueville and England.* Cambridge, Mass.: Harvard University Press, 1964.

Driver, C. H. "Morelly and Mably," pp. 217–52. In F.J.C. Hearnshaw, ed., *The Social and Political Ideas of Some Great French Thinkers in the Age of Reason.* New York: E. S. Crofts, 1930.

Durkheim, Emile. *Montesquieu and Rousseau: Forerunners of Sociology.* Trans. Ralph Manheim. Ann Arbor: University of Michigan Press, 1960.

———. *Socialism and Saint-Simon.* Ed. and introduced by Alvin W. Gouldner. Trans. Charlotte Sattler. Yellow Springs, Ohio: The Antioch Press, 1958.

Egbert, Donald D. *Social Radicalism and the Arts: Western Europe.* New York: Knopf, 1970.

D'Eichthal, Eugène. *Alexis de Tocqueville et la démocratie libérale.* Paris: Calmann Lévy, 1897.

Einstein, Alfred. *Music in the Romantic Era.* New York: Norton, 1947.

Eitner, Lorenz, ed. *Neoclassicism and Romanticism, 1750–1850.* Englewood Cliffs, N.J.: Prentice-Hall, 1970.

Elsen, Albert E. *Purposes of Art.* 2d ed. New York: Holt, Rinehart & Winston, 1967.

Evans, David Owen. *Social Romanticism in France, 1830–1848.* London: Clarendon, 1951.

Faguet, Emile. *Politicians and Moralists of the Nineteenth Century.* London: Ernest Benn, 1928.

Fénelon, Meffire François de Salignac de La Mothe. *The Adventures of Telemachus.* No trans. given. 3d ed. Dublin: n.p., 1777.

Fernier, Robert. *Gustave Courbet.* New York: Praeger, 1969.

Flaubert, Gustave. *Madame Bovary.* Trans. Francis Steegmuller. New York: Modern Library, 1957.

———. *Salambo.* Trans. E. Powys Mather. New York: Berkley Medallion Books, 1955.

———. *Sentimental Education.* Trans. Robert Baldick. Baltimore: Penguin, 1964.

Flint, Robert. *History of the Philosophy of History.* London: W. Blackwood, 1893.

Flores, Angel, ed. *An Anthology of French Poetry from Nerval to Valéry.* New rev. ed. Garden City, N.Y.: Doubleday, 1958.

Fourier, Charles. *Design for Utopia: Selected Writings of Charles Fourier.* Trans. Julia Franklin. New York: Schocken, 1971.

Friedlaender, Walter. *David to Delacroix.* Trans. Robert Goldwater. New York: Schocken, 1968.

Furet, François. *Interpreting the French Revolution.* Trans. Elborg Forster. London: Cambridge University Press, 1981.

Gargan, Edward T. *Alexis de Tocqueville: The Critical Years, 1848–1851.* Washington, D.C.: The Catholic University of America Press, 1955.

———. "The Formation of Tocqueville's Historical Thought." *Review of Politics* 24 (January 1962): 48–61.

———. "Reply to Wyndham Lewis." *The Sewanee Review* 55 (1947), supp.

———. "Some Problems in Tocqueville Scholarship." *Mid-America* 41 (January 1959): 3–26.

———. *De Tocqueville.* New York: Hillary House, 1965.

———. "Tocqueville and the Problem of Historical Prognosis." *American Historical Review* 68 (January 1963): 332–45.

Gassner, John, ed. *A Treasury of the Theatre.* Rev. ed. New Haven: Yale University Press, 1967.

Gay, Peter. *The Enlightenment: An Interpretation. The Rise of Modern Paganism.* New York: Vintage Books, Knopf, 1968.

———. *Voltaire's Politics: The Poet as Realist.* Princeton: Princeton University Press, 1959.

George, Albert Joseph. *The Development of French Romanticism: The Impact of the Industrial Revolution on Literature.* Syracuse: Syracuse University Press, 1955.

George, William Henry. "Montesquieu and de Tocqueville and Corporate Individualism." *American Political Science Review* 16 (February 1922): 10–21.

Gianturco, Elio. "Joseph de Maistre and Giambattista Vico." Ph.D. dissertation, Columbia University, 1937.

Gibert, Pierre. *Tocqueville, égalité sociale et liberté politique.* Paris: Aubier, Montaigne, 1977.

Gillies, Alexander. *Herder.* London: Basil Blackwell, 1945.

Giraud, Jean. *L'École romantique française: Les doctrines et les hommes.* Paris: Librairie Armand Colin, 1927.

Goethe, Johann Wolfgang von. *The Sorrows of Young Werther.* Trans. Victor Lange. New York: Holt, Rinehart & Winston, 1949.

Goldmann, Lucien. *The Hidden God.* Trans. Philip Thody. New York: Routledge & Kegan Paul, 1970.

Goldstein, Doris S. "The Religious Beliefs of Alexis de Tocqueville." *French Historical Studies* 1 (December 1960): 379–93.

———. *Trial of Faith: Religion and Politics in Tocqueville's Thought.* New York: Elsevier, 1975.

Gombrich, E. H. *The Story of Art.* 11th ed. rev. New York: Oxford University Press, 1966.

Gooch, G. P. *History and Historians in the Nineteenth Century.* New York: Longmans, Green, 1920.

Graña, César. *Bohemian versus Bourgeois: French Society and the French Man of Letters in the Nineteenth Century.* New York: Basic Books, 1964.

Grant, Elliott Mansfield. *French Poetry and Modern Industry, 1830–1870.* Cambridge, Mass.: Harvard University Press, 1927.

Guizot, François Pierre Guillaume. *The History of Civilization in Europe.* Trans. William Hazlitt. New York: A. L. Burt, n.d.

Halévy, Elie. *The Growth of Philosophic Radicalism.* Trans. Mary Morris. Boston: Beacon, 1955.

Hauser, Arnold. *The Social History of Art.* Trans. Stanley Godman in collaboration with the author. Vols. 3 and 4. New York: Vintage Books, Knopf, 1958.

Hazard, Paul. *The European Mind, 1680–1715.* Trans. J. Lewis May. London: Hollis & Carter, 1953.

Hearnshaw, F.J.C., ed. *The Social and Political Ideas of Some Great French Thinkers in the Age of Reason.* New York: E. S. Crofts, 1930.

Helvétius, Claude-Adrien. *De L'Esprit, or, Essays on the Mind and Its Several Faculties.* No trans. given. New ed. London: Albion Press, 1810.

Hemmings, F.W.J. *Culture and Society in France, 1848–1898: Dissidents and Philistines.* New York: Scribner's, 1971.

Herder, Johann Gottfried von. *Reflections on the Philosophy of the History of Mankind.* Ed., abridged, and introduced by Frank E. Manuel. Trans. T. O. Churchill. Chicago: University of Chicago Press, 1968.

Herr, Richard. *Tocqueville and the Old Regime.* Princeton: Princeton University Press, 1962.

Hobbes, Thomas. *Leviathan.* Oxford: Clarendon, 1909.

Hobsbawm, E. J. *The Age of Revolution, 1789–1848.* New York: Mentor, 1964.

Hodges, H. A. *The Philosophy of Wilhelm Dilthey.* London: Routledge & Kegan Paul, 1952.

Holbach, Paul Henry Thiry, Baron d'. *The System of Nature, or Laws of the Moral and Physical World.* Ed. and with notes by Denis Diderot. Trans. H. D. Robinson. Boston: J. P. Mendum, 1889.

Holt, Elizabeth Gilmore, ed. *A Documentary History of Art,* Vol. 3, *From the Classicists to the Impressionists.* Garden City, N.Y.: Doubleday, 1966.

Horowitz, Irving Louis. *Claude Helvétius: Philosopher of Democracy and Enlightenment.* New York: Paine-Whitman, 1954.

Horwitz, Morton J. "Tocqueville and the Tyranny of the Majority." *Review of Politics* 28 (July 1966): 293–307.

Hugo, Victor. *Les Misérables.* Trans. Charles E. Wilbour with assistance from Frederick Mynon Cooper. 2 vols. in one. New York: A. L. Burt, n.d.

Iggers, George G., ed. and trans. *The Doctrine of Saint-Simon.* New York: Schocken, 1972.

Jardin, André. *Alexis de Tocqueville, 1805–1859.* Paris: Hachette, 1984.

Johnson, Douglas. *Guizot: Aspects of French History, 1787–1874.* Toronto: University of Toronto Press, 1963.

Johnson, Lee. *Delacroix.* New York: Norton, 1963.

Jones, R. A. "Fénelon," pp. 70–103. In F.J.C. Hearnshaw ed., *The Social and Political Ideas of Some Great French Thinkers in the Age of Reason.* New York: E. S. Crofts, 1930.

Keohane, Nannerl O. *Philosophy and the State in France: The Renaissance to the Enlightenment.* Princeton: Princeton University Press, 1980.

Kirk, Russell. *The Conservative Mind, from Burke to Eliot.* 6th rev. ed. Chicago: Regnery/Gateway, 1978.

La Fournière, Xavier de. *Alexis de Tocqueville: Un monarchiste indépendant.* Paris: Librairie Académique Perrin, 1981.

Lamberti, Jean-Claude. *La Notion d'individualisme chez Tocqueville.* Paris: Presses Universitaires de France, 1970.

————. *Tocqueville et les deux démocraties.* Paris: Presses Universitaires de France, 1983.

Lamennais, F. *Paroles d'un croyant* et *Essai sur l'indifference en matière de religion.* Paris: Gillequin, 1912.

La Mettrie, Julien Offray de. *Man a Machine.* Trans. M. W. Calkins. La Salle, Ill.: Open Court, 1912.

Lang, Paul Henry. *Music in Western Civilization.* New York: Norton, 1941.

Langer, William L. *Political and Social Upheaval, 1832–1852.* New York: Harper & Row, 1969.

Larg, David Glass. *Madame de Staël: Her Life as Revealed in Her Work, 1766–1800.* Trans. Veronica Luca. New York: Knopf, 1926.

Larkin, Oliver. *Daumier: Man of His Time.* New York: McGraw-Hill, 1966.

Laski, Harold J. "Alexis de Tocqueville and Democracy," pp. 100–15. In F.J.C. Hearnshaw, ed., *The Social and Political Ideas of Some Representative Thinkers of the Victorian Age.* London: George Harrap, 1933.

————. *Authority in the Modern State.* New Haven: Yale University Press, 1919.

Lavedan, Pierre. *French Architecture.* London: Pelican Books, 1944.

Leberruyer, Pierre. *Dans l'intimité d'Alexis de Tocqueville.* Cherbourg: n.p., n.d.

Lefebvre, Georges. "A propos de Tocqueville." *Annales historiques de la révolution française* 27 (October–December 1955): 313–23.

————. *The Coming of the French Revolution.* Trans. R. R. Palmer. Princeton: Princeton University Press, 1947.

————. *The French Revolution,* Vol. 1, *From Its Origin to 1793.* Trans. Elizabeth Moss Evanson. New York: Columbia University Press, 1962.

————. *The French Revolution,* Vol. 2, *From 1793 to 1799.* Trans. Elizabeth Moss Evanson. New York: Columbia University Press, 1962.

Leichtentritt, Hugo. *Music, History, and Ideas.* Cambridge, Mass.: Harvard University Press, 1939.

Lerner, Max. "Tocqueville's *Democracy in America:* Politics, Law, and the Elite." *Antioch Review* 25 (Winter 1965–66): 543–63.

Leroy, Maxime. "Alexis de Tocqueville," pp. 472–500. In William Ebenstein, ed., *Political Thought in Perspective.* New York: McGraw-Hill, 1957.

————. *Histoire des idées sociales en France,* Vol. 1, *De Montesquieu à Robespierre.* Paris: Gallimard, 1946.

————. *Histoire des idées sociales en France,* Vol. 2, *De Babeuf à Tocqueville.* Paris: Gallimard, 1950.

Levin, Harry. *The Gates of Horn: A Study of Five French Realists.* New York: Oxford University Press, 1963.

Lewis, W. H. *The Splendid Century: Life in the France of Louis XIV.* Garden City, N.Y.: Doubleday, 1957.

Lewis, Wyndham. "De Tocqueville and Democracy." *The Sewanee Review* 54 (Autumn 1946): 557–75.

Lipset, Seymour Martin. *The First New Nation.* Garden City, N.Y.: Doubleday, 1967.

_____. *Political Man: The Social Bases of Politics.* Garden City, N.Y.: Doubleday, 1963.

Lively, Jack. *The Social and Political Thought of Alexis de Tocqueville.* Oxford: Clarendon, 1962.

Longyear, Rey M. *Nineteenth-Century Romanticism in Music.* Englewood Cliffs, N.J.: Prentice-Hall, 1969.

Löwith, Karl. *From Hegel to Nietzsche: The Revolution in Nineteenth-Century Thought.* Trans. David E. Green. Garden City, N.Y.: Doubleday, 1967.

Loy, J. Robert. *Montesquieu.* New York: Twayne, 1968.

Lucie-Smith, Edward. *A Concise History of French Painting.* New York: Praeger, 1971.

Lukács, Georg. *Studies in European Realism.* No trans. given. New York: Grosset & Dunlap, 1972.

Lukacs, John. "The Last Days of Alexis de Tocqueville." *Catholic Historical Review* 50 (July 1964): 155–70.

McGowan, Margaret M. *Montaigne's Deceits.* Philadelphia: Temple University Press, 1974.

Machiavelli, Niccolò. *The Prince* and *The Discourses.* Trans. Luigi Ricci and E.R.P. Vincent (*The Prince*), and Christian E. Detmold (*The Discourses*). New York: Modern Library, 1950.

Maistre, Joseph de. *On God and Society.* Ed. Elisha Greifer. Trans. Elisha Greifer and Laurence M. Porter. Chicago: Henry Regnery, 1959.

Manent, Pierre. *Tocqueville et la nature de la démocratie.* Paris: Julliard, 1982.

Manuel, Frank E. *The New World of Henri Saint-Simon.* Notre Dame, Ind.: University of Notre Dame Press, 1963.

_____. *The Prophets of Paris.* Cambridge, Mass.: Harvard University Press, 1962.

Marceau, Félicien. *Balzac et son monde.* Paris: Gallimard, 1955.

Markham, Felix. *Napoleon and the Awakening of Europe.* London: The English Universities Press, 1954.

Martin, Kingsley. *French Liberal Thought in the Eighteenth Century.* New York: Harper & Row, 1963.

Marx, Karl. *Class Struggles in France, 1848–1850.* No trans. given. New York: International Publishers, 1964.

_____. *The 18th Brumaire of Louis Bonaparte.* No trans. given. New York: International Publishers, 1963.

Matthews, Brander. *French Dramatists of the 19th Century.* 5th ed. New York: Scribner's, 1914.

Mayer, J. P. *Alexis de Tocqueville: A Biographical Study in Political Science.* Gloucester, Mass.: Peter Smith, 1966. (Originally published in 1939 under the title *The Prophet of the Mass Age.*)

_____. *Political Thought in France: From the Revolution to the Fifth Republic.* 3d rev. ed. London: Routledge & Kegan Paul, 1961.

Mellon, Stanley. *The Political Uses of History: A Study of Historians in the French Restoration.* Stanford: Stanford University Press, 1958.

Menczer, Béla, ed. *Catholic Political Thought, 1789–1848.* London: University of Notre Dame Press, 1962.

Mesnard, Jean. *Pascal.* Trans. Claude Abraham and Marcia Abraham. University: The University of Alabama Press, 1969.

———. *Pascal: His Life and Works.* Trans. G. S. Fraser. London: Harvill Press, 1952.

Michelet, Jules. *History of the French Revolution.* Trans. Charles Cocks. Ed. and introduced by Gordon Wright. Chicago: University of Chicago Press, 1967.

———. *Le Peuple.* In *Société des textes français modernes.* Paris: Librairie Marcel Didier, 1946.

Mill, John Stuart. "Democracy in America." *Edinburgh Review* 72 (October 1840): 1–48.

———. "De Tocqueville on Democracy in America." *London Review* 2 (October 1835): 85–129.

Montaigne, Michel de. *Essays.* Trans. and selected by J. M. Cohen. Baltimore: Penguin, 1958.

Montesquieu, Charles de Secondat, Baron de. *Considerations on the Causes of the Greatness of the Romans and Their Decline.* Trans. David Lowenthal. Ithaca: Cornell University Press, 1965.

———. *The Persian Letters.* Ed., trans., and introduced by J. Robert Loy. New York: World, 1961.

———. *The Spirit of the Laws.* Trans. Thomas Nugent. 2 vols. in one. New York: Hafner, 1949.

Moreau, Pierre. *Chateaubriand: Collection tels qu'en eux-mêmes.* Bordeaux: G. Ducros, 1969.

Moulinié, Henri. *De Bonald.* Paris: Librairie Félix Alcan, 1915.

Mras, George. *Eugene Delacroix's Theory of Art.* Princeton: Princeton University Press, 1966.

Musset, Alfred de. *Seven Plays.* Trans. Peter Meyer. New York: Hill & Wang, 1962.

Neff, Emery. *The Poetry of History.* New York: Columbia University Press, 1947.

Nerval, Gérard de. *Selected Writings of Gérard de Nerval.* Trans. and ed. Geoffrey Wagner. New York: Grove Press, 1957.

Nisbet, Robert. *Twilight of Authority.* New York: Oxford University Press, 1975.

Pascal, Blaise. *Pensées.* (Brunschvicg ed.) Trans. W. F. Trotter. Introduced by T. S. Eliot. New York: Dutton, 1958.

———. *The Pensées* and *The Provincial Letters.* Trans. Thomas M'Crie. New York: Modern Library, 1941.

Pevsner, Nikolaus. *An Outline of European Architecture.* Baltimore: Penguin, 1961.

Pierre-Marcel, R. *Essai politique sur Alexis de Tocqueville.* Paris: Librairie Félix Alcan, 1910.

Pierson, George Wilson. *Tocqueville and Beaumont in America.* New York: Oxford University Press, 1938.

Plutarch. *Lives of the Noble Greeks.* Trans. John Dryden and Arthur Hugh Clough. Selected and ed. Edmund Fuller. New York: Dell, 1968.

_____. *Lives of the Noble Romans.* Trans. John Dryden and Arthur Hugh Clough. Selected and ed. Edmund Fuller. New York: Dell, 1969.

Pocock, J.G.A. *The Machiavellian Moment.* Princeton: Princeton University Press, 1975.

Poggi, Gianfranco. *Images of Society: Essays on the Sociological Theories of Tocqueville, Marx, and Durkheim.* Stanford: Stanford University Press, 1972.

Rabelais, François. *Gargantua and Pantagruel.* Vol. 24 of *Great Books of the Western World.* Chicago: Encyclopaedia Britannica, 1952.

Raynal, Guillaume Thomas François, The Abbé. *A Philosophical and Political History of the Settlement and Trade of the Europeans in the East and West Indies.* Trans. J. O. Justamond. Vol. 1. 2d ed. London: n.p., 1789.

Raynal, Maurice. *Goya to Gauguin.* Cleveland: World, 1951.

Read, Herbert. "De Tocqueville on Art in America." *The Adelphi* 22 (October–December 1946): 9–13.

Redier, Antoine. *Comme disait M. de Tocqueville . . .* 2d ed. Paris: Librairie Académique Perrin et Cie, 1925.

Richter, Melvin. "Toward a Concept of Political Illegitimacy: Bonapartist Dictatorship and Democratic Legitimacy." *Political Theory* 10 (May 1982): 185–214.

_____, ed. *Essays in Theory and History: An Approach to the Social Sciences.* Cambridge, Mass.: Harvard University Press, 1970.

Robespierre, Maximilien. "Speech on the Moral and Political Principles of Domestic Policy," pp. 129–43. In Philip Dawson, ed., *The French Revolution.* Englewood Cliffs, N.J.: Prentice-Hall, 1967.

Rougemont, Denis de. *Love in the Western World.* Trans. Montgomery Belgion. Rev. ed. New York: Harper & Row, 1974.

Rousseau, Jean-Jacques. *Collection complète des oeuvres de J.-J. Rousseau,* Vol. 1, *Considérations sur le gouvernement de Pologne.* Geneva: n.p., 1782.

_____. *Confessions.* No trans. given. New York: Modern Library, n.d.

_____. *Eloisa.* No trans. given. 4 vols. London: T. Becket, 1776.

_____. *Émile.* Trans. Barbara Foxley. London: J. M. Dent, 1911.

_____. *The Government of Poland.* Trans. Willmoore Kendall. New York: Bobbs-Merrill, 1972.

_____. *Politics and the Arts: Letter to M. d'Alembert on the Theatre.* Trans., ed., and introduced by Allan Bloom. Ithaca: Cornell University Press, 1968.

_____. *The Social Contract* and *Discourses.* Trans. and introduced by G.D.H. Cole. New York: Dutton, 1950.

Sachs, Curt. *World History of the Dance.* New York: Crown, 1937.

Saint-Simon, Henri de. *Social Organization, The Science of Man, and Other Writings.* Trans. and ed. Felix Markham. New York: Harper & Row, 1964.

Salomon, Albert. "Tocqueville, Moralist and Sociologist." *Social Research* 2 (November 1935): 405–38.

_____. "Tocqueville, 1959." *Social Research* 26 (Winter 1959): 449–70.

_____. "Tocqueville's Philosophy of Freedom." *The Review of Politics* 1 (October 1939): 400–431.

Sartre, Jean-Paul. *Baudelaire.* Trans. Martin Turnell. New York: New Directions, 1950.

Sayce, Richard Anthony. *The Essays of Montaigne: A Critical Exploration.* London: Weidenfeld & Nicolson, 1972.

Schapiro, J. Salwyn. "Alexis de Tocqueville: Pioneer of Democratic Liberalism in France." *Political Science Quarterly* 57 (December 1942): 545–63.

Schleifer, James T. "Alexis de Tocqueville Describes the American Character: Two Previously Unpublished Portraits." *The South Atlantic Quarterly* 74 (Spring 1975): 244–58.

———. *The Making of Tocqueville's "Democracy in America."* Chapel Hill: University of North Carolina Press, 1980.

———. "Tocqueville and Religion: Some New Perspectives." *The Tocqueville Review* 4 (Fall-Winter 1982): 303–21.

Schwartz, Joel. "The Penitentiary and Perfectibility in Tocqueville." *Western Political Quarterly* 38 (March 1985): 7–26.

Sennett, Richard. *The Fall of Public Man.* New York: Vintage Books, Knopf, 1978.

Sérullaz, Maurice. *Corot.* Paris: Fernand Hazan, 1952.

Sewell, William H., Jr. *Work and Revolution in France: The Language of Labor From the Old Regime to 1848.* London: Cambridge University Press, 1980.

Shklar, Judith N. *Men and Citizens: A Study of Rousseau's Social Theory.* London: Cambridge University Press, 1969.

Simon, G.-A. *Histoire généalogique des Clérel, seigneurs de Rampan, Tocqueville, etc.* Caen: Imprimerie Ozanne, 1954.

Skinner, Quentin. *The Foundations of Modern Political Thought,* Vol. 1, *The Renaissance.* London: Cambridge University Press, 1978.

Soboul, Albert. *The Sans Culottes.* Trans. Rémy Inglis Hall. Garden City, N.Y.: Doubleday, 1972.

Soltau, Roger Henry. *French Political Thought in the 19th Century.* New York: Russell & Russell, 1959.

Staël, Madame de. *De la littérature considérée dans ses rapports avec les institutions sociales.* Paris: Charpentier, 1887.

Stanton, Stephen, ed. *Camille and Other Plays.* Trans. J. R. Planché et al. New York: Hill & Wang, 1957.

Stearns, Peter N. *Paths to Authority: The Middle Class and the Industrial Labor Force in France, 1820–1848.* Urbana: University of Illinois Press, 1978.

Stendhal. *The Charterhouse of Parma.* Trans. Margaret R. B. Shaw. Baltimore: Penguin, 1958.

———. *Lucien Leuwen,* Book 1, *The Green Huntsman;* Book 2, *The Telegraph.* Trans. Louise Varèse. New York: New Directions, 1961.

———. *Scarlet and Black.* Trans. Margaret R. B. Shaw. Baltimore: Penguin, 1953.

Sterling, Charles, and Margaretta Salinger, eds. *French Paintings.* Vol. 2. New York: The Metropolitan Museum of Art, 1966.

Strout, Cushing. "Tocqueville and Republican Religion: Revisiting the Visitor." *Political Theory* 8 (February 1980): 9–26.

———. "Tocqueville's Duality: Describing America and Thinking of Europe." *American Quarterly* 21 (Spring 1969): 87–99.

Strunk, Oliver, ed. *Source Readings in Music History: The Romantic Era.* New York: Norton, 1965.

Sykes, Rev. Norman. "Bossuet," pp. 39–69. In F.J.C. Hearnshaw, ed., *The*

Social and Political Ideas of Some Great French Thinkers in the Age of Reason. New York: E. S. Crofts, 1930.

Tacitus. *The Complete Works.* Ed. Moses Hadas. Trans. Alfred John Church and William Jackson Brodribb. New York: Modern Library, 1942.

Taylor, Charles. "Interpretation and the Sciences of Man." *Review of Metaphysics* 25 (September 1971): 3–51.

Thorburn, David, and Geoffrey Hartman, eds. *Romanticism.* Ithaca: Cornell University Press, 1973.

Topazio, Virgil W. *D'Holbach's Moral Philosophy: Its Background and Development.* Geneva: Institut et musée Voltaire, 1956.

Toussaint, François Vincent. *Manners.* Translation of *Les Moeurs;* no trans. given. 3d ed. London: n.p., 1752.

Turnell, Martin. *Baudelaire: A Study of His Poetry.* New York: New Directions, 1972.

———. *The Novel in France.* New York: New Directions, 1951.

Van Tieghem, Paul. *Le Mouvement romantique.* Paris: Librairie Vuibert, 1940.

Vigny, Alfred de. *The Military Necessity.* Trans. Humphrey Hare. London: Cresset, 1952.

Virtanen, R. "Tocqueville and the Romantics." *Symposium* 13 (Spring 1959): 167–85.

Voltaire, Jean François Marie Arouet de. *The Age of Louis XIV.* Trans. Martyn P. Pollack. London: J. M. Dent, 1961.

———. *The Philosophy of History.* No trans. given. New York: Citadel, 1965.

———. *The Portable Voltaire.* Trans. H. I. Woolf et al. Ed. Ben Ray Redman. New York: Viking, 1963.

Wach, Joachim. "The Role of Religion in the Social Philosophy of Alexis de Tocqueville." *Journal of the History of Ideas* 7 (January 1946): 74–90.

Walker, Mack, ed. *Metternich's Europe.* New York: Harper & Row, 1968.

Wickwar, William H. "Helvétius and Holbach," pp. 195–216. In F.J.C. Hearnshaw, ed., *The Social and Political Ideas of Some Great French Thinkers in the Age of Reason.* New York: E. S. Crofts, 1930.

Wilenski, R. H. *French Painting.* Rev. ed. Boston: Crales Branford, 1949.

Williams, Raymond. *Culture and Society, 1780–1950.* New York: Harper & Row, 1966.

Wilson, Arthur. *Diderot.* 2 vols. in one. New York: Oxford University Press, 1972.

Wilson, Edmund. *The Triple Thinkers.* New York: Oxford University Press, 1948.

Woodcock, George. *Pierre-Joseph Proudhon: His Life and Work.* New York: Schocken, 1972.

Zeitlin, Irving. *Liberty, Equality, and Revolution in Alexis de Tocqueville.* Boston: Little, Brown, 1971.

Zetterbaum, Marvin. *Tocqueville and the Problem of Democracy.* Stanford: Stanford University Press, 1967.

Zuckert, Catherine. "Not by Preaching: Tocqueville on the Role of Religion in American Democracy." *Review of Politics* 43 (April 1981): 259–80.

Index

Library of Congress Cataloging-in-Publication Data
Boesche, Roger.
    The strange liberalism of Alexis de Tocqueville.

    Bibliography: p.
    Includes index.
    1. Liberty.   2. Liberalism.   3. Tocqueville, Alexis de,
    1805–1859.   I. Title.
    JC585.B575   1987   323.44   86-29141
    ISBN 0-8014-1964-6 (alk. paper)